"No one has inspired the Jewish community to perform acts of kindness more than Danny Siegel, and this comprehensive collection of his most radiant works sings out to us all. *Radiance* is a spiritual masterpiece!"

—RABBI DAVID ELLENSON,
chancellor emeritus, Hebrew Union
College–Jewish Institute of Religion

"This volume is a unique mix of prose, poetry, classic texts, Torah insights, models of good deeds, portraits of Mitzvah heroes, and Danny Siegel's unflagging affirmation of the good in people and in living. In a classic comic book trope, a hitherto ordinary person is hit by a powerful, mysterious ray and becomes endowed with superpowers. If you allow yourself to be hit by this collection's rays of love and life wisdom, you will emerge a Mitzvah superhero."

—RABBI YITZ GREENBERG,
author of *For the Sake of Heaven and Earth: The
New Encounter between Judaism and Christianity*

"It's impossible to think about Mitzvah heroes and the way they inspire others to change the world without the work of Danny Siegel. Through his poetry, his stories, and perhaps most of all his *person*, Danny helps us to believe in the possibility of tikkun, healing and repair, for everything that is broken. *Radiance* is aptly named —this beautiful collection fills the reader with light and hope!"

—RABBI YOSHI ZWEIBACK,
Stephen Wise Temple, Los Angeles

"In today's world Siegel's *Radiance* is a much-needed guide—each text becomes a source of action, and any Mitzvah, no matter how ostensibly small, changes the world."

—HARLENE APPELMAN,
executive director, Covenant Foundatio

"Danny Siegel was one of the first people in the 1960s to call for a new approach to Jewish communal life: seeking out ways to give and 'do' Tzedakah. Within a short time, young people, their parents, and entire communities were thinking differently about Tzedakah. *Radiance*, the best of Siegel's transformational teachings through the years, is a welcome volume that continues to challenge and teach us today."

—DEBORAH E. LIPSTADT,
Dorot Professor of Modern Jewish History
and Holocaust Studies, Emory University

"Danny Siegel is that rare writer who dazzles us by spelling out time-less values and inspiring suggestions that can change our lives—and the lives of those who may need our help."

—WILLIAM NOVAK,
coauthor of the best-selling memoirs of
Lee Iacocca, Tip O'Neill, Nancy Reagan,
Oliver North, Magic Johnson, and others

"My father, Rabbi Noah Golinkin z"l, was one of Danny Siegel's Tzedakah rebbes; Danny Siegel is my Tzedakah rebbe. We have learned in the Talmud: 'Greater is one who convinces others to do [Tzedakah] than one who does' (*Bava Batra* 9a). 'One who learns in order to do, they enable him to learn and to teach, to observe and to do' (Avot 4:5). Danny Siegel has taught tens of thousands of people how to do Tzedakah. May he continue to learn, to teach and to do—*ad meah v'esrim*, until 120."

—RABBI DAVID GOLINKIN,
president, Schechter Institutes, Jerusalem

© 2020 by Danny Siegel. New and updated essays © 2020 Jewish Publication Society. Foreword © 2020 by Joseph Telushkin. All rights reserved. Published by the University of Nebraska Press as a Jewish Publication Society book. Manufactured in the United States of America.

∞

Library of Congress Cataloging-in-Publication Data
Names: Siegel, Danny, author. | Gold, Neal, editor. | Telushkin, Joseph, 1948–, author of foreword.
Title: Radiance: creative mitzvah living / Danny Siegel; edited by Rabbi Neal Gold; foreword by Rabbi Joseph Telushkin.
Description: Lincoln: University of Nebraska Press; Philadelphia: The Jewish Publication Society, [2020] | "Published by the University of Nebraska Press as a Jewish Publication Society book." | Includes bibliographical references. | Summary: "This first anthology of the most important writings by Danny Siegel, spanning and modernizing fifty years of his insights, Radiance intersperses soulful Jewish texts with innovative Mitzvah ideas to rouse individuals and communities to transform our lives, communities, and world."—Provided by publisher.
Identifiers: LCCN 2019030004 (print)
LCCN 2019030005 (ebook)
ISBN 9780827615021 (paperback)
ISBN 9780827618404 (epub)
ISBN 9780827618411 (mobi)
ISBN 9780827618428 (pdf)
Subjects: LCSH: Jewish way of life. | Jewish ethics. | Charity laws and legislation (Jewish law). | Commandments (Judaism). | Jewish religious poetry, American.
Classification: LCC BM723 .S5825 2020 (print) | LCC BM723 (ebook) | DDC 296.7—dc23
LC record available at https://lccn.loc.gov/2019030004
LC ebook record available at https://lccn.loc.gov/2019030005

Set in Merope by Laura Ebbeka.

JUN 2 5 2020

RADIANCE

RADIANCE

Creative Mitzvah Living

DANNY SIEGEL

Edited by Rabbi Neal Gold

Foreword by Rabbi Joseph Telushkin

University of Nebraska Press
Lincoln

The Jewish Publication Society
Philadelphia

In memory of
The Rabbanit Bracha Kapach, the
classic Tzaddeket of Jerusalem;
Myriam Mendilow, founder
of Life Line for the Old;
and
Jöel Dorkam, director of the
Maimon Volunteers;
and in honor of
Hadassah Levi, founder
of Ma'on LaTinok

The first Mitzvah heroes I met on my
initial Tzedakah trip to Israel in 1975

A *Rebbi's Proverb*

If you always assume
    the person sitting next to you
    is the Messiah
    waiting for some simple human kindness—
You will soon come to weigh your words
    and watch your hands.
And if that person so chooses
    not to be revealed
    in your time—
It will not matter.

CONTENTS

Teaching Goodness

RABBI JOSEPH TELUSHKIN

The problem with writing about goodness is that the topic is generally seen as rather unexciting, often dominated by clichés, and sometimes even boring. Rabbi Moshe Chaim Luzatto pinpointed this problem in his introduction to *Mesillat Yesharim (The Path of the Upright)*, the eighteenth-century text that is probably the most influential work of Musar (ethical self-improvement) ever written. Luzatto explained that most people think they already know all they need to know about being a good person and believe the subject is so self-evident that only the most simple people devote themselves to the study of basic ethics and kindness.

Nor does kindness seem to intellectually engage and intrigue most people. The Nobel Prize–winning author Isaac Bashevis Singer used to say, "Even good people don't like to read novels about good people."

Part of what has made Danny Siegel so significant a figure in Jewish life is that he makes the subject of being a good person compelling, both in his prose and in his poetry, and in the activities he uncovers and supports.

I remember reading a Ziv Tzedakah Fund annual report that listed some of the Mitzvah heroes' efforts his organization was helping to fund. Lists like this can often be boring to read. Not Danny's listing, which reminded me of the infinite ways of doing good. Let me cite just a few examples:

> Merrill Alpert of Encino, California, runs, under the auspices of her synagogue, infant car-seat drives, which are donated to agencies that pass them on to families that cannot afford to buy them.

Donni Engelhart of Chicago collects new and used wigs for individuals with cancer.

"The King of the Bagel People," Herman Berman of Los Angeles, solicits bagels from bagel stores that would normally throw away their unbought, hours-old bagels and helps distribute them to poor people.

Kathy Freund of Portland, Maine, has created the Independent Transportation Network, a network of three hundred volunteer drivers who transport elderly people where they need to go.

Iqbal Masih of Pakistan, an international children's rights activist, visited the students of Broad Meadows School in Quincy, Massachusetts. He inspired them to establish a school for child laborers in Asia and to launch a global campaign on behalf of children's rights.

The fifth-grade class at the Ramaz Yeshiva of New York City, under the supervision of Victoria Ginsberg, has collected and donated more than 250,000 pounds of food in six years.

Danny specializes in finding strangely specific Jewish sources and then identifies strangely specific fulfillments of these very sources. Thus, the Torah commands us to give a poor person "sufficient for whatever he needs" (Deut. 15:8). Jewish law understands this to mean that we should try to provide precisely what the person lacks: "If he is hungry, he should be fed. If he needs clothes, he should be provided with clothes. If he has no household furniture or utensils, furniture and utensils should be provided.... If he needs to be spoon-fed, then we must spoon-feed him" (*Shulchan Arukh, Yoreh De'ah* 250:1).

Regarding this last example, Danny recalls an incident related to him by a medical resident. A prominent physician was taking the resident and some medical students on morning rounds, offering insights at the bedside of each patient. They soon came to an older woman, whose complex ailments made it impossible for her family and friends to care for her. The woman was depressed and withdrawn, and she refused to eat. To the students' astonishment, the professor stopped the rounds and spent twenty minutes spoon-feeding the woman. Siegel concludes, "[The woman] was capable of feeding herself, but she refused to do so. So, with deliberate and gentle care, the teacher taught a lesson in kindness. He did not do it as a demonstration to the students. No . . . he spoon-fed this old woman because those were the demands of the hour." It was the very specific and unexpected nature of the doctor's act that so moved me.

Some years ago, I wrote a book on Hillel, the first-century BCE rabbinic Sage who I believe remains a particularly vibrant model for twenty-first-century Jews and for all humanity. In large measure the volume serves as an extended commentary on Hillel's fifteen-word summation in Aramaic (twenty-six words in English) of Judaism's essence: "That which is hateful unto you, do not do unto your neighbor. This is the whole Torah; all the rest is commentary. Now, go and study" (Babylonian Talmud, *Shabbat* 31a).

Some twelve hundred years after Hillel, Maimonides—in commenting on the verse "Love your neighbor as yourself"—defined the Golden Rule in these terms:

> Whatever I wish for myself, I should wish the same for that [other] person. And whatever I do not wish for myself or for my friends, I should not wish for that [other] person. That is the meaning of the verse, "Love your neighbor as yourself." (*Book of the Commandments*, positive commandment #206)

Danny Siegel is one of the preeminent disciples of the ethics of Hillel and of Maimonides in our generation. He has written of what both their teachings mean in concrete terms: "As I would not want to suffer hunger, homelessness, joblessness, ill health, and disease, and personal tragedies of every kind, so too I would not wish that on others. And I would have to act to prevent these misfortunes happening to them." And, regarding Maimonides's words, "Whatever I wish for myself, I should wish the same for that person. . . . If I wish to have peace of mind, security, a decent living, friends, family, good health for myself, I am to wish that for others also, and to act in such a way as to allow others to have those blessings."

Danny, I believe, equally offers specific examples of kindness as a form of commentary on the most famous words of the most widely read Jewish martyr of the twentieth century, Anne Frank: "How wonderful it is that nobody need wait a single moment before starting to improve the world."

When you're faced with a particularly hard issue and people tell you "nothing can be done," Danny reminds us that in almost every circumstance we can still do something. And if we continually excuse inactivity with the claim that nothing can be done, then what is the purpose of our lives? Rabbi Nachman of Bratslav said, "If you are not going to be a better person tomorrow than you were today, then what need do you have for tomorrow?" As I like to say when quoting Reb Nachman, "I wish you a good today and an even better tomorrow."

As you read *Radiance*, I believe you too will discover new ways to help people in need. Together, with this volume as our inspiration and charge, we can meet that ideal and challenge of Anne Frank: "How wonderful it is that nobody need wait a single moment before starting to improve the world."

ACKNOWLEDGMENTS

I am deeply grateful to Rabbi Barry Schwartz, director of The Jewish Publication Society (JPS), who enthusiastically agreed to this project of bringing together selections from my works into this single volume.

My thanks to Joy Weinberg, managing editor at JPS, whose steadfast interest and encouragement guided the transformation of this book from being merely a retrospective into a volume that, I hope, will be relevant and meaningful today for readers old and new alike. She pored through this material line by line, word by word, and guided the process with wisdom and patience. I am deeply grateful for her loving and passionate commitment to shaping this work.

My thanks, as well, extend to the University of Nebraska Press for their fine, professional work in publishing this book.

The following list includes categories and time references to the people in various settings who have molded me as a person and, as a result, produced my writings. My debt to all would fill another entire book.

My family; my synagogue, the Arlington-Fairfax Jewish Center (now Etz Hayim) and the late Rabbi Noah Golinkin; Hawthorne, the small, creative private high school in Washington DC; United Synagogue Youth; various individual professors at the Joint Program of Columbia University's School of General Studies and the Jewish Theological Seminary; friends, blessedly too numerous to count; rabbis and Jewish educators numbering more than five hundred, most notably my ultimate Rebbi in this field, the late Dr. Abraham J. Gittelson; Rebbis in Tzedakah; the doctor (and friend) who diagnosed my attention deficit disorder, telling me that I was a classic case; that person (who specifically I have forgotten now) who told me, "You should be writing poetry"; the individuals who encouraged and guided my writing—early on, most notably Elie Wiesel; William Novak, who first put my poetry and prose in print; Arnie Draiman, my resource person in Israel for more than two decades, who did research and fact-checking for us in the preparation of this book; the more than one hundred inspired and inspiring Mitzvah heroes and Tzaddikim; and the many thousands of students, young and old, in my classes and seemingly out-of-the-blue strangers at my lectures who told me their lives' dazzling Mitzvah stories, among them more than ten thousand United Synagogue Youth Israel pilgrims I have worked with in the USY Tikkun Olam program over the last forty-four years.

Finally, a word about my student, teacher, and friend Rabbi Neal Gold: He first suggested publishing this book a long time ago. I was ambivalent and hesitated, until he made a connection with the director of The Jewish Publication Society, who expressed interest. Since then, he has done the vast majority of the work on this book: communicating directly with JPS, writing the proposal, reviewing the entirety of my writings with me and discussing what to include and exclude, preparing the manuscript, reminding me at every turn that this is *my* book, and gently pushing me along the way to stay the course. I am so grateful that I cannot find sufficiently appropriate words to express my thanks, but let the following line be a hint of what I want to say: Most assuredly, there is no scale that can chart, measure, or weigh my debt to him.

—DANNY SIEGEL

I am honored and humbled that my teacher and friend Danny Siegel entrusted this project to me. He guards and protects his writings with the fervor of a mother hen watching her nest, but he trusted me—even when we disagreed. His teachings and his outlook on the world have profoundly shaped the person who I am struggling to become, and it is a privilege to bring his words to a wider audience, to encourage a new generation of students to find their unique niche in doing the work of world repair.

My deep appreciation goes to Rabbi Barry Schwartz, who when I proposed this project simply said, "I love Danny—let's do it!" Joy Weinberg's tireless and confident guidance has made this a much better book, and I thank her for her support, enthusiasm, and intuitive understanding of the full potential of this collection.

It is an honor to be associated with University of Nebraska Press, which produces such beautiful and high-quality books.

My friend Dr. Ricky Blocker, z"l, a consummate Mensch, offered important technical advice while I was preparing the manuscript, and I am saddened that he did not live to see the final product.

I would like to express my infinite gratitude to my parents, Bob and Barbara Gold, for their boundless support and affection. In the summer of 1992, as I was headed to Israel for a year, my father handed me a box of hearing aids to donate to various medical Tzedakah projects. He had the foresight to say, "Find Danny Siegel in Jerusalem, and ask him for guidance about giving them away." And so our friendship was born.

To my children, Avi and Jeremy: I can only hope that you inherit and help shape a world marked by the love, kindness, and soulful Jewish values found in this book.

And to Heidi, my life's partner and constant source of inspiration: I can never fully express my gratitude for your presence in my life and for your unceasing love. To you I dedicate all my efforts in bringing this work to fruition.

—RABBI NEAL GOLD

INTRODUCTION

Seeking Out Places Where Light Is Hidden

It was summer in Jerusalem in the mid-1990s, and a group of us—
friends and students of Danny Siegel—were gathered at the Village
Green outdoor café in the city center. The restaurant was one of Dan-
ny's favorites. The food was fresh and the portions large, but much
more importantly, the owners had built a relationship with a local
home for developmentally disabled adults, several of whom worked
there. It was a place of dignity and independence.

Danny has a way of attracting like-minded travelers, and at the
restaurant that day, we were an eclectic bunch. There was Danny, in
his Hawaiian shirt and shorts, at the center of it all. Next to him was
Shmuel Munk, an ultra-Orthodox rabbi and gentle soul, in his white
shirt, black pants, and full beard; he runs a sheltered workshop for
men and women from across the religious spectrum of Israeli life who
are recovering from mental illness. Alongside Shmuel were several
female rabbinical students, in tank tops and shorts. Beside them was
Joël Dorkam, a secular kibbutznik from the era of Israel's indepen-
dence, who headed the Maimon Volunteers network to welcome and
assimilate new immigrants with honor. Also in the group were some
American friends, in Jerusalem for the summer, joining us now for a
few hours of camaraderie and inspiration. All told, there were a dozen
of us, each reflecting a different part of the continuum of Jewish life.
Together, we were hunched over a Torah text, parsing its words and
discussing its prescription for a more compassionate world.

A tap on the shoulder interrupted me. It was a woman sitting at
the next table. "Excuse me," she said, "I couldn't help overhearing
your discussion. I have to ask you something." A pause. Then: "Who
are you people?"

"Who *are* you people?"—I like that. We're students of Danny Sie-
gel, anxious to glean from him Jewish inspiration about the power
of each individual to create a more compassionate, just, and gener-
ous world. From his decades on the Jewish lecture circuit, Danny's
teachings have profoundly shaped American Judaism. His influence
is felt in any community where Bar/Bat Mitzvah students do Mitzvah
projects as part of their preparation and in any synagogue that runs
a "Mitzvah Day" of collective acts of kindness and generosity. Like-
wise, this is true for shuls and *havurot* that have created Tzedakah
collectives that raise money and wrestle with the most meaningful
ways to distribute it. Danny didn't necessarily invent these concepts,
but more than anyone he popularized them and made them part of
the fabric of Jewish life. By emphasizing the message that each of us
has been created to do Mitzvahs, Danny moves comfortably between
different streams of Judaism and across the borders modern Jews
have invented for themselves. He mines the tradition for a common
denominator of Menschlichkeit, the art of being a good and kind
human being, that speaks to all of us. Boundary lines disappear in
the radiant light of what binds us together—namely, restoring *kavod*,
human dignity, to every person.

"Radiance." It's a powerful and multifaceted term—a poet's word—
for a wide breadth of human experience. It describes daily phenom-
ena, like the sun emerging from the horizon; it also depicts simple acts
of kindness and their effects: "I saw the light come back to her eyes,"
we sometimes say, even offhandedly. In the Talmud, a prayer of Rabbi
Ammi expresses this so beautifully: *May your eyes sparkle with the light of
Torah, and your face be radiant as the radiance of the heavens* (*Berachot* 17a).

"Radiance" also recalls the Jewish mystical notion that the whole
world is embedded with shards of divine light, often deeply hidden.
One task of religious living is to seek out the places where that light
is hidden, raise it up, and restore it to its original, lofty state. Jewish
tradition calls this Tikkun Olam, repairing the fabric of this broken
world.

With all these interpretations in mind, in 1981 Danny incorporated his Tzedakah fund and named it "Ziv," one of the Rabbinic words for "radiance." Over time, Danny developed a reputation for discovering and contributing to people and projects that had a certain light or human radiance about them. During its twenty-seven years of existence, the Ziv Tzedakah Fund distributed $13,630,615.91 to individuals and organizations doing extraordinary work in creative, often unusual ways, with utmost trustworthiness and reliability. The specificity of that number—right down to the 91 cents—is important. After all, a key Danny teaching is that there is no such thing as a small amount of Tzedakah; coins and dollar bills, selectively and strategically deployed, have the potential to make all the difference in the world. And so "Ziv" came to describe the act of Tzedakah itself, the radiance of Mitzvah heroes, and the luminescence of a network of thousands of people around the world doing this good work together.

Today, we have titled this selected anthology of fifty years of Danny Siegel's prose and poetry *Radiance*—hoping that you too will feel and carry forth some of that brightness as you explore or deepen your ability to transform the world.

This book challenges each of us to ask that most fundamental Jewish religious question: What is it that I am supposed to be *doing*? Danny also urges us to seek out *how and why people do good work* as a pathway to cultivating our individual skills to do Tikkun Olam. Investigating these interactions of mind, heart, and hands—and the careful ways that each refines the others—is one of the most important insights he has contributed to contemporary Jewish thought.

Perhaps the most concise summary of his approach can be found in the essay "Three Prongs," in which he describes the dynamic interplay between (1) studying Jewish texts, (2) meeting Mitzvah heroes who are doing extraordinary work, and (3) putting the lessons into action. Danny urges us to see the interactions between these three parts as a chemical equation, incorporating double arrows. Each part of the equation rebounds against the other part—reacting to it, catalyzing it, and deepening its impact. So, too, is the interrelationship between thinking, feeling, and doing in a Jewish system.

A Torah of Kindness underlies these writings, reminding us of the crucial connection between what we *believe* and what we *do*. Danny is instructing us: Philosophy without kindness is solipsism. Science without kindness is irresponsible. Religion without kindness is hypocrisy. In this sense, a deep spirituality—and a sensitive theology—infuses these pages. This is the work of a Jewish thinker whose writing and activism remain crucially relevant for the current and future generations of leaders.

Learning with Danny can be a whirlwind. His lectures are filled with urgency; we realize there are hurting people nearby, right now, waiting for some human kindness or support. His talks are punctuated with challenges: "Okay, we need $300 to get the shul ten large-print prayer books!"... "Who will go to the local nursing home to see if they want three resident parakeets?"... "Who will ask the donut shop across the street what they do with their leftovers and if we can arrange to donate them to the women's shelter?" In many audiences, kids and teens leap into action. Adults, on the other hand, may grumble about the obstacles and liabilities—although, more often than not, they come around.

Eventually they'll all be on board. In Danny's realm, the excitement to do Mitzvahs and Tzedakah is infectious.

About This Book

In preparing this collection, we carefully sifted through a half-century of prose and poetry. We returned to the nearly thirty books that Danny has published. We also looked at anthologies of Jewish writing and articles from magazines such as *Moment*, whose founder and longtime editor Leonard Fein, *z"l*, was one the earliest champions of Danny's writing. We selected pieces based on a variety of criteria. In some cases, we gave preference to essays or poems that have become particularly well known or influential due to their inclusion in prayer books or popular guides to the Jewish life cycle. In others, it was a delight to rediscover older writings that resonate even more power-fully today than when they were originally written. In addition, we have introduced five new essays, each reflecting on what Danny has learned over his career, exploring Danny's current thinking on doing Mitzvahs and Tzedakah, and offering a prescription for the future work that is yet to be done.

Throughout Danny's prose writings lie certain convictions: that Judaism has something radical and countercultural to say about how human beings ought to be treated; that each of us has God-given talents that are uniquely our own; and that some people go far too long without discovering their special occupation in this world. These messages remain as true and as urgent today as they did when Danny first started this work.

The division of the book into topical sections illustrates how Danny has fine-tuned his thinking over time, as he discovered and learned from new Mitzvah heroes.

The first section of writings includes essays about Mitzvahs and how to implement them. Practical ideas waiting to be put into action fly off the page. In short pieces, we discover the questions to ask in order to unlock the Mitzvah-potential within each of us. In his classic "Gym Shoes and Irises," which first appeared in *Moment* in 1975 and later in *The Third Jewish Catalog*, Danny explains how he came to discover these ideas for himself. He was preparing for a trip to Israel when, as many of us have experienced, friends started giving him money to give away upon his arrival. Inspired, he proceeded to ask his acquaintances for more money to bring with him and ended up with $955 to distribute. You can feel his excitement in discovering the joy of giving away Tzedakah money and changing lives at the very genesis of his long career of writing and teaching. The evolution of his thinking about Mitzvahs is traced in the writings of this chapter. Now, in a new essay, "Jewish Optimism—From Radical to Mainstream," Danny reflects on how what was once considered revolutionary has now became standard in the Jewish community, and he suggests priorities for a new generation of students.

Chapter 2 is devoted to Danny's analysis of Torah texts. As a student at the Joint Program of Columbia University's School of General Studies and the Jewish Theological Seminary in the 1960s, Danny studied with some of the most profound Torah minds of the twentieth century. Navigating a path through Bible, Talmud, and halakhic texts, he introduces us to many off-the-beaten-track texts from Rabbinic literature. He knows how to mine religious works for their essential humanity and their urgent messages to us today.

Consider, for example, his essay "*Jewish* Jewish Leadership." The title itself is a confrontation: what passes for "Jewish" in much of our institutional leadership is far too genteel and complacent for the great thirst for meaning in our communities today. Danny guides us through texts from Bible, midrash, and Talmud intended to wake us up. We encounter the little-known Binyamin the Tzaddik, who had already distributed all of the community's Tzedakah money when a starving woman came and said, "If you do not feed me, a woman and her seven children will die." The Talmud continues, "So he fed her from his own money" (*Bava Batra* 11a) — a profound observation that, on occasion, each of us is positioned to make *all the difference in the world* to another human being. Now imagine studying this text with a Federation or synagogue board. Danny insists, "The model for Jewish leaders should be the Tzaddik, before the successful businessperson, attorney, or organizational whiz." To this Danny adds the sages' description of Moses, who carried an exhausted sheep on his shoulders rather than castigating it for running away from the flock. "Since you tend the sheep of human beings with such overwhelming love," God declares to Moses, "by your life, I swear you shall be the shepherd of My sheep, Israel" (*Exodus Rabbah* 2:2). And more: condemnations of arrogance in community leaders; awareness of the almost unbearable strain that leadership can put on spiritual leaders and their families; the need to place Torah at the center. None of this is presented in a self-righteous or angry way; all of it is mined for the deep, human values the sages understood so well.

Mitzvah heroes themselves are the subjects of chapter 3, portraits of some of the extraordinary people Danny has encountered on his travels. For instance, Samantha Abeel of Traverse City, Michigan: A teenager when they first met, Samantha wrote about the challenge of her learning disability (specifically, her dyscalculia, an inability to work with numbers). Her poetry and teaching inspired Danny and countless others to reevaluate and—finally—confront their own disabilities, whatever they may be. Through her story and teachings, she convinces Danny that his learning difficulties are, in fact, a source of his creativity. Danny describes Samantha as a Rebbi: that sort of individual who possesses keys to opening up a world of potential for people confronted with seemingly insurmountable obstacles. It's no coincidence that Danny's first poetry anthology was called *Unlocked Doors*; after all, removing barriers that restrict people from discovering their purpose is a big part of what Mitzvah work is all about.

Chapter 4 is a collection of similar but harder-to-classify writings with the common theme of how to live a life of Menschlichkeit—a life marked by sensitivity, kindness, love, and generosity. We read of Passover sedarim with developmentally disabled children, of the delicacy with which a medical mentor treats his patients, of an obtuse college interviewer who asks all the wrong questions. And there are elements in this text that engage with the bleakest moments of the Jewish past—where the resounding pain of our history also calls us to act. For instance, here we encounter the sublime, luminescent "Frumka," a prose-poem soaked in Jewish suffering that will haunt you long after you close the book.

Tzedakah—how to give money away so it does the most good—is the theme of the final prose chapter. Danny cuts through Jewish tradition's legal and homiletical materials to answer urgent questions: Why isn't Tzedakah "charity"? Is it really supposed to be done anonymously? What are my investigative responsibilities before I give money away? He also brings these teachings into the Internet age:

How does social media enhance our opportunities to do Tzedakah? Conversely, what are the challenges for a new generation of tech-Tzedakah givers?

And then there's the poetry. Danny's contributions as a Jewish educator have been so significant that his gifts as a poet occasionally have been overlooked. The sensitive, lyrical writing in this collection should remind readers that he is one of the most exquisite Jewish poets of his generation. When I read "The Four Children," "A Blessing," "Above All, Teach This Newborn Child," among many others, it stirs something deep within my soul. Some of the poems are so personal, they are almost too delicate to touch. Consider "The Crippler," a devastating indictment of the bestial antisemitism of the Old Country and the harrowing lengths to which Jews would go just to survive. Often when I've shared this poem with classes, I've found myself unable to read through the entire piece without breaking down. There is simply that much Jewish pain packed into its stanzas.

Other poems are offered for specific occasions: prayers and blessings for baby namings, adult Bar/Bat Mitzvah ceremonies, the Shabbat dinner table, the removal of the Torah from the ark on Shabbat, toasts to a newly married couple. Many of these have found a home in Reform, Conservative, and Jewish Renewal liturgies — not to mention untold numbers of services for youth groups, synagogue retreats, and *havurot*. As Danny explains, "I did not want my poems to be enjoyed only as aesthetic experiences or academic exercises and analyses, but also to be *useful*." They are — and his words have uplift, grandeur, and spiritual excitement.

How to Get the Most Out of This Book

One of the most valuable aspects of Danny's writings throughout the years is that they have been so eminently practical. Sometimes, ideas for Mitzvah projects seem to leap off the page. His poetry, too, is often designed for specific occasions in the life of a community or on a path of the Jewish life cycle, and often he commemorates unheralded moments that have not been marked before with rituals or blessings.

Radiance is designed to be useful. Boards of trustees of synagogues, Jewish schools, and Jewish nonprofits will find plenty of material for study, reflection, commemoration of milestones, and of course taking action. Rabbis, cantors, and Jewish educators will discover scores of classical Jewish texts on Mitzvah living from both well-known and off-the-beaten-path sources. Likewise for religious and day school faculty, youth directors, and camp counselors: much material here will be valuable as you raise up a generation of Menschen. And of course, all collectives that do Tzedakah/Tikkun Olam/social action will encounter new insight, inspiration, and ideas.

On a more personal level, we encourage readers with whom certain essays and poetry resonate to use them ritually, as part of your commemoration of special life moments. Some readings here are meant to amplify life's joys. Other are likely to soften painful moments. Still others will speak in particular ways to readers at different moments along life's path.

Toward these ends, we are offering guidance for using the selected works in this book. The following "Using This Book in Your Personal and Organizational Life" chart is organized into four major sections: "The Life of the Community," "The Jewish Life Cycle," "Shabbat and Festivals," and "Essential Jewish Themes." "The Life of the Community" offers suggested works for use by boards, Tzedakah/Tikkun Olam/social action committees, teachers/schools/camps, and universities and seminaries. "The Jewish Life Cycle" suggests prose and poetry for weddings and anniversaries, birth and baby namings, Bar/Bat Mitzvah, graduation and other education milestones, late adulthood and retirement, and death and mourning. "Shabbat and Festivals" suggests works for Shabbat, Passover, and Rosh Hashanah. Finally, "Essential Jewish Themes" suggests compositions on Israel, in memory of Jewish suffering, wrestling with God, and radical amazement. Certainly, these are just suggestions; different readers will find illumination and motivation from different passages of prose and poetry. Most importantly, we hope you will read and return to your favorite passages again and again as you pursue and refine your own approach to the world of Mitzvah living.

Using This Book in Your Personal and Organizational Life

THE JEWISH LIFE CYCLE

SHABBAT AND FESTIVALS

Notes on Language and Utility

Danny's teachings can be so unique that he has developed his own Torah-inflected vocabulary. These terms appear throughout this book:

"Mitzvahs"—with the Yiddish pronunciation, so much gutsier and more deeply rooted than "community service" or "social action." Mitzvahs are acts of caring and decency grounded in Jewish values, more to the point than the traditional term *gemilut hasadim*. Danny explains it this way: "I consistently translate the plural of 'Mitzvah' as 'Mitzvahs' and not 'Mitzvot' because I want it to mean 'doing good for others, for the world.' I am *not* implying that the other Mitzvot—Shabbat, Torah study, etc.—are not important, but I want to make sure people understand I am talking about being good by doing good and that there is a connection between Mitzvahs and meaning and deep happiness in life."

"Mitzvah heroes"—Perhaps Danny's greatest genius is identifying people from all faiths and backgrounds who are doing Mitzvahs in creative and grassroots ways and pointing to them as teachers. By using the word "heroes" Danny is teaching that we should not put these individuals on pedestals or turn them into something superhuman; indeed, when we do encounter them, we respond to their very humanity. One of Danny's favorite quotes, from educator John Holt, is "Charismatic leaders make us think, 'Oh, if only I could do that, be like that.' True leaders make us think, 'If they can do that, then I can too.'" In encouraging us to meet Mitzvah heroes and become their students and partners, Danny teaches us again and again, "Mitzvah heroes are everywhere, as the midrash says (*Sifrei Devarim*, 'Ekev 11, 47), 'Just as the clusters of stars are so numerous they cannot be counted, so, too, are the Good People/Mitzvah heroes/Tzaddikim.'"

"Rebbi"—the primary mentor from whom one learns the essence of life. Despite the similarity to "rabbi" or the Hasidic "rebbe," Danny's use of "Rebbi" does not necessarily mean an ordained clergyperson—for that matter, the Rebbi need not even be Jewish. Furthermore, and this is important, the status "Rebbi" bears little or no connection to graduate degrees, titles, or other markers of so-called success.

In their original contexts, many of these pieces included citations from classic Jewish literature in Hebrew or Aramaic, as Danny is a scholar of Torah literature, with intimate knowledge of these texts. We regret that we were unable to reproduce those sources here in their original languages and encourage readers to seek out the classic literature.

Readers familiar with Danny's previous work may notice certain differences between the original and the current versions of the essays and poems. Where possible, many works have been updated to reflect egalitarian language in regard to gender and contemporary terminology relating to age. Likewise, the vocabulary regarding disabilities has evolved, and the revised pieces strive to reflect this sensitivity. In other cases, however, the original language has been retained in order to accurately convey the historical context of the essay or poem. We hope sensitive readers will understand.

The original essays have also been selectively edited to make them relevant for today's readers. Some original observations, notable in their time but expected today, were determined not to merit inclusion. Some references to outmoded technology, such as VCRs, were retained as period elements in otherwise classic pieces.

Certain selections in this book describe Mitzvah heroes and projects of historical enduring significance. Some of these individuals may now be retired, deceased, or no longer doing their specific Mitzvah work described here; some of the projects may no longer exist. While many of the original articles included contact information, we have generally deleted phone numbers and email addresses that were unlikely to be accurate today. We have also added some updated project URLs, sometimes to the body of the text, other times to the notes. When that contact information has not been provided, it does *not* mean that this project is no longer continuing. We strongly encourage readers to follow up with the ideas in this book that move them most by searching the Internet and social media.

Danny and I hope that this collection will be both a catalyst and a valuable resource for you and your community to diversify and amplify the ways in which you change the world. It is our deepest desire that a new generation will be inspired to explore their own unique abilities and gifts, restoring a bit more radiance to a world that is desperately waiting for it.

RADIANCE

PART 1

PROSE

1

Mitzvahs and How to Implement Them

The Dress (1981)

I am about to deliver a talk on Tzedakah. The local United Synagogue Youth group has invited me to their synagogue, and the flyer mentions that we are looking for wedding dresses to send to Israel, to lend to brides who cannot afford to purchase them.

Before the talk begins, a young woman comes up to me outside the sanctuary. She is carrying a long white gown in a plastic casing. She explains, "I can't stay for your talk, but here is my wedding dress."

It is a magnificent dress. By now—almost a year later—no doubt it has been used by a number of different brides. The lending-library of dresses is supervised by certain Mitzvah people I have met in Jerusalem.

I cannot even remember the woman's name, but the radiance of her face has left a strong impression on my memory. I think about her frequently, about her enthusiasm as she handed me the dress. I believe that women are entitled to keep their wedding dresses— that all of us should be allowed to preserve things that hold great sentimental value for us. It is a part of life, an attachment, a hold on meanings and memories—and yet—this woman gave hers away, with an open hand and full heart.

Our conversation lasted only a minute, perhaps two.

"Here is the dress."

It was a magnificent gown.

Gym Shoes and Irises (1982)

Last fall friends and acquaintances began gathering for Israel; crisis, again, as usual, was hanging in the air. It seemed apparent that millions of new pages would be written in papers and analyses about whatever chunk of History was going to come crashing down on the Holy Land, any day. For myself, The Urge began to tear away at me, the Psalm-craving to go back to *Eretz Yisra'el*, though I had just finished a year in Jerusalem that previous August. I would go, I decided, *stam*—just because I wanted to go (or had to, or should go, or whatever). To me this was kosher Jewish thinking . . . the more reasons given for the trip, the less chance of gathering the aromas and sounds and stirrings of Holiness waiting to be ingested in the Holy Land.

My tenth trip. You know how you feel when people tell you, "Oh, I've been there eighteen times. Just last year I was over for Sukkot, Purim, and the summer. Ho, hmmm, hum." It is the Repetition Syndrome which teachers, assembly-line workers, and secretaries suffer from (to say nothing of occasional neurosurgeons, professional fundraisers, and other assorted busy individuals). What I would do while in Israel was unclear to me, though a month in Jerusalem, if correctly unplanned, could be awesome, enjoyable, or, at the least, fun.

As was my custom, I visited my well-wishers, telling them to "give me a buck for Tzedakah." I would give it out as the occasion presented itself *somewhere* in Israel. Apparently some friends adjusted their palms to the cost-of-living index, as $5s and $10s and $20s and $25s began inundating my pushka. I usually consider $10 a nice sum to take with me, but by the time of Trip #10, I was rated by Dun & Bradstreet at well over $150. So I decided to steamroll a little, making the rounds of aunts, cousins, parents, in-laws, friends, and passers-by, saying, "I'd really like a thousand."

No one I asked felt that s/he was being "hit." Each considered it a privilege to take part in the Mitzvah with me. No receipts, no questions of income-tax deductions, no hesitations like, "Well, I already did my ten to twenty percent for the year."

A family of eight in Oklahoma spent the better part of a late evening working out how much they could send me.

Oh there might have been one or two who play-grumbled. But

I assured them (taking the last $7 from their hand) that even the most grumbly give, handed over with the most obnoxious intent, is still moving Heaven and Earth. And I threw in a quote and some trumped-up page number from the Talmud to bolster my argument.

So it was that friends and relatives and strangers created a kind of *Mitzvah Chevrah* (a group of like-minded people devoted to doing good together) that would go wherever I went, speaking with (really through) me and giving me some insight into the work at hand. Except for three people who specified where I should give their money, I was on my own, the Chevrah's *shaliach* (messenger) to the Holy Land. I assured everyone I would stretch every bill and coin. I would try to sanctify their money by giving exclusively to those who were reliable, hated bureaucracy, and would use it as directly as possible to bring some assistance, joy, and a sense of *Mah Rabbu Ma'asecha*, How great are Your Creations, O Lord, to the recipients.

I left with $900-plus, and counting what arrived while I was there, we reached $955, or 5,730 Israeli pounds. That "we" was I, Dan Quixote against the Montefiore Windmills; the thirty-five or so of them; and a few others, including my rabbi, my forebears, and some Russian Jews.

About my rabbi, Noah Golinkin: When—I think it was in the 1940s—he was in love, having finally found the woman with whom he wanted to live his life, he gave $1,000 to Israel in place of buying his fiancée an engagement ring. His ring of love was a gift to Israel. (He told me that story. All those years ago, I was his favorite, his hope, his most intimate prayer to God.)

About my forebears: Sometime in the last century, Usher Zelig Siegel took to wife a certain Sarah Golda, whose family name is forgotten. They begot a multitude of children, among them Zev Dovid, called Velvel, my Zeyde. I once pilgrimaged to Keansburg, New Jersey, to supplement the old pictures and conversations with my father and aunts and cousins. His drygoods store is now a gun and ammunition shop, but the cop who grew up with my father said, "He would take a nickel on a pair of gloves, and let them pay the rest whenever they could. He was a kind man." I remember that.

His son, my Abba, has carried on where Velvel left off. It is fit and proper to praise his generosity. Now that I am past the age of rebellion and crankiness toward my parents, we can sit and recall and work out insights into Tzedakah, because he is my Rebbe-Master in this domain of Menschlichkeit. I am his child and again and again return to childhood when I wonder how his vision and foresight have been acted out by me, whether I am worthy of him and his parents and grandparents, all the way back to Abraham. When I bring to mind my years of knowing him, a constant flow of Tzedakah acts-and-intimations gushes forth.

About some Russian Jews: Crossing into Russia from Finland, the border guards took half, more than half, of our *siddurim* and calendars and *mezuzot* and Magen Davids. They were entitled to them — they are Russians and we are Jews, sixty-four Jews with a pittance of thing-gifts for our friends in the Soviet Jewish community. Stripped to the bare heart. I remember that feeling of being scared. Twenty Yiddish phrases and a few tchotchkes to give. Over There, you give someone a $3 prayerbook, and your thanks are in tears. Whoever gave me a $3 gift that moved me so much? *That* question has stuck in my kishkas.

These thoughts and questions are everyone's, I thought.

I thought, as the plane approached Lod, *Ki tireh arom v'chisito!* When you see the naked, clothe them! Isaiah, I hear you, we hear you. The thousand one-shot Tzedakah-slams that had whipped by Big Think brain over thirty years were waiting to explode.

Being a shaliach is an ego-safeguard. Wherever you go and however you choose to distribute your funds, you are constantly aware of the fact that you are just the representative of those who sent you. When speaking to the recipients, you simply say, "It's my friend's."

What Happened to the Gelt?

It immediately became clear to me that there are two distinct psychologies of giving out Tzedakah money: BigGelt and SmallGelt. If you have $500,000, rather than $955, to distribute, you go to different places, talk to different people, and give out different proportions and quantities. With SmallGelt, you are constantly aware of the fact that $50 too much here means next week there may not be anything left to give, just when you are discovering that next week's encounter is the one that needs the $50 the most. As a result, I determined to carefully watch each grush, and to proceed with a sharpened sense of spontaneity vs. overprudence.

Just as I had chosen to collect the money through straightforward, friendly means, so, also, I decided to search out the people and places of my mission. I would listen to my friends, and whoever else I knew or got to know well enough to be touched by his or her grasp of what I was trying to do.

I started with flowers at Life Line for the Old. My mother had discovered Life Line (Yad LaKashish) about five years ago. During one of my previous visits, she, the Mitzvah-Searcher-Outer *par excellence*, put her JewishMotherly food down and declared that I *must* go — in the tone of voice of "No questions, no wise remarks, kiddo!"

"Tell Mrs. Mendilow I sent you," she said.

Life Line is workshops for the elderly. It is food for invalid-old people who are unable to get out. It is a choir and tree-planting, and a Chevrah of Dignity. None of the pathetic foolishness of basketweaving is to be found in its precincts, and, indeed, the handiwork they produce has won awards in various countries, not because a bunch of doddering old fools made them, but because they are joy-forever things of beauty. My Shabbas tablecloths are from their workshops, as are my sweaters and a few of my toys.

The American custom of stashing away aging parents in (ugh) Convalescent Homes to let them die out-of-the-way, stripped of their well-deserved majesty and treated like infants — all this is foreign to Mrs. Mendilow. Anyone who would wish to learn what *menschlichkeit* is would do well to visit her and the other people of Life Line.

So, a friend of mine and I march in with a flower for each individual to take home for Shabbas.

Big man, you say! One lousy rose or chrysanthemum or iris per person. Tzaddik! Righteous One! Ten lousy bucks and he thinks he's turned the world on its ear!

To spite my cynic-self, the next day I did the same for my Chevrah at Hadassah Hospital. There's a certain woman on the Life Line staff who for the last seven years has made the rounds of the Israeli soldiers at the hospital, bringing fruit and cigarettes and candy and other things. After being introduced to the people in the Military Office and obtaining a list of who was in what ward, the lady, my friend, and I, bundled in flowers, began to walk the corridors.

It couldn't hurt, could it? I know they're soldierboys, and tough, and Israelis, and this is sort of twinkie, but the lady said, "Don't worry. It's all right."

Big Man — Tzaddik, with a wad of gelt in his pocket, doing cheap-ticket-to-Paradise Mitzvahs. Flowers for everyone!

Until you talk to the boy (that's all he is, a boy) in the eye clinic, with a bandage, and he tells you he writes and you say, I write too. And he tells you he wrote a story about a soldier who was badly wounded, the only survivor in his tank, and his girlfriend comes to see him in the hospital. But he dies. And she never makes peace with it all. And cracks.

And then he says, "It's the other way around. My girlfriend died in a car crash, and I don't know what to do."

Big Man!

And the mother, who is all War Mothers, standing over her son (the one with the head wound, the paralyzed one), trying to feed him.

Here.

Here are some flowers for your son.

See, Shimon, she says, they brought you flowers (who? oh just some friends from America). See, Shimon, say thank you.

Is there anything we can do?

Pray.

Tears.

Hers, I think.

Big Man. A dime's worth of flowers!

I decided then not to do any of these Mitzvahs alone. I wanted others, preferably three or four others, standing with me, because I am not so sure I can stretch myself that far—even for the Chevrah.

By Sunday I had called my friends and flipped through the note cards of Recommended Tzaddikim, adding here and there a few names my people in Jerusalem had suggested. Spontaneously (I would try spontaneity again, see how far it would go), I picked Mrs. Eva Michaelis. My mother had given me her name, knowing she was *edel*—refined, devoted, kindly; a decades-long crusader for people with developmental disabilities. It was my mother's nature to seek out people like her; she told me how to find her, and I called. I simply *had to* reach her.

Mrs. Michaelis's most recent project is Magen, making a home for developmentally disabled adults whose parents are too old and ill to take care of their children.

I was absorbed by everything she said. I began to like our one-way conversation: "Speak to me, Mrs. Michaelis. Say anything."

And so she continued . . . her struggles with the government and Welfare Department to get proper funds for Magen . . . then passing to some miracles, her having saved children from the Nazis at the outbreak of the War . . . she met Eichmann. (You mean Eichmann's henchmen? No, Eichmann.) Then she stepped out and returned with coffee and cookies.

"I cannot give to your building fund," I explained. "My Chevrah wants more direct, more immediate results, and the funds to be under your personal control." We gave her 250 pounds for anything she liked, like cab fare for Irene Gaster, seventy-seven, who is a little shaky on her legs.

Ms. Gaster: founder of almost everything in Israel having to do with people who are developmentally disabled, denouncer of psychiatrists who are too quick to label, thereby condemning someone to retardation, anathema-hurler at agencies and institutions-gone-bad. Lover of Children Class-A. When she was sent a child who could not learn to feed him/herself, more likely than not she taught the child how to do it. If the child was a bed-wetter at age ten (and therefore disturbed), she stopped the bed-wetting (said with absolute humility and a tinge of modest pride). And, she said, *I never took a penny from anyone*. And, *this is all I own* (hand sweeps the air around the apartment on Ramban Street). And, *when I first arrived, Miss (Henrietta) Szold said I would never get anywhere—now we have this Magen* (take some more tea) *project*.

I reckoned I was doing well. In the course of less than one Jerusalem-week I had discovered three of the thirty-six Righteous People, rubbed my hands in theirs, felt warmth and hope and the mysterious glory of what it is to be a Creature of God. If I could just find two or three more, I would fulfill my mission.

By now I had seen with my own eyes that there are two kinds of these all-the-time Holy People: the quiet, soft-spoken, unannounced Tzaddik, and the other—overpowering, energetic-to-exhaustion, piling adrenaline on adrenaline, not shying away from the Obstreperous of the Earth, fighting and shouting when necessary to actualize their vision, convinced and justified in their Rightness, because it was for the sake of others. They are formidable, and for the unprepared, more difficult to be with, these Tzaddikim, because they are so right. You wonder how you ever thought of the million million wrong ways to do this thing, Living. And *they* know they are converting you to menschlichkeit, and that you might not be able to keep up their pace. But they also know you will make something of the encounter, and that is enough for them. They are reliable, trusted individuals, and you become willing and inspired to give them anything they want, even if they won't tell you what they will do with your gift. Their wisdom and understanding of what is happening in the hearts of human beings is sufficient. And since they have revealed themselves to you entirely and unabashedly, there is, thank God, never any room for doubt.

Back to the stories. I will skip around, including and selecting and excluding, since there are too many, and not every one involves a Tzaddik. I planted trees, eight of them, for births and deaths and friends, and for my eighty-two-year-old *Zeyde* Shmuel, who last planted one for his eightieth birthday, when I prayed I would do the same on my eightieth. There was also a *bris* my friend Mickey said would be nice, but there would only be cookies and juice and soda and some wine, though a bottle or two of schnapps would go really well. So 50 Israeli pounds became some fancy-schmancy schnapps, though I don't know whose *bris* it was, and the parents certainly never heard of the family in Oklahoma.

I also Tzedakah-alchemized one hundred pounds into gasoline. Boris is my only friend in Jerusalem who has a car. I said, "Here's one hundred pounds for benzene — put yourself at Bracha Kapach's disposal till the gelt runs out." Rebbetzin Kapach (or as the Yemenites and non-Ashkenazi Jews would say, *HaRabbanit*) is the Ultimate Yemenite, the woman I was looking for but didn't know she was until I watched her walk around Jerusalem doing her acts of gentle-loving-kindness. Four of the Chevrah had asked me to find someone to whom they could send clothes, so this was a priority. The Rabbanit gives clothes, Shabbas food, love, weddings, a jar of hot sauce and Yemenite bread, books, whatever is needed, all over Jerusalem and into the boondocks on the Hillsides of Judea . . . She is the most extensive farstretching private Mitzvah-Matchmaker I would meet, coordinating the Givers and the Receivers with enthusiasm and uplift as I had never seen before. Mickey and I went Shabbas-flowering with her, into the homes of large-families-in-two-rooms that are around, if you look for them. On the way back to her house she saw some children she knew who should have been in school. *Why not?* she asked. *No gym shoes*, the two girls said. I don't know if they needed gym shoes for gym class or whether it was teenage fashionable to wear the casual style and, therefore, embarrassing to come to school in some other shoe. Either way, the 25 newly arrived dollars were searing the seams of my pockets, and I understand that within two days, as if by magic, they were transformed into sneakers for the girls.

Through another lead I entered the bowels of Israeli bureaucracy (just once, to see what it was like): the Department of Welfare. An assistant director understood the Chevrah and me immediately. With 350 pounds from the fund now in hand, he assured me that it would be used individually, directly, and personally for anything that might come to him that would not be taken care of by the Red Tape Machine.

A widow needed a loan. Okay. The money will be recycled when she has finished with it.

Sara Pearl, Mother of the Soldiers all over Galilee. I couldn't get to Safed, but I called and told her husband the Chevrah believes in her. The check is for whatever she wants.

Hadassah Levi's daycare center for young people with Down syndrome in Ramat Gan. Swings for them. Let me call her the Most Loving Person in the World. Take my word for it.

Ya'akov Maimon, inventor of Hebrew shorthand, recorder for the Government, seventy-two-and-a-half, short, dressed like out of a movie, rumpled hat, thick glasses, shlepping me up and down and up and down steps visiting families (Iranian, Algerian, Moroccan) to whom he brings tutors in English for the children. For over twenty years he has been doing this, bringing truckloads of student volunteers from Hebrew University and others from around town, dropping them off, picking them up, remembering each name, and making sure each one is working well, becoming a part of the family. I would have wished him *"ad me'ah v'esrim*—may you continue your work til you are 120—" but it seemed a shade insulting. He will no doubt do this much longer, with the same vigor and grandheartedness.

Mickey's cousin, Rabbi Mordechai Gimpel HaKohen Wolk, scion of great rabbinic houses, devoted to children, particularly of large families, placing them in good yeshivas, throwing weddings and simchas, and worrying for their welfare. He is the full embodiment of the Life of Torah. Listening to his talks, his quotes, following his hands, you understand a hint of Hillel.

The list is longer. This is not a lyrical exposition or high falootin' dissertation. If you want more, you'll ask, or you'll go.

Getting Your Jollies and Shaking Your Kishkas

Everyone should be a shaliach-messenger sometime. Even if you will be in Israel only a week. Even if you won't be in Israel for a while but want to do it in Minneapolis, L.A., or Aberdeen, South Dakota. The moral insight and imaginative investment will be proportional in at least a 100:1 ratio to the quantum of money put in the pot. By giving your own money, you treat yourself to the feeling that you are not as tight-fisted as you thought you were, Recession or no Recession. You will become more aware of the privilege of Mitzvah-doing and of allowing others to join you. As the Talmud informs us: those who encourage others are even greater than those who do the Mitzvah themselves

So you will say: *Well I'm not all that good. I'm only part time, and Wolk and Kapach and Maimon and Levi and Gaster and Michaelis are too much . . . I'm not those people.* Which is exactly right, and exactly the point. Part time is good enough.

You can play disguises: In one place, you can assume such-and-such a name, and in another (wearing a different hat, sunglasses, and shirt), you can be someone else, from Norman, Oklahoma, instead of Chicago. It is a Purim-play of the highest order. Your latent bravado, naïveté, and flair for romance can come out to your heart's desire; you can swagger and swashbuckle your way into a Grand Old Time of It for the Sake of Heaven. It is a real *zetz* in your soul, a kick in your spiritual life. You're entitled to feel good about it.

And you may never consider despair again.

The next step is to do BigGelt projects. To raise $1,000,000 to be put at your disposal, all you have to do is convince two hundred people to throw a $5K-not-$10K wedding for their kids, or four hundred people to throw a $2,500-not-a-five-grand whopper of a bar/bat mitzvah. With the remaining money, you take the whole family, husbands and wives, sons and daughters, grandpas and grandmas, and all their dear ones to Israel for a Tzedakah-junket.

Next: find yourself a local millionaire and surprise him with a $10 proposal. Tell him you are not a foundation, institution, or home for anything, but on the contrary, you think you can get a lot of Mitzvah-mileage out of $10. If you get $1,000, don't panic. Just check your Matchmaking files and start asking more friends about more people.

Heavy Conclusions

Too few people consider that a hat, a hand gripped firmly on someone's arm, or a cheap $3 prayerbook can give a sense of startling and sublime joy to another person.

For nine trips, I loved wandering the streets and alleys of Jerusalem. I used to watch the sun throw different shadows and light-cartoons on the buildings and street corners and trees.

On the tenth visit, though, I believe I saw an entirely different city . . . a city shimmering with an extraordinary glow of Holiness I would have missed without the Chevrah's help.

When we at long last re-curriculum our Sunday schools and Hebrew schools and day schools, we must include—aside from courses on risk, joy, fear, loss, uncertainty, failure, BigThink, and death—lectures and labs on menschlichkeit and Tzedakah. By the very fact of having reached bar or bat mitzvah, a Jewish child becomes obligated to fulfill the Mitzvah of Tzedakah. Why should we spiritually orphan our children, sending them insensitive as the cattle of Nineveh into the world, only to have them discover at age twenty-five or thirty-three or forty-one that they have missed out for years on this most unique privilege? Let them begin with their 10–20 percent from the earliest age, and let us teach them the ins-and-outs of finding the Righteous Ones and the creativity of giving. Menschlichkeit should be a word in every Jewish child's vocabulary.

According to the Torah, each of us is required to write our own Torah. By doing these acts, by being a shaliach-messenger or Mitzvah-doer or just plain old part-time giver, by the conscientious and energy-charged consideration of the swirl of people around us, and by retelling the signs and wonders of the people we meet along the way, we can do just that.

Proposed Course Titles (1987)

Over the years, sometimes slowly, at other times in a rush of thoughts, it occurred to me that there were many subjects that relate Judaism and Jewish texts to life and living a Jewish life.

I offer here some suggestions for teachers, principals, and rabbis to develop the necessary teachable course materials to bring these subjects to the awareness of our students:

Needed for the Jewish community, urgently: Prepare and disseminate reams of curriculum material, based on Talmudic and other sources, that will deal with *gutsy* Jewish values and human behavior. If necessary, set up a research institute called the National Jewish Institute for the Research of Gutsy Jewish Values in Talmudic and Post-Talmudic Literature for the Teaching and Enjoyment of Adults. Some of the courses might include:

A. Laughter

B. Dreamers

C. The Changeability of People

D. Infinities and Eternals

E. Loneliness, Intimacy, and Suicide

F. Life's Meaning

G. Fear, Breakdown, and Crisis

H. Integrity and Prostitution

I. Craving and Envy

J. Cynicism and Paganism (*Avodah Zara*)

K. Failure and Self-Image

L. Money

M. Sensitization and Desensitization: For doctors, lawyers, social workers, and other professionals; and, separately, for nonprofessionals

N. Limits

O. Tears and Sadness

P. "Defects" and "Blemishes"

Q. Anger

R. Hope and Despair

S. Dignity and Humiliation

T. Arrogance

U. Choosing

V. Will-and Ethical Will-Writing

W. Commitment

X. Life and Death, Killing and Saving

Y. Lyricism in Day-to-Day Living

Z. Righteousness and Self-Righteousness

Alef: Psychiatry and Torah

Beit: Profession vs. Family

Gimel: Bitterness

Dalet: Joy

Heh: The Body

Vav: Hellos and Good-Byes

Zayin: Evanescence

Chet: Making a Living, and Living (Winston Churchill said it best: "We make a living by what we get, but we make a life by what we give.")

Tet: Stealing, Theft, and Robbery

Yud: Repetition and Boredom

Yud-Alef: Gutsy Mitzvahs

Yud-Beit: Easy Mitzvahs

Yud-Gimel: Passion

Yud-Dalet: Passionate Torah

Tet-Vav: Swans and Cheetahs: A Day at the Zoo

Tet-Zayin: Kindness

Yud-Zayin: Origins and Beginnings

Yud-Chet: Endings

Yud-Tet: Simple People

Kaf: Aphorisms, Maxims, Truths, and Half-Truths

Kaf-Alef: Making a Difference

Forty-eight courses. That's for starters.

Why People Who Are Blind Should Own Their Own Cars or, How to Think Mitzvahs (1995)

I. Cars for Blind People

First, we must begin with microwave ovens for blind people. Blind people might benefit from having microwave ovens because:

1. They are safer.
2. They go "bing" when the cooking, baking, defrosting, or reheating is finished and the popcorn or soup or casserole or baked apple is ready.
3. Everyone else has microwave ovens.
4. Many new microwavable foods are coming out which allow for a wider range of nutritional benefits.
5. *Everyone* has microwave ovens.
6. It is easy to put Braille on the keyboard.
7. If you have a microwave oven, you don't have to plan meals so far ahead of time, and why should blind people—just because they cannot see—have to plan their meals differently than people who can see?
8. There are probably fifteen other good reasons why, which anyone can figure out if he or she just sits down and thinks about it, or sits down with a friend and talks about it.

Problem Solved: by John Fling, Mitzvah hero, Columbia, South Carolina, who makes sure his many blind friends have microwave ovens. Who would have thought of it? All of us.

Now, to the cars. Here are some reasons why blind people might want to own cars:

1. Everyone else has one.
2. They might need to go somewhere, and a friend or neighbor who usually drives them to that somewhere might have his or her own car tied up at that moment.
3. In case of emergency, there *has to be* an available car. It is life-saving, an issue of *Pikuach Nefesh*.
4. The car owner, who happens to be blind, can lend the car out to someone else who needs it, just like everyone else does in similar situations. The right to lend is a matter of *kavod*, human dignity. The only difference is that one car owner can see and the other cannot.
5. Once, when I was giving a talk, one of the audience members mentioned that this is a matter of personal property protection: when someone goes away on a week's vacation, he or she cancels the newspaper or asks the neighbors to take it off the lawn so a potential burglar won't come by. If some disreputable persons cruise the neighborhood looking for a likely break-in candidate, if they see a car in the driveway of every house except the one where the blind person lives, the blind person is much more likely to become a victim.
6. The best one of all—from a teenager: *Everyone has to have a place to make out.*

Problem Solved: again by John Fling, Mitzvah hero, Columbia, South Carolina.[1] He bought a car for his blind friend, Emily McKinsey (she could not afford one for herself), so she could do errands, go to the store, the movies, a picnic, anywhere she needed to go, without having to ask the neighbors to drive her around in *their* cars. It so happens he got there first, but who would have ever thought of it? *Any one of us.*

2. Introduction, i.e., Conclusion

The answer to the question, "Who would have thought of it?" is not, "Mr. Mitzvah Hero X or Ms. Mitzvah Hero Y." That is too easy an answer. The correct answer is always, "*I* would have thought of it." *All* of us would have thought of these things, these grand Mitzvah schemes, these solutions to problems, had we only spent some time using our minds, imaginations, and talents thinking about them. And once we *think* of these new ways to do some Tikkun Olam, the next step—the critical one—is to *do* it, to make these imaginative breakthroughs happen in real life.

3. Body Casts and Heart Attacks

The Problem:

1. Someone, somewhere, sometime, somehow has an accident, falls, and breaks a bone in his or her back. It happens.
2. Prescribed therapy: a body cast.
3. Let's say the patient also has a bad heart.
4. And let's say that three weeks later the person has a heart attack.
5. And let's say that the average time needed to remove a body cast so that the emergency medical team can begin pounding the heart back to life or shooting epinephrine right into the heart muscle or using a defibrillator to give it the life-saving charge is 4 minutes and 29 seconds.
6. The result of the brain being deprived of oxygen for 4 minutes and 29 seconds: potential brain damage.

This doesn't have to happen. People with brain damage and deceased human beings should be much fewer in number than the way things are. Too high a percentage of people become brain damaged or die for the wrong reason, like being wrapped in the wrong body cast.

Problem Solved: by Dr. Jesse Lipnick, Rosemont, Pennsylvania, Resident in Rehabilitative Medicine. He designed exactly what the patients needed: a body cast that allows the emergency team to get to a troubled heard in 15 seconds.[2] Who would have thought of it? *Any one of us.* One would allow a certain kind of expertise on the details, but the broad strokes, the general picture—all of us could have figured this one out. In retrospect, it's so obvious.

4. The Mitzvah Menagerie

(Once you start on this one, there's no end.)

The Problem: Finding ways to have animals make the lives of human beings happier, healthier, and more fun, plus a few other ways to do some Tikkun Olam with our furry, feathery, and finny friends.

Bunches of Solutions:

1. Getting animals into residences for elderly people, either as part of a visiting or resident pet program. It is happening already in many old age homes.

The best of the best: An old age home in New Berlin, New York, that has more than one hundred birds, two dogs, four cats, two rabbits, one rooster, many hens, plus hundreds of plants to take care of, plus an abundance of visiting kids of all ages, plus a summer camp for kids *on the grounds of the home.* This is where Dr. William Thomas established his first Eden Alternative program, an experiment in Menschlich living for elders in old age homes. *Of ultimate significance — and to be remembered when everything else in this article is forgotten: in under 2½ years, this home cut the quantity and cost of medications in half.* Any statistician or social scientist who wants to do a rigorous study of the relationship of pets, plants, children, etc. to a reduction of medication in old age homes is invited to start with the concept of the Eden Alternative. Contact Dr. Thomas and ask him how he did it.[3]

2. Getting animals into hospitals —
    A. Visiting pets: animals in hospitals who, by their very presence, provide comfort and calm to patients who may need them terribly (Cindy Niemetz at Huntington Memorial Hospital in Pasadena, California).
    B. A Pet Room, i.e., having a special room set aside so family members and friends can bring in *the patient's own pet* (e.g., Beverly Hospital on Boston's North Shore).

3. Getting birds to lonely people (e.g., Carol Hutton, referred to by some people as the Bird Woman of Indianapolis).[4]
4. Getting videos of animal shows (*National Geographic*, PBS specials, commercial movies on video) to lonely individuals who love animals but (a) aren't well enough to care for them, or (b) are allergic to them. Bring popcorn, friends, the video, and make an afternoon or evening of it.
5. Training animals to assist individuals with disabilities —
   A. Dogs (e.g., Canine Companions for Independence).[5]
   B. Monkeys (Helping Hands, Dr. M. J. Willard).[6]
   C. Horses (in Israel: the Israel National Therapeutic Riding Association [INTRA]; in the United States and Canada, PATH International [Professional Association of Therapeutic Horsemanship International]).
6. Giraffes, i.e., finding Good People doing good things in this world, and who take risks while doing these good things for the benefit of others, designating them as Giraffes for sticking their necks out, and publicizing their work (the Giraffe Heroes Project).
7. Saving injured birds of prey (e.g., the Birds of Prey Foundation, Broomfield, Colorado, founded by Sigrid Ueblacker).
8. Saving all kinds of endangered species (call any animal shelter, any veterinarian, any wildlife foundation).

Solved By: many people whose lives and work we might want to study: Lis Hartel (Denmark, twice an Olympic Silver Medalist), founder of modern therapeutic horseback riding worldwide; Anita Shkedi, founder of the Israel National Therapeutic Riding Association, and all therapeutic horseback riding in Israel; Dr. Bonnie Bergin, founder of Canine Companions for Independence; Ann Medlock, founder of the Giraffe Heroes Project; and a few of the others listed above. But we must remember, these programs had to start somewhere, sometime, had to get their first push into reality by Someone.

Now, who would have thought of these things? *Any one of us.*

5. Wheelchairs on the Beach

The Problem: Getting on to the beach—all the way to the water's edge—in a wheelchair.

The Solution: Make a wheelchair with giant, balloon-sized wheels that roll easily on sand. And eventually refine the design with easy-to-change wheels for a regular wheelchair, and refine it another way so that if people in wheelchairs don't want to be pushed by someone else, they can manage the oversized wheels by themselves.)

Solved By: Someone already. I have a picture of such a balloon-wheel wheelchair, a sun-flooded picture from one of the beaches on the Maryland shore.[7] Whoever did it simply got there before we did. But—

Who in his or her wildest imagination would have thought of it? Allowing for some expertise here, *any one of us.*

6. Leftover Food from School Lunches

The Problem:

1. The kid comes to school with a sandwich, a bag of pretzels, another bag with carrots and celery and other healthy munchies, and a big orange.
2. The kid snarfs down the sandwich, goes for the carrots and celery and orange, but decides not to eat the pretzels.
3. The kid throws out the bag of pretzels.

The Solution:

1. A collection box in the cafeteria.
2. One person takes the leftovers at the end of the school day to a local shelter or soup kitchen.

The Results:

1. Less food is wasted.
2. Many hungry people are less hungry or not hungry at all.
3. Money used by shelters and soup kitchens for food can be used for other things like job training, social workers working

to find new living arrangements, computer equipment for retraining residents, cars to transport people who need to get to their new jobs.

Problem Solved: In a Jewish day school—by four fifth-graders at a Solomon Schechter Day School in Baltimore.[8]

In the public schools—by David Levitt, a sixth-grader from Pinellas County, Florida. From an article I read, it appears that it took fewer than six weeks from the time David wrote to the Superintendent of Schools to change the school policy.[9] When I saw him again a few years later at the University of Florida, where he was studying, *the school system had already donated more than one million pounds of food!* All this happened because of David's bar mitzvah Mitzvah project.

In the Baltimore Orioles ballpark—Steve Chaikin, a Jewish law student in Baltimore, approached the Orioles as they were opening their new ballpark at Camden Yards. He asked if it was okay if he and friends came by at the end of the games to pick up and donate any leftover food. The Orioles agreed, and an average of *one thousand pounds of food was donated after each game!*

Who in his or her right mind would have thought of it? They did. But *any one of us* could have.

Everyone is talking and writing about right brain/left brain performance. Perhaps it is time to talk about and write about the Right Mind and the Other Mind. The Other Mind is the one that deals with our everyday, familiar goings-on. The Right Mind is the Mitzvah Mind.

Follow Up: Once you get started with leftovers, the possibilities are everywhere . . . bakeries and grocery stores; the White House,[10] Congress, Supreme Court, State Department, Treasury Department, and Pentagon dining facilities; the governor's and the mayor's offices; the city council dining room; stadiums and arenas; pizza parlors, greasy spoons, and burger joints; university cafeterias and kosher eating clubs;[11] hotels, motels, and resorts (we could get in an extra Mitzvah while we are on vacation); catering halls; airlines, Amtrak, and charter boat companies; art museum and symphony hall and corporate headquarters cafeterias; overnight camps, day camps (Camp Ramah in California does it, despite the erroneous claims that the health code states that you can't donate food from camps), retreat and conference centers, and anywhere else there might be food and a likelihood of leftovers.

7. Interlude: Some Historical Perspective

1. *Someone* had to be the first person to "invent" fire for heating and cooking. Now all of us take fire for granted.

2. *Someone* had to be the first person to invent a wheel. Now we take wheels for granted. How could we live without wheels?

3. Along the way, Louis Braille (1809–52) took a previously known system of raised dots, adapted it, and developed a method that enabled blind people to read. Now we take Braille, and sign language, for granted.

4. Somewhere along the way someone figured that dogs could be trained to lead blind people. No one is surprised when a guide dog walks by with his/her blind owner.

5. Microchips. It's the same story as fire, the wheel, Braille, and the guide dog.

6. Dr. Ignaz Semmelweis (1818–65) solved a serious problem in Vienna in the late 1840s.[12] Childbed fever was killing mothers at a frightening rate in the hospital where he worked—a much higher rate than in the countryside. Indeed, it was happening everywhere. The joy of giving birth was being destroyed by the tragedy of the mother's death, again and again and yet again. Noticing that the students and doctors were going directly from working with bodies in anatomy classes and the morgue to doing their gynecological and obstetric work, Semmelweis urged the doctors to wash their hands. The number of deaths from childbed fever went down dramatically. Some members of the hospital staff listened to him, and some didn't. As occasionally or often

happens with scientific breakthroughs, Semmelweis spent years fighting to prove his theory. *To wash their hands!* What doctors in their right mind nowadays, wanting to keep their license, would ever begin any medical procedure or examination without washing their hands? Such a simple thing.

8. The Little Shampoos

The Problem:

1. In any given town of 50,000 people or more, lying around the house are at least 47,983 little shampoo bottles, hair conditioner bottles, soaps, sewing kits, shoeshine rags, shower caps, hand lotion bottles, and other tiny useful items people pick up at hotels.
2. They are just sitting there in the closet or medicine chest or in a cute little display on the bathroom sink.

The Solution:

1. Gather all these items.
2. Distribute them to individuals on limited income through food banks, shelters, and soup kitchens.
3. Save them thousands of dollars, which can be used for all kinds of other, more important things. (See 6: The results, 3 above.)

Solved By: Elana Erdstein[13] (now Rabbi Elana Erdstein Perry) but— Who would have thought of it? *Any one of us.*

9. Mitzvah Clowning

The Problem: Unhappy kids, sad kids, kids whose hair has fallen out because of cancer therapy; unhappy adults, sad adults, adults whose hair has fallen out because of cancer therapy; all kinds of other sad and unhappy people in hospitals and institutions.

The Solution: Learn clowning, dress up as a clown, and go into the hospitals and institutions and make people happy.

Solved By:
1. Many, many clowns, including Debbie Friedmann in the Washington area.
2. Mike and Sue Turk, aka Sweet Pea and Buttercup.[14] They teach clowning in the religious school. Their graduates go into hospitals and institutions to make people happy.

Follow Up:
1. Make a study of accelerated recovery rates.
2. Calculate the millions of dollars saved because of earlier discharge from the hospital, medications no longer needed, and all other related costs.

10. The Elbow Brace

The Problem: Someone with cerebral palsy has a problem with an arm. It tends to lock up against the body, interfering with this individual's daily activities and overall welfare. And it is certainly detrimental to this human being's sense of *kavod* (dignity).

The Solution:
1. Get an engineer or work groups of engineers together to talk to this person. Take the human needs into account and work collectively on the mechanical problem.
2. Figure it out, do it right, and do it inexpensively.
3. Let the person with cerebral palsy live an easier, more pleasant, and more dignified life.
4. Just out of curiosity, submit the project for bids to commercial firms that develop and manufacture these devices for profit.
5. Publicize the results to make a good point.

Solved By: A Case Western Reserve University's School of Engineering graduate who belongs to the Case Engineering Support Group, founded by one Professor Jack Daly.[15] The group's purpose is to solve problems exactly like the elbow brace — or, in our terms, to do some Tikkun Olam, World Fixing.

1. The elbow brace designed by the Case group member cost $16.20. The commercial firm put in a bid for $8,000 to design and produce a similar device.

Now, who would have thought of it? *Anyone* with a good eye for mechanics, some training in engineering, a fine and fine-tuned human heart, and a little time, insight, will, good will, and willpower to make it happen.

Addendum: "Handy technology" (or "universal design") is a rapidly growing line of products. Some bathroom scales have large numbers for visually impaired people. Some bathtubs are installed with a door in the side, so the person with limited mobility doesn't have to climb over the side to get in. There are also pill bottles with caps that record the time the medication was taken.[16] Surely, we could ask, "Who would have thought of these things?" Obviously, many people are thinking of these things, and it would be good to meet some of them and learn from them.

12. Interlude #2: The Optometry of Mitzvahs

1. We should train ourselves to look at any given object and think, "Aha! This is how it can be used for Mitzvahs." They may be real or imagined objects, including strange-looking things that just pop into our heads. They may be big or small, ugly or beautiful, normal or weird: airplanes, candy bars, erasers, trees, parking lots, inner tubes, tubes of toothpaste, the human face, old tires, bread crumbs, movie houses, gum wrappers, Karate uniforms in the closet, spatulas, balls of string, rubber bands lying around in a drawer, toothpicks and umbrellas, to name a few, each one with Mitzvah potential. Dollar bills, $50 bills, pennies and quarters are also, of course, among those objects.
2. We should exercise our Mitzvah imaginations by juxtaposing any given object with any person or any situation and seeing what this proximity might yield in the way of new Mitzvahs. A particularly colorful example would be Mitzvah Manicures, i.e.,

getting manicurists to donate their time and come to the syna-
gogue, with all the event proceeds donated to Tzedakah (Ethel
Shull, Tampa, Florida).[17]

3. We should look at any given human situation and think,
   "Is this, can this be, or can it become a Mitzvah situation, an
   opportunity for some act of Tzedakah-Justice?"

4. We should take any moment, beginning with Now, on to One
   Moment From Now, all the way to Way Into The Future, and
   think about the possibilities for Mitzvahs that could happen at
   any of those times.

5. Consider, for example, all the human hours used to solve
   higher theoretical math problems. If we asked twenty-one
   mathematicians to take 9–17% of the time they spend thinking
   math and to transfer it to solving Mitzvah problems, we'd be
   ahead—we, all of us, the human population, the Earth itself,
   Life. Or, think: if we took 3–12% of the time we spend on cross-
   word puzzles, board games, or tinkering with our many toys,
   and used it to apply Mitzvah principles to human situations . . .
   Or think of what we might come up with if we took just 0.639
   of 1% of the time we spent looking at our cellphones and did
   some Mitzvah thinking and planning and acting instead.

6. The end result will be a new and astonishingly impressive
   sum of Mitzvahs, and, without a doubt, a staggering number
   of Mitzvah-breakthroughs: new ways to fix up the world no
   less significantly than when the light bulb was invented, or the
   internal combustion engine, or the telephone.

7. In another context, the *Shulchan Aruch* (*Yoreh De'ah* 249:1) says
   that giving away less than 10 percent of our income to Tzeda-
   kah is considered *ayin ra'ah*, which may be translated as "weak
   eyesight." Using our eyes to consider objects, time, and human
   situations as possibilities for Mitzvah work would help us over-
   come that same visual problem, and would most certainly save
   us many hours of filling out the medical insurance forms when
   we visit the Mitzvah optometrist in our neighborhood.

12. A Bunch of Miscellaneous Items (In No Order of Importance)

Problem #1: Integrating individuals with Down syndrome into the army.

Solved By: Tzahal, the Israeli Army. Many young people, in uniform, work on army bases once a week.[18]
   Who would have . . . ? *Any one of us.*

Problem #2: The enormous amount of paper used in our business uses up too many trees.

The Solution: Plant trees to replace the paper the company uses.

Solved by: Working Assets. They do it figuring a ratio of seventeen trees/ton of paper.[19]
   Who would . . . ? *Any one . . .*

Problem #3: What to do with prom dresses the day after the prom.

The Solution:
   1. Get people to donate them.
   2. Open a second-hand prom dress store for next year's proms, with discounts, and a portion of the profits donated to Tzedakah.
   3. Call it Project Promise or whatever you like, but have a catchy phrase to advertise the project, like "A second chance at the dance."

Solved By: Ellen Barth, high school junior, Howard County, Maryland.[20]
   Who . . . ? *Any . . .*

Problem #4: How to inform the Jewish and general community about what facilities and services are available to individuals with disabilities.

Solution: Hold a Disabilities Faire (they spelled it that way in LA), with displays, booths, programs, and speakers to inform, teach, and publicize the services and facilities.

Solved By: The Commission on Jews with Disabilities of the Council on Jewish Life of the Jewish Federation Council of Greater Los Angeles.[21]
   ...?... *us/we/I/me.*

Problem #5: Unwanted Chanukah presents.

The Solution: Mitzvah Mall or, How to Give Mitzvah Chanukah Presents Instead of Silly or Useless Toys—e.g., Shabbat dinners for people who are unable to leave their homes, inoculations for children in danger of the most common diseases, shares of a cow on a kibbutz, food for guide dogs, etc. The Mitzvah Mall is connected to a group called "the Committee for the Prevention of the Purchase of Tchotchkas."

Solved By: Distinguished educator Sharon Halper.[22]
   ...?... *any ONE...*

Problem #6: The high cost of catering Mitzvah meals.

The Solution: Set up a co-op of families to do the catering themselves.

Solved By: A certain Marilyn Moses and her friends.[23]
   ?!

13. Pre-Conclusion

And now we say, "It's so obvious." The Torah lesson would then be: let us do some cosmically and universally astounding things with our lives that will have students and observers think—"How obvious! Now, why didn't I think of that?"

To which we can reply—

"Who would have thought of it? *Any one of us.*"

And, if someone wanted to, she or he could do some of this professionally:

1. Lawyers could do a nice percentage of free (*pro bono*) work, or

2. Ombudspersons for a variety of institutions or agencies could cut through bureaucracy and snarled-up communications lines, or

3. Columnists for radio, TV, newspapers, or magazines could report on "Action Lines," publicizing complaints such as "Merchant Ploni sold me a faulty blender and wouldn't refund the money when I brought it back to the store." Or worse: "The medical team refuses to allow X, Y, or Z." Or, less seriously, "I went to Melbourne, FL, but my suitcases went to Melbourne, Australia, and the airline says it'll take six days to get them back to me."

4. Employees of Better Business Bureaus or watchdog organizations could keep tabs on everything from crooked government contracts to the honesty of charitable organizations to the fair labeling of food and drugs.

And this is just to mention a few possibilities of how to be a full Tikkun Olamnik. And, of course, you could bring some refreshing creativity to the job, using your Right Mind all the time you are on the job.

14. Conclusion, i.e., Introduction

The answer to the question, "Who would have thought of it?" is not, "Mitzvah Hero X."

That answer is much too costly for all of us.

The correct answer is always, "*I* would have thought of it."

All of us could have thought of these things, these grand Mitzvah schemes, these solutions to problems, if we would only spend some time using our minds, imaginations, and talents thinking about them.

Many pieces of reality are beyond our powers to change, right? So let's:

1. Determine which ones they are.

2. Take on one of those we thought was beyond us, sit with some friends and solve that problem.

3. And after that first one is laid to rest, solved, done, and the solution is out there in reality doing wonders, pick another, and then another.
4. After three of them, take a weekend up in the mountains or down at the shore. Have fun, nothing but fun.
5. Then come back and start all over again, now that we know that the answer to the question,

"Who would have thought of it?," is *Any one of us.*

Holy Balloons (1997)

Aha! At last, after an extensive campaign to make their synagogue more inclusive, the members of Beth El Synagogue Center of New Rochelle, New York, put the finishing touch on their vision of what makes a congregation a *true* community of worshippers.

They had already installed ramps and chair lifts and accessible bathrooms, plus purchased large print and Braille prayer books and Torah texts, as well as a special sound system for hearing-impaired people. But this year, 5757 according to the Jewish calendar, they used their creativity during Rosh Hashanah and Yom Kippur to complete the picture.

At the suggestion of Naomi Brunn, a young woman who has worked with deaf people for a number of years (and who has raised the consciousness of the hearing community about the needs and way of life of Jewish hearing-impaired people), the congregation provided balloons for people who could not hear the sound of the shofar blowing. By gripping the sides of the balloons when the shofar was sounded, and by feeling the vibrations from the sound waves radiating outward from the ram's horn, the hearing-impaired people in the sanctuary could derive even greater meaning from the service.

According to my friend, the superb, sensitive, and creative Jewish educator Jack Gruenberg, who told me this story, the look on many of their faces was so profoundly moving, it was glorious, revelatory.

I would assume that those who witnessed the moment, by which I mean those congregants who had the ability to hear, were also uplifted by the sight, and for a few moments a great holiness permeated the sanctuary. The true meaning of the holidays had been achieved by means of the power of Thinking Mitzvahs and the purchase of a few balloons.

So my old friend Jack told me, and in his telling of the tale his face was radiant.

And Rabbi Charles Kroloff of Temple Emanu-El in Westfield, NJ, told me that in some places, deaf people put their hands on the shofar itself, so they can feel the vibrations.

And when I told the story to my friend, Janis Knight, she pointed out to me that perhaps we should give out balloons to *everyone* in the congregation. Perhaps it will allow *hearing* people to become more *feeling* people.

And the people at Saturn caught on, too. Saturn's sales are based on the principle that, if you really care about the customers, they will buy the car and remain loyal customers long into the future. I'm not certain if they give the customer a box of chocolate chip cookies when they drive off into the sunset, but they do have an annual barbecue, and everyone I've spoken to who owns a Saturn tells me they keep calling to make sure everything is all right and, *is there anything else they can do to make the customer happy?* Some of the owners say Saturn people (as we would say in Yiddish) *hock them a tchynik*, which, roughly translates to, "they are a wee bit too enthusiastic." But they *really* do want to know if their customers are having a satisfactory relationship with their vehicle.

The title of a recent *Saturn* magazine begins with a left quotation mark (") and a right quotation mark ("), and in between are twenty-one letters reproduced in standard finger spelling with no translation. The story goes that a certain Holly Daniel complained to her dealer about the stereo in her '92 Saturn. The ad continues, "Of course, we don't normally get stereo complaints from owners who use sign language." Ms. Daniel explained that it had to do with *the vibrations* from the music. The Saturn people got it, did what they had to do in Ms. Daniel's car to make her happy, and subsequently made significant changes in future models.

Aha! See how much can be accomplished if we just use our minds, imagination, hearts, and souls to make Mitzvahs happen just right!

Which is precisely why the biblical root שמע-Shin-Mem-Ayin so often means more than just "to hear." It really means "to understand."

Songs of Love (1997)

I was in the Magic Kingdom yesterday. Thousands of people — many thousands — were having a good time. The sounds of at least a dozen foreign languages were in the air. Screams of delight could be heard from the kids and adults on the rides. Whirling shapes to the left, strolling people munching on popcorn and hot dogs smothered in mustard, onions, and relish to the right. Every so often there was a show or parade: a marching fife and drum corps, floats, costumes galore. Distinctly Disney colors, straight from the cartoons of my childhood, filled my eyes. I must have seen four Goofys and at least a dozen Minnies and Mickeys in the space of fifteen minutes. Merry, oversized chipmunks were in abundance.

It was December 24th, one of the busiest days of the year. Though the wait for some rides approached two hours, it didn't seem to matter to the tourists. Northerners were enjoying the pure pleasure of being in shorts and short sleeves. Everyone was having fun, great fun.

Some of them were probably having the time of their lives.

Disney's Anaheim and Orlando sites are easily the most popular destinations for kids with cancer. Many of these kids want to meet movie stars or sports heroes, others have very personal requests, but the greatest number want to go to Disney's parks. Looking around, you couldn't tell which of the happy kids were there on a last wish and which were destined to live into their eighties or nineties in full health.

It's a wonderful Mitzvah making kids happy.

It's a Mitzvah in a category beyond words to make dying children happy.

John Beltzer's Mitzvah Project

John Beltzer has an ever-growing group of friends, and friends of friends, and friends who know people, and people he doesn't know who know other people ... all professional songwriters and musicians. They write individualized, personalized songs for children with life-threatening diseases. First they gather information about the children: family facts, hobbies, whether they like to draw or play baseball, the color of their eyes, nicknames, their pets, anything that can go into a song. They write it, orchestrate it, produce it, and send the tape to the child. It is a simple-enough idea and a perfect use of the songwriters' talents.

They call the project Songs of Love.

The following two letters will give you an indication of just how awesome this project is.

Dear John,

Please accept this check as a donation to Songs of Love in memory of our son Sam.

You wrote and sang a song for Sam at Easter time. The song brought him many smiles and he listened to it over and over. Sam passed away May 28 and as there were no words to capture the specialness of Sam, your song was played at his funeral in lieu of a eulogy. We hope this donation helps in some small way so that you can continue to bring joy to other sick children.

Fondly,
Michelle and Barry Johnson

Dear Mr. Beltzer,

On behalf of the staff and patients at . . . Children's Center for Cancer . . . I would like to extend my sincerest thanks to you and everyone at Songs of Love for creating a song for our patient Julie. If it had not been for your dedication, Julie would never have heard her inspirational song.

As you know, Julie and her family were able to hear her song together the day before she died. We are so appreciative that you were able to compose the song and hand deliver it to the hospital in less than 24 hours when you were informed of the urgency of the situation. Julie's song served as a therapeutic tool in her last day of life to help recapture who she was before her illness took over. It is very kind and considerate individuals such as yourself that help make the patients' treatments more endurable. . . .

Gratefully yours,
Betsy Carlson, CCLS,
Child Life Specialist

Each year Songs of Love expands its reach. Such is our intimate world nowadays: an e-mail from Paris about a five-year-old child dying of cancer pops up on John Beltzer's computer screen, a songwriter writes, the musicians record, the song is delivered to the child. How very awesome all this is!

Update

As of 2019, Songs of Love is going stronger than ever. More than a thousand songwriters and musicians have contributed to nearly thirty thousand songs for children around the world who are facing life-threatening diseases.

Wouldn't it be wonderful if *every* child in such a catastrophic situation could have his or her own song?

Three Prongs (2000)

How to fix the world? Over the years of teaching Tikkun Olam, I have come to determine that there are three prongs, which, in combination, work best:

1. Meeting, learning from, and working with Mitzvah heroes.
2. Learning Jewish texts about Tikkun Olam — Fixing the World.
3. Doing it.

#1: The Mitzvah heroes are our teachers. We learn best by watching them at their work, listening to their teaching, and even paying attention to their commonplace conversation. Over twenty years ago, Hadassah Levi gathered more than forty infants with Down syndrome who had been abandoned in the hospitals and raised them to young adulthood. She knows things that nobody else in the world knows. She has much to teach us.

#2: Jewish texts give us a thousands-years-long connection to our roots. We are performing Mitzvahs as our ancestors have done for centuries before us, and as others are doing simultaneously around the world. Jewish texts often give us a different perspective on Fixing the World than those presented by general, secular, or humanitarian society. We need to live in all of these worlds, so they can better interact with each other.

One well-known text (Mishnah, *Sanhedrin*, end of chapter 4) is worthy of remembering throughout our lives. It is a fundamental motivating force for all our attempts to make Tikkun Olam a reality. *Whoever saves a single life — it is as if that person had saved an entire world.*

#3: In the final analysis, we cannot "talk" Tikkun Olam; we have to *do* it. We get a sense of its power and wonders when it brings together all human elements: body, mind, heart, and soul.

All three elements — texts, heroes, and the doing — interact with each other, sometimes more or less intensely. Sometimes one or two of the three are most prominent.

It is like three prongs of a fork, which enable us to enjoy our food, or a pitchfork used for hard labor in the fields. Some have likened this concept to a braid, such as in a challah or a Havdalah candle, interwoven and blending together. The important thing is that *all three elements* are essential.

Occupation: Mitzvahs (2000)

> Living is not a private affair of the individual.
> Living is what man does with God's time,
> what man does with God's world.
> —Rabbi Abraham Joshua Heschel, z"l

Why would anyone take a serious cut in salary, leave a comfortable job, and go into full-time Mitzvah work?

Because they then experience the *Ziv*, the exceptional Radiance of doing Mitzvahs.

Because they become students of Mitzvah heroes, the Great Ones, the Awesome Teachers, day in and day out.

Because they feel good about themselves.

Because they feel positive that the world is getting to be a better, more Menschlich place.

Because they love living simultaneously in the worldly fray of human endeavor and the Upper Worlds of the Sublime and the Ineffable.

And because "living" becomes "Living."

A Jewish text articulates this idea beautifully:

"Open the Gates of Righteousness [Justice, Victory] for me. . . ."
[At the Time of Judgment] in the Future World,
everyone will be asked, "What was your occupation?"
If the person answers, "I used to feed hungry people,"
they will say to that person,

"This is God's gate, you, who fed hungry people, may enter." . . .
"I used to give water to thirsty people,"
they will say to that person, "This is God's gate, you,
who gave water to those who were thirsty, may enter." . . .
"I used to give clothing to those who needed clothing,"
they will say to that person, "This is God's gate, you,
who gave clothing to those who needed clothing, may enter." . . .
and, similarly, those who raised orphans,
and who performed the Mitzvah of Tzedakah,
and who performed acts of caring, loving kindness.
—Psalm 118:19; *Midrash on Psalms*, 118:17

So, no matter how that person earns a living, everyone's personal bio should include entries such as: (1) life-saver; (2) dignity-restorer; (3) everyday-miracle-worker; (4) Mitzvah-magician; (5) hope-giver; (6) dream-weaver; (7) star-gazer; (8) solution-maker; (9) tool-user-for-Mitzvahs; (10) soul-repairer; (11) broken-body-fixer; (12) Mitzvah-power-hungry-person; (13) creator-of-radiance.

Apparently, the *Occupation: Mitzvahs* phenomenon is playing itself out in some rabbinical schools and degree-level departments of Jewish education. First-year classes have many students who are clearly not right out of college. There are some in their thirties and forties and fifties, most on their second careers, a few already on their third. Obviously they did some very serious thinking, looked deeply within themselves, and asked what *really* was important in their lives. They were uncomfortable in their present jobs and began to feel that their True Life's Work lay somewhere else. Then they acted on it.

I call this process *ikkar* and *tafel*. These terms originate in Jewish law's system of *berakhot* (blessings) for various foods. For example: a tuna sandwich. Bread—the staff of life—is the *ikkar*, the predominant element, and the tuna is *tafel*, secondary to the bread. So the blessing to be recited is the one for bread, *ha-Motzi*, and the tuna is "covered."

In a way, these older rabbinical students went through a serious evaluation of the *ikkar* and *tafel,* and concluded that they needed to make a bold move. (A common term in modern Hebrew is *ikkar ha-ikkarim,* i.e., *the absolutely most important thing* under consideration.) The older students found the *ikkar ha-ikkarim* of their own lives.

Where the more personal and human addendum to the biographical "facts" of one's life may lead depends on the individual. It may lead to a change of occupation or possibly a minor, medium, or major re-ordering of priorities in that individual's personal Life of Mitzvahs. In all instances, with the appropriate faith, it will surely be all for the good.

David Copperfield (2000)

> Rabbi Simla'i explained in a public discourse: The Torah begins and ends with acts of caring, loving kindness.
> —*Sotah* 14a

> The meaning of man's life lies in his perfecting the universe. He has to distinguish . . . and redeem the sparks of holiness scattered throughout the darkness of the world.
> —Rabbi Abraham Joshua Heschel, z"l

"For all his accomplishments, David Copperfield insists that his greatest work to date is Project Magic. He developed this rehabilitative program over a decade ago to strengthen dexterity and motor use in disabled patients by using simple sleight-of-hand magic. As Copperfield explains, 'It motivates a patient's therapy and helps to build self-esteem.'"

Project Magic is currently being used in one thousand hospitals in thirty countries around the world, from Belgium to New Zealand, Iceland to Singapore.

What I like most about this is David Copperfield's additional statement on his website, dcopperfield.com, *"There is nothing I do that is more important"* (my italics).

The Copperfield Principle: No matter what we "do" as an occupation, we should remember that there is nothing more important than our Mitzvah work.

I would add that while Copperfield's talents are awesome, we *all* have absolutely unique talents. No one else in the world can do what we can do. So, a corollary to the Copperfield Principle would be: We should use our absolutely unique talents to fix the world the way absolutely nobody else can fix it. In some situations, this involves our professions, but it can also include our avocations, and even our ostensibly peripheral interests. As a consequence, we should pursue training in all areas that will expand our capabilities and horizons and allow us to use our talents and skills even more for Tikkun Olam.

The Starfish (2000)

Someone strolling along the beach sees hundreds of starfish that have been washed ashore. A young girl picks one up and throws it back in the water. The adult says to the child, "Why are you doing this? There are hundreds of starfish on the beach. What difference does this make?" As the girl throws another starfish into the water, she replies, "It makes a difference to *that* one!"

Many of us have read or heard this popular and simple story or seen it on the Internet. Sometimes, it is just an undefined "someone" strolling and "someone" else putting the starfish back in the water. Other versions say it is an adult and a child. Still other versions have an interesting twist—a teacher asks the child, "What difference does it make?"

A story from Jewish tradition expresses the very same idea. When Moses was a shepherd, one young lamb ran away. Finding the sheep sipping from an oasis some distance away, Moses gently carried it back on his shoulders and returned it to the flock. In response, God told Moses he had earned the right to be the shepherd of Israel (*Exodus Rabbah* 2:2).

What can we learn from stories like these? By definition, since every human being is made in God's Image, everyone, every one, every single human being is valuable. "Usefulness to society" is not a valid criterion. There is a certain arrogance to those who maintain that the mover-and-shaker, the orchestra conductor, or the research geneticist is of greater importance than the cashier at TJ Maxx, the UPS person, or the synagogue custodian. God chose Moses because Moses cared about every single individual in the flock.

In the world of Jewish tradition, *no one* gets left out.

By extension and possible analogy, a curious section of Jewish law hints at this. The background: for certain prayers to be recited, a minimum of ten adults must be present. This quorum is called a *minyan*. In the Shulchan Arukh (Code of Jewish Law), section *Orach Chayyim*, 55:6, it states: "*If one of them is asleep, even so, that person is counted.*"

Some commentators disagree, but the plain text says that, even asleep, the person is part of the *minyan*.

I have discussed this ruling with several people over the past few months, and their interpretations vary:

There are many people in society who are, as it were, "asleep," unaware or unresponsive to their own situation. They are most certainly part of our community.

Perhaps the sound of the prayers themselves will awaken the person. Stories are legion about people in comas waking up from the most likely to the least likely stimuli . . . a piece of music, petting a dog, a familiar smell, a touch or stroke on the arm. It is all very mysterious, and while not everyone is capable of "waking up," certainly many more do than we might initially assume.

Medical personnel in operating rooms are ever-more-aware of how much an anesthetized person can hear and remember. While the person may not visually or aurally respond, clearly the person is definitely absorbing the words.

To summarize: (1) Everyone who is alive is part of the community, and (2) We can never know how little or how much or what in particular will "wake someone up."

A story: My mother, my teacher, *zichronah livracha* (may her memory be for a blessing), was in the hospital for about a month. Though she was unresponsive, I remember many occasions when her cardiologist, Dr. Warren Levy—May he live a long, happy, and full life!—came in, and before examining her, would whisper into her ear, "Now, Edythe, I am going to check..." even when he only had to lift her eyelid to check her eyes. It was so gentle, so very, very moving. It was the perfect human touch.

The Butterfly (2000)

> Please make sure my red bear gets a good home.
> —Lisa, a Jewish communal worker, donating
> one of her favorite stuffed animals during her
> agency's campaign to provide for others.

When a butterfly flutters its wings in China, it can cause a storm in Los Angeles. That's what the ninth-grade science teachers used to teach us about the physical world.

The same is true with Mitzvahs: any Mitzvah, no matter how ostensibly small, changes the entire world. We learn from God's gorgeous ever-so-fragile creature: *There is no such thing as a small Mitzvah.*

Now add some of your own examples to the following list:

1. Paul Newman gives away to Tzedakah all of the after-tax profits from the sales of his food products. As of 2018 Newman's Own products have generated more than half a billion dollars for Tzedakah. Still, from the first dollar he donated, the whole world was changed for the better.

2. For his bar mitzvah, a young man collected seventy-five used, out-of-service cellphones people had lying around the house because the owners had changed carriers or upgraded. Victims and potential victims of domestic violence could still use them to dial 911 free of charge. The first one alone changed the world.

3. Ray Buchanan, founder of Stop Hunger Now, had hoped to provide $500,000 of international relief in his organization's first year of operation. As it happened, he provided $7,500,000 worth of relief. One of our favorite aspects of his work is funding the purchase of anti-worm medicine that prevents malnutrition and possibly death for adults and children in Central America. To quote from Ray's e-mail, "The $1,500 from you translates into thirty thousand doses of life-saving worm medicine with a fair market value of $75,000!" That comes out to 5¢/dose. One nickel is only one step removed from the least valuable coin in America! Is 5¢, then, a small Mitzvah? To the contrary, I think the Mitzvah-energy of this 5¢ carries to the very ends of the universe.

4. One of Linda Tarry's Project People Foundation's many programs is the manufacture of black dolls. Beginning with unemployed women in South Africa (where these innocent objects were outlawed under Apartheid), and now including an employment program in rural Georgia, it affords the workers an opportunity to make a living. And . . . the dolls are distributed in many other parts of the world where they make black children happy, including Ethiopian children in Israel. Project People's workers have made thousands of them. *Every single doll* in the hands of a child offers profound warmth and comfort. A doll, such a small thing? To use a phrase from my Southern upbringing, "Not hardly!"

5. When preschoolers paint primitive designs on simple pads that they bring as placemats for Elders at a nursing home, is that such a small Mitzvah?

6. A letter I received in 1992:

I am sorry I can not donate any money. My husband has been laid off since Sept. and I can not give—Your work is very important. I am sorry. H.S.

This letter is so filled with passion! While I do not agree that the author needed to apologize, nevertheless, her words moved me then, and have guided me ever since in my own Tzedakah work.

If we keep in mind the Butterfly Principle, we will avoid a number of pitfalls:

1. There is no reason to feel guilty or have a sense of inadequacy about our own Mitzvah work. All too often when people meet Mitzvah heroes or hear stories about their Mitzvah work, they feel guilty that they have not done enough. This is not about guilt. *Every act of Tikkun Olam makes a difference. We* do whatever *we* are capable of doing.

2. Tikkun Olam is not about charisma, as it is commonly misunderstood. None of the Mitzvah heroes have any magical powers or are in some way different than we are. They are just "regular people." Indeed, one of the basic meanings of the Greek word "charisma" is "a gracious gift [of the gods]." Jewishly speaking, everyone has the Divine Gift. We express our gratitude by doing acts of Tikkun Olam, and every act changes the entire world for the better.

There is no such thing as a small Mitzvah.

Wow!→Duh! (2000)

When I describe grand Tikkun Olam to others, I often hear half-words and an assortment of exclamations: Wow! (the most common sound), Ah!, Oh!, Oh my!, Oy!, Ugh!, Feh! (a Yiddish word expressing extreme disgust), or sometimes a simple gasp. The Wow!→Duh! principle simply states: *Through the power of Tikkun Olam, that which is astonishingly radical can become the common rule.* In retrospect, all of it makes sense; this is the way things should be, and most certainly can be.

1. David Levitt's bar mitzvah project urging public schools to donate leftover food from the cafeteria led to the donation of six-hundred-thousand-plus pounds of food in the first three years. First his own county's school system agreed, and ultimately the entire state has joined the effort. Why not *every* state?

2. An organization called Casting for Recovery organizes wonderful retreats where they teach women who have had breast cancer surgery how to fly fish. This is exercise-appropriate for their needs, and provides a means to get away and talk in a sheltered, comfortable environment. After the retreats, almost 100 percent of the women have emotionally internalized the feeling that life is not about cancer. It is about Life.

3. Naomi Berman-Potash's Project Debby finds hotels that have unoccupied rooms which may be used to provide safe haven for victims of domestic violence.

4. A most extraordinary project called "Dying with Dignity" illustrates the Wow!→Duh! principle exceptionally well. One aspect of the program is "Five Wishes," an eight-page document that a person may fill out long before dying seems a possibility. Part of the third wish states:

I wish to have warm baths often . . . to be kept fresh and clean at all times. . . . I wish to have personal care like shaving, nail clipping, hair brushing and teeth brushing, as long as they do not cause me pain or discomfort. I wish to have a cool moist cloth put on my head if I have a fever. I wish to have religious readings and poems read aloud when I am near death.

A section of the fourth wish states:

I wish to have pictures of my loved ones in my room, near my bed.... I wish to be cared for with kindness and cheerfulness, not sadness. I wish to have my hand held and to be talked to when possible, even if I don't seem to respond....

This document, or a similar one written in the same spirit, should be made available to everyone. In retrospect, it is such an obvious and necessary part of Life.

5. In Albemarle, North Carolina, the residents of Stanly Manor Nursing Home regularly party with members of the local Harley-Davidson biker club. (Think of the postcards and e-mails to friends: "Having a wonderful time. Wish you were here!")

6. Why don't most hospitals keep a supply of hearing aid batteries on hand? If the batteries wear down, the patients might not respond properly to questions or could miss some critical instructions for their present and future recovery.

7. A photography teacher gets a request from blind people to teach them how to use a camera. At first glance, this doesn't make any sense. Among the reasons for the request: People ask them out on dates—they want to know what they look like. Photography for blind students . . . Why not?

8. Petting a cat or a dog can relieve stress. My student and teacher Samantha Abeel suggests that such common pets be made available to students at exam time (or any other time when they get stressed out). Why not?

9. Joe Lejman of Gas City, Indiana, dressed in a tuxedo, borrowed fine china and crystal and served as a butler for a day in a shelter for battered women. To quote Lejman, "The ladies have such low self-esteem. Some of them have never felt special for any reason. During the course of the day, I was serving one of the clients coffee, and then lighted her cigarette, and she started crying. She said, 'This is the first time I could ever cry because someone's been so nice to me.'"

10. Voicemail for homeless people—to help them find work. A free service provided by Chris Petty of Littleton, Colorado.

11. All those people who did a stint in the Peace Corps and VISTA back in the sixties. . . . They were wowed, for sure, about how much of a difference they could make in the lives of other people. When they came home, if you asked them, "Did you make a difference?" the response would have been clearly, "Duh!" (We should commission a study to see how much those experiences have played a part in their lives *today*: how much are they presently involved in active Tikkun Olam work and in their commitment to protest against All Things Wrong in the World?)

12. Once upon a time on Wall Street, a young clerk misplaced $900,000,000. He knew exactly where he had put it, but it was the wrong place. His immediate problem was how to correct the situation. The young man's boss, known as "a screamer," had ruled her division of the corporation by intimidation and fear. So, understandably afraid to admit the error, the clerk began to move the money over several days—$50,000,000 at a time—to the appropriate account. The problem was: the flow of money crossed into the next calendar month. Government regulators discovered the irregularity and reported it to my friend, Marc Sternfeld, the young man's boss's boss's boss. Sternfeld fired the clerk's boss and kept the young clerk on the job. His reasoning was that *the clerk* had made an honest (if rather enormous) mistake. *His arrogant boss* was the flaw in the system.

13. A teenager arranges for leftovers from a bagel shop to be taken regularly to the waiting room outside the intensive care unit at the hospital . . . for all those people who need a pleasant diversion and bit of nourishment amid the horrible stress.

14. The Pure Food and Drug Act of 1906, Brown v. Board of Education, 1954 (desegregating the public schools), the Civil Rights Act of 1964, the Americans with Disabilities Act of 1990, the Bill Emerson Good Samaritan Food Donation Act of 1996

(providing liability protection for donors of food to nonprofit organizations feeding hungry people), laws eliminating sex, race, ethnic, and age discrimination, and various child-labor laws—all thought to be radical when introduced into law, but now the norm.

15. At one point in his career, the eminent psychologist Abraham Maslow, z"l, turned away from the study of pathological phenomena in the human personality and, instead, devoted years of research to investigating what makes people *good* human beings.

Let us not dwell on the embarrassment or dismay that these breakthroughs were not made long, long ago. Instead, let us place our creative and emotional energy into making more Tikkun Olam *a matter of routine.*

The Pedestal (2000)

Mitzvah heroes. Just plain everyday people who made big-time Tikkun Olam happen. The good thing to do is to meet them, watch them at their Mitzvah work, listen to them, and learn from them. Draw close to them, not as a fawning, unquestioning disciple, but rather as one who shares their vision. The not-so-good thing to do is to put them on a pedestal and admire them and stand in awe of them. It separates us from them, keeps us at a safe, but unfortunate, distance.

Though I have used the educator John Holt's quote in a number of my books, I use it again here, because it is so apropos:

Charismatic leaders make us think, "Oh, if only I could do that, be like that." True leaders make us think, "If they can do that, then . . . I can too."

Mitzvah heroes *are* awesome because their Mitzvah work is awesome. For example, Kathy Freund, concerned about the dangers of some Elders who were no longer able to drive safely, established the

Independent Travel Network (ITN) in Portland, Maine. It provides (mostly) volunteer drivers to transport Elders to the market, doctor, hairdresser, wherever they need to go, all for a very nominal fee. This *very* impressive program benefits so many Elders, particularly those who are unable to use public transportation, cannot afford cabs, or don't have relatives or friends to drive them.

If we stand back and merely admire Ms. Freund and others like her, we miss the point. "If they can do that, then . . . [to whatever extent I, myself, am able], I can, too." *They* don't want to be on a pedestal, so don't feel a need to put them there.

In November 1999 my Ziv Tzedakah Fund sponsored its first "Mitzvah Heroes Conference." Gathered together were ninety people, fifteen of whom were the very personalities whose stories I have been telling and retelling for years. All of this was packed into a day and a half. It was *extremely* intense. But the participants knew we were there together to see what we had in common with the teachers, and then to apply our own talents and time and energy to do as they do. No pedestals!

Whatever I Want for Myself, I Want for Other People (2000)

Maimonides succinctly defines the meaning of loving others as we love ourselves:

> This is the commandment that we were commanded to love each other just as we love ourselves. That is to say . . .
> Whatever I want for myself,
> I want the same for that other person.
> And whatever I do not want for myself or my friends,
> I do not want for that other person.
> This is the meaning of the Most Sublime One's verse,
> "And you shall love the other person as yourself" (Leviticus 19:18).
> —Maimonides, *Sefer HaMitzvot*, Positive Mitzvah #206

"*Want* for that other person" means, of course, "want so much, I will do something to make certain they receive it. They are entitled to it."

We should make a list of things we want in our own lives: a sense of meaning and fulfillment, love, to be cared about and cared for, good health, protection from the elements, food (including holiday goodies, fun food, a little pure junk food, and enough food to entertain guests), Menschlich shelter (including pictures you like on the wall and paint colors you enjoy), and clothing (including fancy clothes for celebrations and holidays, comfortable lounge-around-the-house clothes that you would never wear outside, and fancy fancy clothes to boost your sense of self-image, like a homburg or stylish suit or dress). Then, keeping in mind Maimonides' two briefly stated criteria—I want/don't want for myself—we will have a better understanding of where our efforts on behalf of Tikkun Olam lie.

A short letter accompanying a $2.00 contribution to a local Jewish federation is one of the most eloquent in my files. I believe this says it all:

> Dear Sir: Enclosed, two dollars. I hope the hungry will be fed. I have enough food. I live off of Social Security. Yours truly, . . .

24 Questions Parents May Wish to Ask Themselves (2004)

> Do not hold back from doing good for others
> When you have the power to do so.
> —Proverbs 3:27

Raising a child is lived in small time units. It is so much a day-by-day, hour-by-hour, and even minute-by-minute affair. It is time-consuming beyond anything you imagined when your daughter or son was born, and has been filled with pleasures and worries, highs and lows. Mostly, though, it has hopefully been essentially "normal," even-flowing.

Now, though, bar/bat mitzvah is approaching. It may have caught you off guard; it may give you a feeling of all-of-a-sudden. This is hardly like the routine of buying new shoes for Rachel, shlepping Max to a baseball game, driving Shira to school because she overslept and missed the bus, or taking Miriam to Hebrew school even when she is whining that she doesn't want to go.

Bar/bat mitzvah is a different class and magnitude of life experience, not only for your child ... also for *you* as a parent. Simchas, joyous family celebrations, are ideal opportunities to consider and re-think certain momentous real-Life topics that you may not have thought about since your child's birth.

The following are just a few of the possible questions that may be somewhere in the back of your mind and which you might want to *actively* think about as your child is about to enter a brand-new stage of Jewish life. Your Glorious Child is about to become a Mitzvah Person. Note: "Mitzvah Person" is in fact the grammatically correct translation of bar/bat mitzvah—it is *not* "son/daughter of a commandment." What does it all mean?

The questions are listed in no particular order of importance:

1. What do I want my child to be when he or she grows up? This question is *not* about the usual categories of "occupation," "field of endeavor," or "ways to make a living," but rather, what kind of human being and Jew do I want my daughter or son to be? Often there is a degree of overlap between "making a living" and "the kind of person" someone is. You are asking the question *now* in order to get to the very heart of the matter: Is being a Mitzvah Person and a Mensch the highest priority or of secondary importance?

2. Have I ever asked myself, "Is my child gifted in Tikkun Olam-type Mitzvahs?" Everyone in the child's life—parents, grandparents, friends, teachers, etc.—is already watching for promise in music, math, sports, computers, and the like. Taking note of Mitzvah-talent is of no less importance. If everyone

looked for this kind of talent in children as well, the sum total of Mitzvahs and Tikkun Olam in the world would increase exponentially.

3. When I think about the future development of my child, what do I mean when I say—"There are no guarantees"? In the larger sense, this cliché (as with all clichés) is only a partial truth. "No guarantees" is obviously an aspect of the nature and flow of life. However, even though there are no guarantees, it is possible to ask yourself how you would change the odds, offering your child a better chance to become a Mitzvah-doing-Mensch.

4. What do I mean when I say to myself, "I want the best for my child"? What does "the best" mean? In what contexts and in relation to what other things, people, and events in life do you want your child to be "the best"? What are the ultimate reasons for being "the best"? In which ways is being "the best" an authentic Jewish value, and in which other ways is it not? (Note: There are no Talmudic terms for "excellence," "well-rounded," "achievement," or "competitiveness.")

5. What do I mean when I say, "I want my child to be happy"?

6. What do I mean when I say, "I want my child to be successful"?

7. What aspects of my child's personality and activities make me particularly proud?

8. What do I mean when I say, "I want my child to have what I never had"? Perhaps writing out a list of these opportunities and items will help you to answer this one more completely. Your own list might include things such as "I want them not to be lonely" and "I want them to have a close, loving relationship with me" if these were missing in your own life. Asking this question and the previous one should help parents focus more on their child as a separate person, and avoid the pitfall of "living through their children."

9. When I say to myself or to my child, "Count your blessings," what exactly do I mean? The Talmud (*Menachot* 43b) teaches

that every Jew should recite one hundred blessings every day. It might be worthwhile at this time to make a list of what you consider to be one hundred of your personal blessings . . . and to ask yourself, "Does my child understand what these blessings are in my life and *why* I consider them to be blessings?" You might also ask your child to make a list of her or his own life's blessings.

10. Have I discussed my own Mitzvah work with my child and other family members?

11. Have I spoken to my child about where I give my Tzedakah money, and how I decide where and how much to give? Have I taught this child that there are two different *kinds* of money in his or her life: (a) personal money and (b) Tzedakah money?

12. Have I told my child that I am donating to Tzedakah in honor of his or her becoming a Mitzvah Person?

13. What is the relationship between my child's secular education and what kind of a person he or she is and will possibly become? Does it contribute to his or her Jewish and human character (in Yiddish—Menschlichkeit)?

14. What is the relationship between my child's Jewish education and what kind of a person he or she is and will possibly become? Does it contribute to his or her essential character (in Yiddish—Menschlichkeit)?

15. Do you expect your child's bar/bat mitzvah and bar/bat mitzvah Mitzvah Project to contribute toward her or his becoming a Mensch? Is there an *automatic, potential,* or a *possible* connection between doing Mitzvahs and becoming/being a Mensch?

16. If my child came home with a 97 or 98 on an exam or paper, did I ever ask him or her, "What did you get wrong?" (And did my parents do the same to me, too?) Is this the best approach to teaching my child The Ultimate Meaning of Education, Menschlichkeit, Torah, Mitzvahs, Tikkun Olam, Being Jewish? What would be a healthier approach to getting good grades?

17. Jewish tradition teaches, "Mitzvahs were given in order to refine human beings" (*Leviticus Rabbah* 13:3). As my child becomes a bar/bat mitzvah, what qualities would I like to see "refined out" of her/his personality? What qualities would I like to see remain, appear, or become predominant in my child?

18. Who are my child's heroes? Does my child understand that Mitzvah heroes can play a crucial part in his or her life? Is my child open in some way to becoming a Giant of Tikkun Olam when he or she "grows up"?

19. Who are my child's friends? What kind of *chevra*—the group he or she spends the most time with—is this group of friends? Are they "into" doing Mitzvahs?

20. Complete this sentence: "You should use all of your [God-given] gifts for. . . ." Ask your child to complete it as well. Then discuss your individual answers.

21. Finish the sentence: "Life is short, therefore. . . ." Again, have your child do the same and compare and discuss your answers. (Friends and students have also suggested that it may be equally productive to finish the sentence, "Life is long, therefore. . . .")

22. How seriously do I take my own commitment to Judaism and things Jewish? For example, in the area of Torah study, does my child see me engaged in personal study and Torah classes? (Jewish tradition actually teaches that adult education takes precedence over that of children; see Shulchan Aruch, *Yoreh De'ah* 245:2. There are many reasons for this ruling, but one of the most important ones is that without Torah knowledge, how will a parent teach the child?)

An appropriate analogy from air travel comes to mind. The flight attendant says, "In the event of loss of oxygen, put on your oxygen mask first, *then* put one on your child." When we first hear this, it doesn't sound right. On second thought, though, we understand that this makes perfect sense and is really the "right" way to react in an emergency. A dysfunctional adult deprived of oxygen is of no use to the child.

As we know, children are very perceptive. They learn very quickly if Mommy or Daddy just drops them off at Hebrew school and picks them up afterward. It "feels" to them like it's a burden for the parent to *shlep* them back and forth. And when religious school classes take second place to other outside activities, they also very quickly get the message.

23. How seriously do I take my own dedication to Tikkun Olam, and if I am serious about it and actively commit to Mitzvah projects, do I do it alone, or with my family, or both?

24. Does my image of being a role model for my child approximate my child's perception of me? A classic example of a child "getting" it is the story of a fisherman named Tuck Donnelly. While he was working as a manager on a commercial fishing vessel, one of his crew members told him how distressed he was about how much fish they had to throw back—dead or alive. Because of government regulations, they were allowed to keep only pollock and cod. Perfectly good protein that could feed hungry Americans was therefore being wasted. After many meetings and long negotiations, Donnelly succeeded in having the government change the regulations. Now, his Mitzvah project, SeaShare, has become a supplier of millions of pounds of fish to food banks, soup kitchens, and shelters around the United States. Commercial vessels and processors have come "on board," and many thousands of Americans are eating more healthy food due to SeaShare's efforts.

The question remains, do Tuck Donnelly's children "get it"? Do they know what Daddy is "all about"? The answer is a most definite Yes. Here's the proof. One day, Tuck Donnelly's wife, Jax, overheard a conversation between their daughter, Rachel, and two friends. The first one said, "My Dad's a lawyer, and he makes a lot of money." The second one said, "My Dad's a doctor, and he makes a lot of money." Rachel's words said it all— "My Dad feeds hungry people."

100 Possible Reasons Why You May Have Decided to Do More Tikkun Olam—in No Particular Order of Importance (2006)

> I figure, what good's a clean house if your county's radioactive?
> —Barbara Howell, Wilson, North Carolina, as quoted by the Giraffe Heroes Project

> Realize that if you have time to whine and complain about something, then you have the time to do something about it.
> —Anthony J. D'Angelo, motivational speaker

There's nothing earthshaking about writing that people act the way they do for a variety of reasons. In fact, they are usually motivated by a tangle of thoughts and emotions. This is true not only for "regular" life, but also for doing Mitzvahs and Tikkun Olam. Fortunately, Jewish tradition teaches that a person's reasons for doing Mitzvahs are secondary to performing the Mitzvah-deed itself. As long as the Mitzvah is done in a manner that has the welfare and dignity of the recipient in mind, the Mitzvah itself is validated.

Below, in no particular order, is a long and still-partial list of reasons why you may have decided to do more Tikkun Olam. Most likely, more than one of the motivating factors is a source for your actions.

I suggest placing a check mark next to any reason that personally resonates with you, whether fully or even partially. The rule is always to go with *whatever works best for you*. If it helps, make notations in the margins. Start anywhere and skip around if that's easier too.

Furthermore, I have most definitely missed many reasons which may apply to you. Recognizing this, I have left four spaces at the end for you to record your own thoughts, making this piece a collaboration between us.

Or, ignore the list completely and write out your own personal thoughts.

This exercise may help you clarify your own reasons, and inspire you further. The end result will be more Tikkun Olam.

1. It's a Mitzvah; God wants me to do it.
2. Doing good is a Mitzvah. It makes me more Jewish, and I want to "be more Jewish."
3. I heard about the Jewish idea that I could be God's partner in fixing the world. In my finer and more humble moments I said to myself, "I like that."
4. The spiritual aspect of Tikkun Olam greatly appealed to me. I wanted more depth and sensitivity in my Jewish soul which I felt I had neglected for too many years.
5. I met a Mitzvah hero and was inspired to go out to do something.
6. The Jewish People is under assault by rabid and frightening anti-Semitism. Some attacks are blatant, some more subtle. Rather than sit idly by and say, "It's always been that way," I said to myself, "I am going to do something about it."
7. Doing that part of my Tikkun Olam work which benefits Jews is an absolute necessity. The Jewish People needs my efforts.
8. My daughter's Bat Mitzvah Mitzvah project so impressed me, I gave it my full moral, psychological, and financial support. I even said to myself, "I am surprised how much I was taken by my child's enthusiasm . . . and by my own support."
9. I kept hearing people talk about the wonderful charitable work of terrorist gangs such as Hamas. Something seemed terribly wrong about this kind of thinking. Most outrageous was the fact that too many journalists wrote about it with similar praise. Some, though they vigorously denied it, justified this terrorism with, "BUT look at what they are doing to provide

food and medical services." Their egregiously misplaced values severely violated my sensibilities. I was horrified that "right-minded" people could say and write such morally repugnant words. Equally appalling were the "right-minded" people who read the articles, nodded their heads, and thereby, in a way, agreed with the terrorists. I said to myself, "I am going to take these people on and disabuse them of their flawed ethical thinking because it leads to more unspeakable suffering. If I don't, more people in Israel may die in terror attacks."

10. My friend's brother was having a cup of coffee with classmates in a café in Jerusalem. He was horribly maimed when a homicide bomber blew himself up nearby. While I had been reading reports about terror attacks for a long time, I had only gone so far as being appalled at the obscenity of the bombings and sympathy to the victims. This changed radically when "it hit home": The War was no longer something distant and abstract. It became very real, and I knew I had to do something about it.

11. I began to think seriously about when I would face the Almighty in the Next World and would have to account for my life. What would I have to show for it?

12. I want to leave the world a better place than when I came into it.

13. When I came across Maurice Sendak's quote, "There must be more to life than having everything," I began to think about what human beings can really call their own in Life.

14. I reached a point in my life when I realized that TV is TV and movies are movies . . . but Real Life is Real Life. On TV and in the movies, those who suffer or die for unreasonable reasons get up when the scene is over and go back to their Real Lives. In Real Life, those who suffer or die for unreasonable reasons are really suffering or dying. If I could help it, I wanted to make certain that this wouldn't happen any more.

15. The line, "I was sad I had no shoes until I met a man who had no legs" struck a very deep chord in me. When this came to

mind as if out of nowhere, I began to seriously consider just how fortunate I am.

16. I got tired of people mouthing the lines, "That's just the way Life is" and "The world never changes and there's nothing you can do about it." Then I got angry. Then I decided I ought to do something about it to prove that they were wrong.

17. A certain person in my community, a fine person, a Mensch who was very involved in Tikkun Olam, passed away. I realized that someone had to carry on that person's work. I said to myself, "I can be that person."

18. While I do not recall specifically what might have brought it to mind, I realized that some Tikkun Olam had to be done *now*, and to wait until tomorrow, this afternoon—or even another ten minutes—would be disastrous.

19. I have always suspected that I could make a bigger difference than I have in the past.

20. My life changed on September 11, 2001, and I want to do something about making the world a better place. I want to do everything to show that terrorist monsters will not win out.

21. The evils in the world have eaten away at me for years. All manner of things bad, morally ugly, and unfair tore at my soul. I thought about this again and again, and talked about it over and over again, until I decided I had to act on it. The moment of revelation came when I heard myself saying to myself, "Enough! This has got to stop, and I am going to stop it!" Now I feel that I want to make a significant, even possibly a formidable, change so that these terrible things will not continue to happen to others.

22. I have never been "good at" philosophy and cannot understand Ultimates such as the Meaning of Life. I need something much more concrete. My intuition tells me that doing Mitzvahs may give me a sense of meaning.

23. After years of receiving a salary for my work, I like the idea of doing something without being paid. I want to get a better

"feel" for what it's like to do things with absolutely no expectation of reward or thank-you. Doing more for the pure goodness of it, and because it is the right thing to do, makes me feel very good.

24. After a few years of gnawing discontent and disappointment with my job, I began to look ahead to retirement when I could hope for something more soul-satisfying.

25. I sense that as I get more involved in Tikkun Olam, I will meet many wonderful people. The thought of having this new and marvelous *chevra* really excites me.

26. I like the feeling that I can make things happen.

27. I always keep a light on wherever I sleep. As far back as I can remember, I have been afraid of the dark. I don't want others to have that fear. Whether the dark is real or imagined, no one should have do go through what I felt as a child.

28. I kept seeing advertisements on TV to join the army. The clever tag line was, "Be all that you can be." I began to wonder if I really am all that I can be. Being involved in Tikkun Olam might be at least a partial solution to my unsettling gut feeling that I have not lived fully because I have not engaged sufficiently in Tikkun Olam.

29. I finally decided to listen to my mother, who kept nagging me, "Quit your whining!"

30. I have always liked—and welcomed—challenges. Tikkun Olam–type challenges really appeal to me.

31. I have always liked doing things that others said couldn't be done.

32. My parents always wanted me to be a doctor, but I chose some other field of endeavor, and now I really want to go out and save as many lives as I can.

33. I have read that doing Tikkun Olam is good for my health. I am told that when I do Mitzvahs, endorphins and all kinds of other good chemicals start flowing through every cell in my body.

34. I like to feel good about myself.

35. I want to feel good about myself.

36. I became old enough to realize that if I wanted a "new me," it would take more than a whirlwind trip to a half-dozen clothing stores.

37. I have been in academia for my entire career. I really do believe in the importance of academic studies, pure research, and theoretical inquiry. Still, deep inside, I began to feel that my academic pursuits were too divorced from real life, and that I was living in an ivory tower. Now I want to be more seriously involved in the everyday struggles of individuals to live a Menschlich life. I really want to do things so that others will be afforded every opportunity to experience life, liberty, and the pursuit of happiness.

38. I (my spouse, child, parent, friend) was once seriously ill. I was extremely impressed with how many people came together to take care of me (them), and how beautifully and gently they related to me (them). As a result, I decided to try, in some way, to do something for others with the same gentle touch.

39. I (my spouse, child, parent, friend) was once seriously ill. I was disappointed at how few people came together to take care of me (them). As a result, I decided to try, in some way, to do something, so that this would not happen to others.

40. I like working with people.

41. I like making others happy, even for a few moments. It makes me happy.

42. I always had a need to achieve excellence, and I sensed that excellence in Tikkun Olam was somehow different than doing well in my job.

43. Doing Mitzvah work gives me a feeling of stability. It keeps me from wasting time on trivial pursuits. It also keeps my mind from running every which way from one end of the universe to the other at lightning speed.

44. I feel empty about my regular work routine, but I think that doing Tikkun Olam will fill this void with meaning.

45. I took stock of how far I had gotten in my job. I thought a lot about how it wasn't as high up as I had wanted, hoped, or dreamed by this time in my life. Somewhere along the way, I came to realize that the best and healthiest way to deal with it is to get over it and to get on with my life. Thinking about it more and more, it made sense that "getting on with my life" meant doing Tikkun Olam, where it doesn't matter any more how highly rated I am by my boss.

46. I admire creative people but have always considered myself to be a non-creative person. I failed at painting, and I wouldn't even try sculpture. Even good friends winced when I played the piano or sang a song I wrote. Maybe I can be creative in another way, namely, by doing Tikkun Olam.

47. Many people risk their lives for the sake of other people. The least I can do is some kind of Tikkun Olam even if there is no great risk involved.

48. I've always been a tinkerer. I have read every biography of Thomas Edison that was ever published. I am sure there is some way I can become a "Tinkerer for Mitzvahs." Maybe I can refine some Tikkun Olam project that others have been working on but couldn't finish.

49. I am an amateur inventor, though I've never patented any of my inventions. (My combination tire iron/automatic espresso machine/shoe shine kit never caught on.) Maybe I can invent some Tikkun Olam project no one has ever thought of before.

50. In some way, I want to make up for things I really messed up in my life until now.

51. I often think of myself as wishy-washy. It took me months to decide Buick or Toyota? Hours of research and indecisiveness—Mac or PC? I am really terrible at Baskin-Robbins. Maybe by committing myself to providing for the needs of others I will become more assertive and decisive.

52. I am tired of people saying to me, "Get a life!"

53. When I was a kid, somebody called me a real loser, saying that I would never amount to anything in life. It still stings. No one is a loser when he or she is doing Tikkun Olam.

54. Even though I've done some good for others all my life, I really want to do more.

55. By nature and training I am a specialist. There isn't a thing about the archeology of ancient Israel, neuro-psychopharmacology, or twelfth-century Hebrew poetry that I haven't mastered. I have a photographic memory and an incredible ability to focus intensely on a problem and solve it. One day, I just said to myself, "With all these gifts and tools, I bet I can make the transition into Tikkun Olam very easily."

56. I love doing diddly tasks like filing papers, stuffing envelopes, washing dirty dishes and greasy pots and pans, vacuuming, changing kitty litter boxes, and scrubbing bathrooms until they sparkle. I realize that not too many other people enjoy this kind of thing, so I thought these particular little joys in my life might be of particular use for various Tzedakah projects.

57. Many times I have heard from others about "doing this Tikkun Olam thing," *and how there's just nothing in Life quite like making someone else happy, healthy, warm, and with enough food to live a good life.* They gave me ideas on how to get more involved, and I decided to take the opportunity.

58. My accountant (lawyer, spouse, child, I myself) looked at my financial situation and decided it would be wise to get more charitable deductions on my tax form.

59. One day it hit me that I was resting on my Tikkun Olam laurels. So I put away all the awards from my walls and display cases, talked to some friends, and got started on a new program to teach Hebrew to adults who never had the opportunity to learn.

60. I kept hearing, "No one is indispensable." It just didn't sound right to me. I decided to increase my efforts to get others to do

Tikkun Olam with me by telling them they were absolutely and totally indispensable.

61. Life has been good to me. Things have generally gone very smoothly: Right out of college I got a well-paying job that I liked; I was never unemployed; I had a comfortable life style, but then I got swept up into materialism a little too much. I got back "heavy" into Tikkun Olam, which quickly cured me.

62. My eyeglasses broke one day. It was a holiday and the optometrist's office was closed, so for twenty-four hours I could barely function. I thought to myself, "If something as simple as a pair of glasses holds others back, this can be easily corrected. And I can do something about it."

63. I like to try new things, and since Tikkun Olam covers every possible aspect of life, there are many new things I could try.

64. I come from a long line of social change activists—real Tikkun Olamniks. Someone in my family was always involved in the fight for freedom for Soviet Jews, the chance for Ethiopian Jews to come to Israel, children's rights in carpet factories, women's rights, civil rights, voters' rights, workers' rights, elders' rights, equitable healthcare legislation, fair housing, fair trade prices for coffee farmers . . . Some of it inevitably rubbed off on me.

65. I wanted to be well thought of by my family and friends. When they think of me, I want them to think, "caring, generous, a Mensch."

66. When I began to receive birthday cards that humorously indicated that I was "over the hill," I got angry and decided it was time to live every day with at least some Tikkun Olam on my agenda.

67. I don't think I have been using all of my brain power. It may very well be that being involved in Things Larger Than Just My Own Life, dormant parts of my brain will become activated and I will function better and approach Life with greater sensitivity.

68. I once heard the line, "Doing good is good," and I thought that made a lot of sense.

69. I am a power-hungry person. I think I can apply this hunger for power to Tikkun Olam. I am sure it will make a significant difference in the lives of many people.

70. I'm tired of "it" — people going hungry when there is enough food in the world to feed everyone, terrorism, anyone who can't get basic healthcare, nursing homes that don't treat their Elders with sufficient dignity and confuse "treatment" for "care." I'm not going to take it any more. I am going to dig in and do something about it.

71. I wanted to be useful.

72. I didn't want to feel useless.

73. I like how, with only a little effort, I can make great changes in the lives of many other people.

74. I began to realize how often a small Mitzvah-gesture can change the lives of other people in a very big way, and I wanted to do more of it.

75. I hate waste: food, recyclables tossed in the trash, or human talents and lives.

76. I hate seeing others waste things, just like in #75.

77. I hate seeing people waste good money that could be used for Tikkun Olam. I went to one-too-many weddings that cost $200,000 and was outraged at the extravagance and waste, I said to myself, "I have to do something about this!" I went on a campaign to encourage others to downgrade their excessive Life-events and to donate the money they saved to Tzedakah. My first victory was convincing a Tzedakah organization to change its annual dinner (which cost $150/person for the food) to a dessert reception ($12/person). As a result, $20,354 more became available for its Tzedakah work.

78. I want to leave a legacy of Mitzvahs for my children/ grandchildren/friends.

79. I have a lot of time on my hands, more than I could possibly handle without something meaningful to do with myself and for others.

80. I have had so many time constraints because of my job, I didn't think I had enough time to do all the Tikkun Olam I wanted, and I began to chomp at the bit. Now—no matter the demands of my job, I am ready to make a BIG difference. Even if I don't think I have the time, I am determined to make time anyway.

81. I see far too many retired people living what appear to be boring lives. I don't want that to happen to me.

82. I used to think building the business (establishing my reputation, becoming The Best in my field) were the most important things in Life. Now I see that while they are important, they aren't that important compared to doing Tikkun Olam.

83. Life expectancy statistics keep getting better and better, and with all of those statistically additional years, it means I will have much more time to do many, many Mitzvahs.

84. The late senator Paul Tsongas once said, "No man ever said on his deathbed I wish I had spent more time in the office." Once I heard this line, it rang a very loud, often distracting, and occasionally deafening, bell in my soul. I cut back on the workload and starting putting more effort into Tikkun Olam.

85. I began to feel that my idealism was slipping away from me. I felt a terrible sense of loss. Somehow I knew that doing Tikkun Olam would restore this idealism.

86. All around me, I kept hearing cynicism and sarcasm. Then I heard myself saying similarly sarcastic and cynical lines. I even disparaged the good things others were doing. This shocked me so much, it really woke me up. By getting more involved in Tikkun Olam I finally stopped myself.

87. All my life I have been a collector. I amassed coffee mugs, old license plates, keys, vintage electric trains, rare wines, dozens of knick-knacks, and what seemed like tons of other "stuff"

from my travels. One day, I suddenly realized I was surrounded by things. Doing my Tikkun Olam work reminded me that (1) things in and of themselves have no real value, and that (2) sometimes some things can be used for Tikkun Olam. Even more—there are times when things are most needed for a specific Mitzvah solution. Now I relate to "things" very differently.

88. Now and again I noticed how some people were more disturbed when a famous painting was destroyed in a fire. They weren't as troubled by the death of the guard who was killed when the flames raged out of control. I wanted to do something to help people re-think their priorities and help restore the value of human life to its proper place.

89. I am frequently asked to donate to a specific Tzedakah program in honor of someone I know. The same is true for donations in memory of relatives and friends I knew. Sometime along the way it struck me that I could use my time and talents to also become involved in one of those programs. This seemed to me to be a particularly fine way to honor, or to honor the memory of, individuals who had been good to me.

90. I like myself more when I do good things.

91. I have experienced social anxiety throughout my life, and am, on occasion, very uncomfortable around people. This often got in my way of engaging with others and participating in community projects. Yet as I got older, something changed; perhaps I just grew more comfortable about myself. Once I started doing Tikkun Olam work, I discovered I was able to connect more easily with others—so I wanted to do more of it.

92. In Robert Dallek's book *Flawed Giant: Lyndon Johnson and His Times, 1961–1973*, the author records a conversation between LBJ and Alabama's racist governor George Wallace. It is the height of the civil rights era, and the president is hammering away at Wallace to desegregate the schools. As Dallek recounts, "He [LBJ] urged Wallace not to 'think about 1968; you think about

1988. You and me, we'll be dead and gone then, George. . . . What do you want left after you die? Do you want a Great . . . Big . . . Marble monument that reads, "George Wallace—He Built"? . . . Or do you want a little piece of scrawny pine board lying across that harsh, caliche soil, that reads, "George Wallace—He Hated"?'"[24] It's a great question: what kind of legacy do I want to leave after I am gone?

93. I used to think there were people who did amazing things in this world—but I was not among them. Then one day I had a good idea. And then I shared with a friend, and suddenly we started working on it together. And eventually, it happened—and I realized that anyone has the power to make changes happen.

94. I have suffered from depression on and off throughout my life. Sometimes I have great difficulty even doing the most basic daily routines. But I discovered that when I am immersed in Mitzvah work, I have fewer "bad days" than I used to have. Tikkun Olam can sometimes be a tremendous antidepressant.

95. I've been involved in Mitzvah work on-and-off throughout my life, and always said I would get around to doing more when I felt more inspired. Then the world started changing so quickly for the bad and I realized I couldn't wait around for the perfect time and the perfect project. I had to take action now because the world depended not only on me but on many other like-minded people—right now.

96. I received a Vision from Above. I know this as a fact, because almost every one of the entries on this list came to me in a single outpouring of high-speed writing. The circumstances were these: I had eaten some weird combination of foods right before I went to bed. Around 1:00 a.m., after having tossed and turned for a couple of hours, and after some spectacular, disjointed, but entertaining dreams, I awoke and the words began to spill out. I wrote until 4:15 a.m. Having experienced The

Glory in its full glory, and having written out all these reasons, I thought it might be time to settle down and do some real-live Tikkun Olam.

97. _____ [My personal reason]
98. _____ [My personal reason]
99. _____ [My personal reason]
100. _____ [My personal reason]

A First Exercise

The Relationship Between Doing Tikkun Olam
Jewishly and Your "Jewishness" (2006)

On a scale of 1–10, 10 being the most or highest, rate the following and explain your ratings:

1. How important to you is doing Tikkun Olam Jewishly?
   Rating:
   Explain:
2. How important to you is being Jewish and living Jewishly?
   Rating:
   Explain:
3. Do you expect/find that your Tikkun Olam work will/does affect your connection, affiliation, and/or commitment to Judaism?
   Rating:
   Explain:
4. Do you believe that doing Tikkun Olam is sufficient to keep you connected, affiliated, and/or committed to your Judaism?
   Rating: (If your rating is between 6 and 10, explain below, but if your answer is between 1 and 5, please move to the next question.)
   Explain:

5. If your rating for Question #4 was between 1 and 5, what else do you believe you would have to do to keep your connection, affiliation, and/or commitment to Judaism strong?
   Explain:
6. How important is it to you that your descendants remain Jewish?
   Rating:
   Explain:
7. Do you expect that your doing Tikkun Olam Jewishly will contribute to your descendants' remaining Jewishly connected, affiliated, and/or committed?
   Rating:
   Explain:
8. Do you believe that your doing Tikkun Olam is sufficient to keep your descendants committed to their degree of "Jewishness"?
   Rating: (If your rating is between 6 and 10, explain below, but if your answer is between 1 and 5, please move to the next question.)
   Explain:
9. If your rating for Question #8 is between 1 and 5, what else do you believe you would have to do to influence their Jewish connection, affiliation, and/or commitment?
   Explain:

The Four Questions (2006)

"The Four Questions" is the most useful stimulus I know for people of all ages who want to match their individual personality with specific kinds of Tikkun Olam.

And, yes, there really are eight questions. But, as the joke goes, there are three kinds of people relating to math — those who can do it and those who can't. Had I had called this section "The 8 Questions," no one would have paid much attention to it.

1. What are you good at?
2. What do you like to do?
3. What bothers you so much about what is wrong in the world that you weep or scream in anger and frustration? What is so terribly wrong that you are at a loss for words . . . and are determined to do something to change it?
4. Who are your heroes, and what is it about them that you admire?
5. Whom do you know?
6. Why not?
7. What can you do right now?
8. What are you not good at, but might do anyway because it would make a big difference in someone else's life?

Comment: The answers to questions #1 and #2 may be identical or two separate categories. For example: You are a fabulous salesperson. Your husband says you could sell double-layered overcoats to Tahitians. Sometime in your career you realize you no longer enjoy it and that it is time to "get on with your life" and do something else. An example of the opposite: You love to play the clarinet, but you have no sense of rhythm and your off-key performances drive others crazy. Worn down by the cacophony, your friends and family politely (but firmly) insist that you play when no one is around. *Hint:* #3 *always* gets the most articulate and deeply felt response.

The Good Stuff and the Crud (2006)

> Rav said: Mitzvahs were given in order to refine human beings.
> — *Leviticus Rabbah* 13:3[25]

"Crud"—it was one of the great versatile words of my youth. "He has the crud" and, worse, "He has the *creeping* crud" needed no further explanation. (When we were younger, "cooties" served a similar purpose, but by age thirteen or fourteen, it was deemed too childish to use.)

Apparently, some adults continue to find the term useful. Some physicians, especially dermatologists, might tell an anxious teenager, "We can get rid of all this crud on your face within ten days." Pimply adolescents no doubt find this particularly reassuring, because the doctor speaks their language, and because it spares them the trouble of dealing with obfuscating Latinized technical terminology. "You've got crud" sounds better and easier to understand than "You've got pernicious dermatitis universalis."

Furthermore, "crud" continues to serve a purpose beyond the medical profession. It is the all-purpose, comprehensive opposite of "the Good Stuff."

Rav's noble Torah insight, above, addresses this very issue of "crud" and "the Good Stuff." In English there are many terms for the refining process: purifying, filtering, distilling, winnowing, brewing, and smelting are only a few. Each refers to separating the Good Stuff from the Crud, the wheat from the chaff, wine from lees, silver from dross. Rav's teaching attributes great power to Mitzvahs, among them Tikkun Olam Mitzvahs. He is speaking, of course, of the power to refine the human personality.

For this exercise, first make a list of your own "personality crud." On the Good Stuff list, record characteristics that you would expect to become prominent once you have eliminated your personal crud. Keep in mind that even if you remove only *a fraction of crud*, more of the Good Stuff will display itself in full glory.

1. Do you believe that Tikkun Olam and Mitzvahs have the power to refine your personality? Circle one. YES / NO
   If no, why not? If yes, how and why do you think it works?

(If you answered "yes" to Question #1 above, proceed with the following:)

2. Next to the items you've listed in the Crud column, rate from 1 to 10 how much of that trait or habit you think can be refined by engaging in Tikkun Olam? ("10" = "all of it," "1" = "just a tad.")
3. For those negative traits—the Crud—that you have rated on the lower end of the scale (1–5), explain why you feel some of this crud will always remain an aspect of your personality.
4. For those positive traits—the Good Stuff—contemplate how your engaging in Tikkun Olam could refine them so that they can be even more prominent in your life.

Jewish Optimism—From Radical to Mainstream (2020)

For all the discouraging polls and studies about the problems for Jewish life today in North America, I believe there is reason to be optimistic.

However wretched the world at times seems to be, the ever-multiplying number of people doing good together should be a vaccine against cynicism. Consider all the innovations of recent years that have made Jewish life more accessible: the rise of *havurot* and alternative minyanim; the integration of children with special needs; the flourishing of family education; adult Bat and Bar Mitzvah; recognition and response to hungry, poor, and homeless Jews; the willingness to embrace the LGBTQ community in Jewish thought and communal life; and perhaps most of all, women's ordination, scholarship, and leadership in every area of Jewish life. We may not yet be in the Promised Land of 100 percent inclusion, but in truth the American synagogue is a much more accessible place for many more people than it was a generation ago. What was once considered radical is now mainstream.

Similarly, just reflect on the proliferation of Mitzvah projects accomplished on community "Mitzvah Days." Contemplate the growth of Mitzvah vegetable gardens on synagogue grounds for donating food to those who need it and the many Mitzvah initiatives integrated into reshaped curricula in our Jewish schools. Just think of the enormous amount of food that is gleaned on Yom Kippur food drives throughout America, as people are urged to donate that which they've denied themselves throughout the fast day. Projects and activities like these, which once seemed peripheral, have become commonplace in Jewish life.

An important case in point is the common expectation that Bar and Bat Mitzvah students engage in Mitzvah projects as part of their preparations. Back in the 1970s and 1980s, this was not part of our communal consciousness — except in one significant way: "twinning" with Soviet Jews. At the time, American Jewry's political consciousness came of age by agitating for the freedom of their brothers and sisters in the Soviet Union. Many young Jews were connected with Russian thirteen-year-olds who, of course, were forbidden from marking Bar/Bat Mitzvah celebrations themselves. So American Jewish kids included their "twins" on their invitations, strove to connect with their families behind the Iron Curtain, draped a tallit over an empty chair on the *bimah* to represent their missing partner, and sang "We Are Leaving Mother Russia" with gusto in the pews.

Today — as a result of the most successful human rights campaign in history — the prisoners of conscience have long been freed, to emigrate or to build meaningful Jewish life in the former Soviet Union. But the consciousness that "twinning" spawned got the ball rolling toward the revolutionary idea of using our *simchas* for the purpose of making other people's lives better — and it remains proof that big-time Tikkun Olam can really happen.

A similar, contemporary phenomenon is the growth of grassroots Tzedakah collectives. To be sure, the idea is related to the Jewish free loan society, the generations-old communal safety net designed to prevent an individual's descent into hopeless poverty. My teacher

Professor Eliezer Jaffe, a founder of Hebrew University's School of Social Work as well as its Center for the Study of Philanthropy, was a scholar of the Jewish free loan society. He also built the Israel Free Loan Association, for years the largest project of its kind in Israel. (The IFLA has continued his life-saving work after his passing in 2017.)

Today's grassroots Tzedakah collectives are perhaps rooted most of all in the "cultural earthquake" of the 1960s: the determination of many American Jews to own, embrace, and personalize their Jewish practice. This trend can also be seen in the rise of the *havurah* movement, the proliferation of customized *siddurim* and other liturgies, and the influence of folk music such as Shlomo Carlebach's and Debbie Friedman's songs. In the same vein, the development of the small, local Tzedakah collective—coordinated by a group of friends in the local community—reflects the rise of what I've called "personalized Tzedakah."

I'd like to think that my Ziv Tzedakah Fund contributed in some measure to this new consciousness. Ziv's power was in its direct and grassroots nature; its supporters sent in money, and we sought out powerful, creative, impactful Mitzvah heroes and their projects that often flew under the radar screen of larger, established systems. Ziv ceased operations in 2008 (Ziv Tzedakah Foundation of Canada remains active), but a proliferation of other Tzedakah funds are operating along similar principles: Kavod Tzedakah Fund, based in Omaha;[26] the Good People Fund in Millburn, New Jersey;[27] Boston's Yad Chessed[28] (which preceded Ziv); Jewish Helping Hands in New York City;[29] To Save a Life in Boynton Beach, Florida;[30] Hands On Tzedakah in Boca Raton, Florida;[31] etc. These are some of the premiere Tzedakah collectives and personalized Tzedakah projects in America today. Yet there are countless more examples of good people banding together, raising as much money as they can, and then making the all-important allocation decisions in accordance with their values.

What do these groups have in common with each other? They all embody a grassroots approach toward their desire to do good. Each is incorporated with a responsible board of trustees, people who are committed to ethical and responsible oversight. While each fund has its own particular flavor and focus, all of them are determined to distribute Tzedakah money in ways where the effectiveness of every dollar donated is maximized to its fullest potential. These people understand how to identify Mitzvah heroes who are doing crucial work in their respective fields, often (but not always) in unheralded and under-the-radar ways. The directors of these Tzedakah funds, especially Naomi Eisenberger at the Good People Fund (www.good-peoplefund.org) and Rabbi Joel Soffin at Jewish Helping Hands (www.jewishhelpinghands.org), can serve as excellent resources for people looking to start their own Tzedakah collectives, fulfilling that do-it-yourself spirit that has sprung up in Jewish life since the 1960s.

God knows, there is still an enormous amount of work to be done. Significant amounts of passivity and entitlement are slowing down the "revolution." Huge realms of Tikkun Olam wait to be explored. And yet, thanks to the growth of these hands-on changes in the Jewish landscape, there are plenty of reasons to be optimistic. Substantial numbers of creative Jewish minds—with ever-expanding technology at their disposal—are engaged in these efforts for the benefit of the present and future Jewish community.

2

Interpretations of Jewish Texts

The Angels (1980)

It all began—as so many of these pilgrimages into Eternity begin—in Jerusalem.

I was boarding a bus, setting out to explore the sights and wonders of the Holy City. It was a long-established custom of mine: I would arise early to examine the faces of the Jews, to make note of the rhythms of their footsteps . . . and their echoes, and to take in the personality of our Yerushalayim as she awoke from a quiet, full-starred night. And though it was only six-thirty in the morning, the bus was already crowded with Jews preparing to begin their sacred tasks of working and buying and selling and shouting Torah of many hues and tenors.

When I approached the driver, I handed him my card, which he punched *three* times. I was puzzled by his caprice. What could he mean by this inexplicable gesture? And so I asked, in my Virginia-drawled Hebrew, some stammered phrase that roughly translates as "For whom and for whom am I to pay His Honor, the Driver, two extra times?" His reply (without belaboring the nuances) could be rendered as something like this, "For *them!*" (He pointed to either side of me.) "Oh, *them!*" I said, looking around, still not knowing who *them* was.

But the driver was bigger than I was, the line behind me and *them* was long, and I did not want to start up with someone as mighty as the driver of an Egged bus. So I rode into town, confused, watching the sights and listening to the sounds of the City of Cities, thinking of *them*.

Toward noon, having completed my rounds of the crowds and alleyways, I wandered into one of the streetcorner yeshivas and began taking the Holy Books from the shelves—a Shulchan Aruch, volumes of the Talmud and Midrash, Bibles and translations in various tongues, many concordances—searching for the meaning of *them* in Jewish tradition. At four-thirty I had my first revelation. It was not as if the Highest Heavens had opened up for me (though this is not an entirely uncommon event in Yerushalayim, I am told). Nevertheless, there before me was the first breakthrough: a passage of Talmud blazing with meanings, hints, intuitions of a reality far exceeding the scope of my previously naïve experience with Judaism. Roughly translated, it looked like this:

> When you go into the bathroom, you should say, "Honorable Holy Ones, Servants of the Almighty, be honored, and give honor to the God of Israel. Wait for me, please, while I enter this place and do what I have to do, until I return to you." —*Berachot* 60b

In retrospect, it is apparent to me that millions of Jews over the centuries must have been talking to someone before going to the bathroom, but I, who had had too superficial and too unprogressive a Jewish education, must have missed knowing to whom I was supposed to address these lyrical remarks. So I re-examined the page and consulted the commentary of the genius of nine hundred years ago, Rashi. He explained: One recites this to the angels who accompany people everywhere, as it says in Psalm 91, "God will instruct His angels to watch over you wherever you go."

Aha! The angels! Now I understood my bus driver—I was paying for my angels.

Now I understood why buses in Yerushalayim were so crowded.

And, beyond that, now I understood why I had always found it so difficult to get through revolving doors and subway turnstiles. There were my two angels.

Now, enthused to the hilt (*farschvitzed* and *farbrennt*, my forebears would have said), I began taking down more and more volumes from the shelves, seeking out angels.

Abraham spoke with angels. They visited him in his pain of circumcision; they announced to him the imminent destruction of Sodom and Gomorrah; they proclaimed his wife's extraordinary pregnancy.

Indeed, an angel stayed Abraham's hand on Mount Moriah, saving that son, Isaac, and all of Jewish history.

Two generations later, Jacob saw angels in a dream, ascending and descending a ladder reaching from earth to heaven and from heaven to earth. And later, he would wrestle an angel all night, winning, but crippled in victory, for a name, our name, Israel.

Angels seemed to appear from everywhere. In the first century, the great Rabban Yochanan ben Zakkai spoke with angels. The Talmud is careful to point out that in addition to his vast expertise in Jewish matters, he knew the conversation of palm trees, of evil spirits, and of angels of every variety.

There were other texts, too.

The Talmud explains that a good and a bad angel accompany us home from synagogue Friday night, and when they see the candles lit, the table set with a white tablecloth, and the challahs, the good angel says, "So may it be next week." The bad angel must then reply, "So be it." You may notice, on Shabbas, how crowded it feels coming through your door, how you sometimes bump your elbow. Again, the angels.

Some Talmud tales relate how, when we are conceived, an angel named Lylah takes the drop of sperm to the Almighty and asks, "This drop—what will become of it? Will it be strong or weak, tall or short, male or female, rich or poor, wise or foolish?" (Lylah does not ask if the persons-to-be will become righteous or wicked; that is in our own hands alone.) This angel guards us through pregnancy, keeping us safe and secure as life takes form. Two other angels remain at the opening of the womb to prevent miscarriages. Another summons the soul destined for this human creature and places it in the sperm-and-egg.

There is more: One of those angels periodically takes the soul of this emerging being to Gan Eden and Gehinnom, Paradise and Hell, warning us of the consequences of our way of life. This angel gives us a Grande Tour of sorts, a preview of all of the glories of life, from where we shall live to where we shall die. And this same angel urges us from the womb, reluctant though we may be to leave the warmth of that world, because there, before birth, we were taught the entire Torah without pain, without struggle. Free and at ease. As we are born, the angel strikes us above the mouth, and we forget everything we learned; we cry our first cry of life over the Torah that is slipping away from us. It is the end of one life, and the beginning of another, a life where we must work hard to relearn all that Torah we once knew. A notch is left on our lip as a reminder of that unique moment, that awesome loss.

And so, too, at the end of life. The same angel comes to us one day and says, "Do you recognize me?" And we reply, "Yes, but why are you here today?" "It is your time." And again we weep, though we are not alone. We are fortunate; God is gracious to us; we never have to pass through the crises of life alone. Always there is this presence, even in death.

And so, Jewish tradition teaches that there are two kinds of angels of whom we are to be aware. One kind is present at the extraordinary occasions in the cycle of living. The other, a pair of angels, is always with us.

This latter category particularly interests me.

The verse Rashi quotes reads as follows, in full, "God will instruct His angels to watch over you wherever you go. They will carry you in their hands to keep you from stumbling." So Jews are never alone.

Existential alienation, so fashionable in the Sixties, still plagues many people. Loneliness is lethal—it squashes our sense of the exquisite in life, sucks our strength and will to respond fully to living. We read accounts of suicides and are confounded, torn with the sorrow of it all. In the eyes of our long centuries of Jewish literature, it is a blindness, an ignorance of the angels' ever-presence and care.

Angels are messengers, and their message, as I understand it, is that grandeur and majesty are not beyond our grasp as human beings. A passage from the Mishnah expresses this: Every single human being is required to say, "The entire world was created just for me" (*Sanhedrin* 37a). Life is arrayed before us in a breathtaking display of possibilities.

In Psalm 139, King David evokes this message, portraying himself as a simple creature made in God's image:

I thank You, O God,
for I am awesomely, wondrously created;
Your handiwork is extraordinary;
I must always be conscious of this. (Ps. 139:14)

And again, in Psalm 8:

When I survey Your heavens,
the work of Your hands,
the sun and the moon
which You have created—
I think—"Of what importance
can people be,
human beings—
of what concern are they to You?"
And yet [such a sublime "and yet"]
You have made them barely lower than divine,
You have crowned them
with infinite dignity and majesty. (Ps. 8:4-6)

And once more, in the Talmud:

All Jews are children
of a Great King. —*Bava Metzi'a* 113b

The presence of angels is our reminder that our connection with the Divine is an intimate one. Where we walk, there are opportunities for holiness, despite the pull of monotonies that deaden our senses.

The angels help us define ourselves: No matter what the specific doubts of identity—lawyer, mechanic, store owner—our *ultimate* definition is clear. The Talmud explains that as we enter the world at birth, we are made to take an oath. The words of this oath are stark, fraught with importance: *Be a Mensch* (*Niddah* 30b). We do not become a part of life as a neutral entity. We are obliged to respond to the messages transmitted ever-so-gently by the angels, to seek out the Menschlich in our selves and to actualize these qualities in our lives. One more text about angels illustrates this in a striking manner:

When the Jews are in distress, and one Jew separates himself from this distress, saying, "I will go home, eat, drink, and enjoy my own peace-of-mind," the two angels that are always with that Jew come and place their hands on his head and recite, "This person who has separated himself from the People of Israel shall not enjoy the comfort of Israel." — *Ta'anit* 11a

This is the moral dimension to God's angels in the life of a Jew, a responsibility, the necessity for commitment. The angels remind us of who we are, and what we must do.

Today, however, we are not accustomed to picturing angels. What can we say to know of them now? Plastic *tchatchkas* we see sitting atop Christmas trees in the Diaspora, Charlie's Angels (they should only enjoy good health), and a mediocre baseball team in California. We have lost much in the passage of time and in the uprooting of ancestors.

Some remnants of angels do remain, though, such as the Friday night ritual when we sing "*Shalom Aleichem, Malachay HaSharet,*" "Welcome to you, O Angels, servants of God." But we don't talk about this out in the real world. How are we—sophisticated moderns that we are—to explain that we are inviting angels to our Shabbas dinner table? (Thank God they don't eat—otherwise how would we explain the incredible food bills?)

As a poet, I have found it fairly easy to reconnect to my angels. I have even given them names: Refael, "Healing," and Nechama, "Consolation." However, for those of us who find it difficult to gain a primary sense of their presence, perhaps there is an alternate way to make sure the angels' messages remain distinct and constant elements in our lives.

We can associate with people who embody angelic qualities, the quiet Tzaddikim, like the lady in Connecticut who has sent five thousand plus packages of clothes to Israel over the past seventeen years, the man in Massachusetts laboring to teach a developmentally disabled man his Bar Mitzvah blessings, the American spending a year in Jerusalem taking tourists to meet these angelic figures, and so many others. They are everywhere, if we but look for them.

The Chasidic Rebbi, Naftali of Ropschitz, once hired someone to ask him every day, "For whom do you work?," to remind him that his labors were ultimately for the Holy One. That is the message of the angels, and the meaning of their presence.

Commentary on *Bava Batra* 8a (1989)

Once, when there was a drought [in Eretz Yisrael], Rabbi Yehuda HaNassi opened the food warehouses and announced, "Let all those who have studied Bible, Mishnah, Gemara, *halakhah*, and *aggadah* come in, but those who are ignorant of Torah should not enter."

Rabbi Yonatan ben Amram forced himself in [without identifying himself] and said to him, "My teacher, feed me!"

He said to him, "My son, have you studied the Bible?"

He answered, "No."

"Did you study the Mishnah?"

He answered, "No."

"If that is the case, how can I feed you?"

He answered, "Feed me as you would feed a dog or a raven."

He fed him.

When [Rabbi Yonatan ben Amram] left, Rabbi Yehuda HaNassi remained troubled, saying, "Woe is me! I have given food to one who is ignorant of Torah."

His son, Rabbi Shimon said, "Maybe that was your student, Rabbi Yonatan ben Amram, who has never wanted to gain any advantage because he has studied Torah?"

They checked and discovered that that was, indeed, the case.

Rabbi Yehuda HaNassi then said, "Let everyone enter." — *Bava Batra* 8a

This tale is 1,800 years old. It is such a troubling story. It could have been edited out of the Talmud because of its harshness, but it wasn't, and the fact that it remains in our literature must mean it was left there to instruct us.

The opening lines make no sense to me: How can Rabbi Yehuda HaNassi, leader of the Jews in Palestine, deny food to starving people simply on the basis of their Torah education? What of the Jews who were so poor they had to work day in and day out to eke out a living, and upon their return home were too exhausted to study? What of the Jews whose minds were unable to grasp the more sophisticated intricacies of Torah study? What of those who showed no interest in Torah study and, like everyone else, felt the pain and suffering of having no food to eat?

I admit that the story does have a comforting solution. But as Elie Wiesel has taught over and over again, the questions are much more significant than the answers and solutions. And these questions do not easily go away just because one of Rabbi Yehuda HaNassi's students forced the crisis to some more humane resolution.

Is the point that—in the face of outrageous injustice and enormous human suffering—we are to use all manner of radical methods to alleviate human suffering?

Is the point that—in the face of hunger and the bloated stomachs of children unfed for days and no hope for even minimal recovery—lesser scholars and less famous Jews are the real teachers of the Great?

Are we to derive from this text that we have been studying Torah all wrong, that while every Talmud student knows the name of Rabbi Yehuda HaNassi—compiler and editor of the Mishnah—the name we should *really* know is that of Rabbi Yonatan ben Amram?

Are we meant to study this text in order to forever remember how shocked we were—or if we were not shocked, how stunned we ought to have been—at what transpired centuries ago in the face of catastrophe in the Holy Land?

It is a troubling and vital story for our times.

Life (1995)

Tzedakah is Life.
Life is Tzedakah.
Tzedakah is even more than Life. It is immortality:

In Tzedakah's way is Life;
on its path is immortality. (Proverbs 12:28)

Life is a road. Tzedakah is a road. The road of Life and the road of Tzedakah are the same.

At times the road of Life may be dark and troublesome to negotiate. At other times it may be slippery, frightening, or treacherous.

Tzedakah clears the way. Tzedakah allows the walker/wanderer to continue on from any starting point to the final destination with confidence, peace of mind, and hope.

Two possibilities: (1) the road of Tzedakah takes us to the right destination; (2) the destination is of secondary importance . . . the very fact that human beings are on this particular road means that they are on the right road.

Three more possibilities: (1) even though it may be a well-worn path, our going that way makes the way smoother for others who come after us; (2) even if the road is paved and our footsteps make no noticeable impression, still, we know we are on the right road; (3) sometimes we are called upon to be trailblazers, opening up new trails for others.

For the person who uses all human powers [for Mitzvahs],
the road of Life leads upward. (Proverbs 15:24)

Say to this people:
Thus says God,
"I offer you the way of Life
and the way of death." (Jeremiah 21:8)

I love your Mitzvahs.
Give me Life through Your Tzedakah. (Psalm 119:40)

The way of Life is Tzedakah. One must be passionate about Tzedakah and Mitzvahs, no less passionate than about the things we crave as human beings that are no more than that: things.

One must love Tzedakah and Mitzvahs, no less than we, as human beings, love other people: spouses, soulmates, friends.

We are to love them no less than we love Life itself.

Teach me the path of Life.
In Your Presence is overwhelming joy;
eternal pleasantness is in Your right hand. (Psalm 16:11)

Torah guides us like a map: which way to turn, how steep the hills, how difficult or dangerous the way on a night of raging storm.

Torah shows which Mitzvah tools work best, and when. Torah teaches the feel of each tool, no less than the expert carpenter knows one saw's blade from another in relation to each particular kind of wood's resistance to the plane, no less than the surgeon knows which blade, scissors, or laser will ease the tumor from the kidney's wall. Torah teaches how to use the tools of Tzedakah to find our way, planting gardens and orchards along the roadside, removing stones from the path so others may walk with greater ease and enjoy the exquisite view.

Tzedakah is Life. Life is Tzedakah.

The act of caring, loving kindness is called "Life,"
as the verse states,
"Truly, Your caring, loving kindness — ever reliable —
is better than Life." —*Avot de-Rabbi Natan* 34, Psalm 63:4

Tzedakah is what gives Life its meaning. The meaning of Life, if we would use such a phrase, is using our Divinely given gifts to serve as God's agents ... to save the lives of those who should not die for the wrong reasons, to renew a sense of the Good Life in those who have lost hope, to give dignity to those who may have forgotten who they are—magnificent people, so important in God's eyes they are barely lower than angels, glorious, the work of God's own hands.

You have made them—at times nearly imperceptibly so—
barely lower than the Divine, gracing them with glory and majesty. (Psalm 8:6)

Your care, Your need to know that this thing called "Life" is truly good, and that these human beings You created will work things out; that we people can be partners with You in making a human-and-divinely decent world—*this* is what gives Life meaning. A Life of Tzedakah is Life.

Life Is the Good People (1995)

Ten are called "Life" ...
A Good Person is called "Life,"
as the verse states,
"The fruit of a Good Person is a tree of Life" (Proverbs 11:30).
—*Avot de-Rabbi Natan* 34

Good People are what makes life Life.

Life is being with the Good People, because they personify Tzedakah in everything they do. They affirm the goodness of Life, the incredible, at-times-miraculous power of human beings to bring sweetness and pleasantness and kindness and justice and decency into the lives of others.

In the verse from Proverbs, it doesn't state, "A Good Person is a tree of life," but rather, "The *fruit of a Good Person....*" Human goodness, righteousness, is defined by a person's acts, not by his or her thoughts. It is what they *do* and not what they *think* that makes them who they are.

They live well; they feel their lives are very rich, because of their relationship to others, tied to the rest of Life by acts of justice and decency . . . and humbly so. They are simply doing what is expected of them.

One such Good Person was the late father of one of my Ultimate Torah Teachers, Shmuel Munk. This man, learned in Torah, held a very important position for many years at a bank in Israel. His job was to get people who were slow to repay their loans . . . to repay them. This immediately conjures up seedy or sleazy images of investigators and heavy-handed tactics, repo people taking back cars purchased with the bank's money.

Not so. Shmuel's father was a person of such stature, so pleasant and sweet a human being, he established a record so impressive that when he retired, the bank could find no replacement. Borrowers repaid their debts because it was the right thing to do, the only thing to do.

The Good People, even though they have passed away,
are referred to as "alive." —*Ecclesiastes Rabbah* 9:4

This is immortality. Shmuel's father is no longer alive, yet he lives . . . through this story, the many other tales of his righteousness, and through his descendants, who live by his ideals and standards of what is humanly possible . . . and through the descendants of all those who benefited from his life of good deeds.

This is immortality. The descendants of the descendants of those who benefited from Shmuel's father will live a different, better life, because of how he chose to live his life.

This is immortality—the cycle continues until the end of time, because of his kindness, caring, and decency . . . like the rings of water that move outward and outward and all the way to the outer reaches of a pool or pond, because of one pebble dropped in the water, even a leaf fallen from a tree.

From such prosaic work—loans and repayment of loans—the fruits of the labors produce grand and everlasting results. It is exactly like the life-giving fruit we eat to give us strength. And if, sometimes, we bring the fruit to one who is starving, who is near death, and this is what restores the body to good health, that person, and all who are touched by him or her, and all those who come afterward who are touched by them, will have benefited.

As the scientists think of it: when the butterfly in Asia moves its wings, the weather in North America changes.

Nothing in Life is static. Whatever we do changes the course of people's lives and of Life itself . . . and history itself. Grand thinking this is, these intimations of eternity and immortality . . . and very Jewish thinking.

As to what makes Good People who they are, I have discovered (up to this point) what appear to be only two of their so-called "secrets," which are not really secrets at all. Both of these insights come from Shmuel Munk, who explained to me the essence of living the Life of the Good Jew:

A Good Person lives by unwavering trust in God. (Habakkuk 2:4)

Shmuel has an extraordinary sense that God always has the best interests of human beings in the forefront of the Divine Plan. While the Hebrew word *emunah* has come to mean "faith" in modern times, in its ancient philological context it really carries the weight of "absolute trust." This does not preclude the need to raise questions, and with great passion at that. Shmuel's kind of *emunah* is not naïveté or simplemindedness; nor does it imply surrendering one's critical powers to become a slave, cultist, or lemming-like person. To the contrary, it allows the Good Person's personality to be fully harnessed to brilliant Mitzvah activities, and it is a wonder to behold.

As best as I can tell, some people seem to achieve this with a degree of ease; others do so after an inordinate struggle; and still others never do reach this ability to trust, though they still never surrender the worthiness of the goal: acquiring the quality of *emunah* deep in the soul.

Shmuel's other "secret" comes from a verse he explained to me:

Cast your substance on God, Who will sustain you,
God will never let the Good Person stumble. (Psalm 55:23)

This verse's interpretation depends on the meaning of the word *yehavkha*, "your substance." Shmuel understands the verse to mean, "Put everything in Life in the Hands of God." Once a human being has done that, recognizing everything is from God, then all human reactions to Life's events, good and bad, uplifting or discouraging, will come as reactions of a person who believes God has the person's best interests in mind.

This, too, is a difficult human quality to acquire. The same statistical spread holds true with this verse as with the one from Habakkuk: Some seem to be able to hand everything over to God with a degree of ease; others after an inordinate struggle; and still others never do so.

Shmuel brought the concept down to very simple imagery for me. It is like a child and a parent at a street corner. They are about to step off the curb to move to the other side. There is a great deal of fast-moving traffic, a din, perhaps wild, frightening sounds coming from the cars and buses. There may even be a reckless or lunatic driver, or a drunk behind the wheel, approaching the intersection. Yet, the child puts his or her hand in the mother's or father's hand, and crosses the street, confident that it is safe to do so . . . the parent will watch out for the wellbeing of the child.

This makes more sense to me. I like the feeling of return-to-childhood. Surely the child is not a fool for trusting the parent. Surely the very shoes the child walks in were bought with the parents' money. Certainly things can go wrong when crossing the street—the light changes suddenly, someone runs a red light, harried pedestrians push and shove from all directions, rain and snow make the terrain slippery for the parent as well as the child.

Surely, Shmuel is teaching us fine Torah. And like all good Torah-insights, we can come back to his again and again, discovering new things each time.

Now, we can also understand two texts from the second century CE. One day, hundreds of years ago, in one of the many great places of Torah study in ancient Israel, in one particular discussion, Rabbi Akiva brought great words of wisdom to the attention of the assembled Rabbis. Overwhelmed with emotion, Rabbi Tarfon responded:

"Akiva, being too far away from you
is like being too distant from Life itself." — *Kiddushin* 66b

So intense was the moment, Rabbi Tarfon realized that simply knowing this man, just being in his presence, brought home to him a grasp of the feel and touch of Life itself. Note that Rabbi Tarfon does not say, ". . . from *the meaning of life* itself." His reaction is more fundamental than "meaning."

In a parallel passage in another part of the Talmud, our printed texts record Rabbi Tarfon's comment slightly differently:

"Akiva, being too far away from you
is like being too distant from one's own life." — *Zevachim* 13a

This phrase is as immediate as the other one, but it is personalized even more. Rabbi Tarfon feels that being close to Rabbi Akiva touches *his own Life* very deeply. He sees that his own Life is defined by his relationship to this genius of Life, Akiva ben Yosef—who, after all, was no more than a simple illiterate shepherd until at age forty, when, through the most unexpected circumstances, he assumed his Self and destiny through Torah study.

This is not magic. Nor is it mysticism, or hokey para-psychology. It is intimacy and connectedness in the highest form.

Rabbi Akiva himself passionately expressed how this teacher-student relationship served Life. It was at a high, joyous moment in his own personal life:

Once, when Rabbi Akiva made a feast for his son,
every time he opened a new barrel of wine
he would offer the toast,
"Here's to the lives of Torah teachers,
and here's to the lives of Torah students." —Tosefta *Shabbat* 7:8[1]

We are accustomed to saying "*L'chayim*—To Life!" as a toast. For Rabbi Akiva, Life is the interactive relationship between teacher and student, and student and teacher.

Returning now to the end of a verse mentioned at the beginning of this article, we read—

Wise people attach themselves to these Good Souls. (Proverbs 11:30)

It would follow that being with the Good People would lead us to Life at its most profound, most intimate and most intense.

And they are everywhere to be found. Commenting on the verse "And those who bring the people to do the right thing / shall be as the stars, eternal" (Daniel 12:3), one Jewish text offers the following insights:

Just as one sees the light of the stars
from one end of the world to the other,
so, too, one sees the light of Good People
from one end of the world to the other.
Just as the stars are sometimes visible
and at other times hidden,
so, too, with Good People.
And just as the clusters of stars
are so numerous they cannot be counted,
so, too, the groups of Good People are innumerable. —*Sifrei Devarim*, 'Ekev 11, 47

This poem of mine may synthesize the place of Good People in the Grand Scheme of Things:

The Good People everywhere
will teach anyone who wants to know
how to fix all things breaking and broken in this world—
including hearts and dreams—
and along the way we will learn such things as
why we are here
and what we are supposed to be doing
with our hands and minds and souls and our time.
That way, we can hope to find out why
we were given a human heart,
and that way, we can hope to know
the hearts of other human beings
and the heart of the world.[2]

This is the heart of the matter.

Jewish Jewish Leadership (1995)

Our topic is basic, vital: educating and training new leaders for the needs of the modern Jewish community. As we, Annie Sullivan/Helen Keller–like, try to locate these leaders, three larger questions emerge:

1. Of all the many talents needed to be a Jewish leader, are the elements of Mitzvah work and Tzedakah merely additional— desirable, but no more critical, than administrative skills? Or, as I contend, are these elements essential—strong unifying forces for the Jewish people?
2. If Mitzvah work and Tzedakah are in fact fundamental and indispensable to our Jewish leadership, shouldn't we be looking for leaders who possess these attributes—now? Can the Jewish community truly afford to choose people whose talents could be applied just as easily to raising funds for a university or restructuring the staff of a lobbying organization . . . as if there were no differences in the purpose of such leadership?

3. How do we get the powers-that-be to change the priorities in hiring practices and the selection of lay leadership?

The basis of this attempt to reorder the Jewish community's priorities in seeking Jewish leadership is, of course, Jewish text.

1. The Ultimate Purpose of the Jewish Leader: Doing Good for Others

Rabbi Levi said,
whoever thinks to himself or herself
before going to sleep at night
"When I wake up tomorrow,
I will do good things for So-and-So."
That person will ultimately share great joy
with the Good People in the Future, in the Next World,
as the verse states,
"For those who plan good, there is joy" (Proverbs
     12:20). — *Midrash Mishlay* (Proverbs) 12:1

We catch a glimpse of the kind of person who constantly plans new Mitzvahs to do in a brief phrase from the Jerusalem Talmud:

There was a certain woman who loved
the Mitzvah of Tzedakah very much. . . . — *Terumot* 8:5

To be in love with the Mitzvah of Tzedakah! That is the beginning of *Jewish* Jewish leadership.

If more and more individuals would do as the text says, planning the night before for the next day's activities of doing good for others, we will have moved that much closer to a Menschlich, Jewish world. Whatever the crises that arise, whatever other skills the leader has, will all be harnessed to that goal.

2. Everyone Counts; Doing Good

Our teachers have said:
Once, while Moses, our Teacher,
was tending [his father-in-law] Yitro's sheep,

one of the sheep ran away.
Moses ran after it until it reached a small, shaded place.
There, the lamb came across a pool and began to drink.
As Moses approached the lamb, he said,
"I did not know you ran away because you were thirsty.
You are so exhausted!"
He then put the lamb on his shoulders and carried him back.
The Holy One said,
"Since you tend the sheep of human beings
with such overwhelming love —
by your life, I swear
you shall be the shepherd of My sheep, Israel." — *Exodus Rabbah*
2:2

Comments:

1. Moses is living with Yitro in Midian because he is a wanted man. While the Children of Israel were enslaved in Egypt, he had killed an Egyptian taskmaster who was beating a fellow Jew. With a price on his head, Moses fled to distant lands, eventually losing his status as Prince of Egypt and becoming a shepherd for this man named Yitro. He eventually married the boss's daughter, Tzipporah.
2. Rather than curse the one stray sheep that is making his work more difficult, he values it, pursuing it into the wilderness. In many communities, the single stray sheep today include: Jews with disabilities and challenges, battered Jewish spouses, poor Jews, Jews with AIDS, and a host of other categories of people who are far from the center of Jewish activity.
3. Finding the thirsty sheep at the pool of water, Moses does not curse the stray sheep. Rather, he humbly admits his own short-comings, admitting that he was not aware that this individual sheep had particular needs beyond that of the rest of the flock.
4. God takes note of Moses's sense of compassion (*rachamim*). But compassion can be a relatively cheap emotion if it remains

just an emotional response to a Mitzvah-situation. It is the fact that Moses *carried the sheep back to the flock*, that he *did* something *to act* on his emotional response to the situation that convinced God that this was the true future leader of the Jewish people.

5. Consider the situation in Montreal. After a demographic study, the Jewish community discovered there were 18,000 of its 90,000 Jews living in poverty. After their initial astonishment at the magnitude of the human needs, the members of the Jewish community immediately put enormous effort and talents toward finding solutions to this devastating situation. No one blamed the victims, the poor Jews, no one recited the standard list of woes, "We are already overwhelmed with work" or "Where shall we find the resources?" Foremost in the minds of the leaders in Montreal was the benefit of their poor Jewish brothers and sisters.

6. On the negative side, sadly: at the Chase Memorial Nursing Home in New Berlin, NY, a Dr. William Thomas has created an extraordinarily human environment for the residents. The actual results are quite staggering, these being just two of them: (1) they have cut the medications in half in the first two and a half years of their program (called "the Eden Alternative") and, (2) in comparison to the residents of a similar home nearby, the Eden residents have experienced half the infections the others have suffered. One would think, with such staggering statistics that Jewish nursing homes around the country would jump to contact Dr. Thomas, at least to ask how he does it, and possibly to go see the Eden Alternative in action. Not so. The suggestion is rarely taken up, not even a thank-you from one director who received Dr. Thomas's book as a present. Imagine, cutting the quantity and costs of medication in half—a solution to all the laments about rising medical costs in nursing homes. How would one explain it?

7. In sum, it is how we *act*, not how we think, that defines us as Jews and as human beings.

3. Juggling One's Emotions

[While Moses was tending Yitro's flocks,
God took note of Moses's concern
for the anguish of the Children of Israel suffering in Egypt.]
... The Holy One said:
Since Moses is so disheartened and distraught
by the woes of Israel in Egypt,
he is worthy to be their shepherd. — *Exodus Rabbah* 2:6

When the Jews are in trouble, no one should say,
"I will go home, eat, drink, and be at peace with myself." — *Ta'anit* 11a

Many North American Jews are living quite comfortably. Why would they want to disturb their peace of mind and comfort by being "disheartened and distraught by the woes of Israel"?

Because it is the Jewish thing to do.

How does one juggle the need to be distressed with the happiness of a well-to-do life? How do those people who do so function "normally"? How do they define "normal"?

This would make a wonderful topic for a psychological/psychiatric study.

4. The Jewish Leader as *Tzaddik*

A story is told of Binyamin HaTzaddik,
who was the supervisor of the community's Tzedakah fund.
Once, when there was little food to be had,
a woman came to him and said, "Rabbi, feed me!"
He answered, "I swear that there is nothing left in the Tzedakah fund."
She said, "If you do not feed me,
a woman and her seven children will die."

So he fed her from his own money. (*Bava Batra* 11a)

And so we learn:

A. The model for Jewish leaders should first and foremost be the *Tzaddik*.

B. A Jew can become a *Tzaddik* more easily than one might think. We should not be frightened by the term, believing it only means "Righteous One." In Jewish literature, *Tzaddik* often means "a good person, a Mensch, *a guter Yid*." While few attain true righteousness, all have the potential to become *Tzaddikim* by striving toward it. *Jewish* Jewish leaders should foster these *Jewish* Jewish leadership skills which are already present in everyone.

C. The Talmudic tale of Binyamin HaTzaddik proves the principle: When nothing else can be done, something can *still* be done. In the story, when the community's resources are not sufficient to solve the problem, the leader takes it upon himself to resolve it.

5. Where the Leaders Are

And those who bring the people to do the right thing
shall be as the stars, eternal. (Daniel 12:3)

Just as one sees the light of the stars
from one end of the world to the other,
so, too, one sees the light of the Good People
from one end of the world to the other.
Just as the stars are sometimes visible
and at other times hidden,
so, too, with the Good People.
And just as the clusters of stars
are so numerous they cannot be counted,
so, too, are the groups of Good People innumerable. —*Sifre Devarim*, 'Ekev 11, 47

From this text we learn that leaders are everywhere, and they are too many to count. Some wish to remain anonymous, doing their work quietly behind the scenes.

We need to find them, learn from them, apply their insights into solving the problems at hand.

6. How Much Power

Rabbi Yehuda used to say:
Ten strong things were created in the world—
A mountain is strong, but iron cuts through it.
Iron is strong, but fire can make it bubble.
Fire is strong, but water puts it out.
Water is strong, but clouds contain it.
Clouds are strong, but the wind [*Ruach*] can scatter them.
Breath [*Ruach*] is strong, but the body holds it in.
The body is strong, but fear breaks it.
Fear is strong, but wine dissipates its effects.
Wine is strong, but sleep overcomes its power.
Death is stronger than all of them.
But Tzedakah saves from death, as it is written,
"And Tzedakah saves from death" (Proverbs 10:12).
 —*Bava Batra* 10a

We can infer at least three teachings here:

A. Tzedakah can save people from dying for all the wrong reasons. A society built on Tzedakah may in fact guarantee that no one is without food, clothing, shelter, medical attention, companionship, self-esteem, and Meaning in Life.

B. Therefore, a person who does Tzedakah wields the power of life and death. This awesome responsibility, and source of great uplift, is what the Talmud calls *Simcha shel ha-Mitzvah*—the Joy of Doing Mitzvahs.

C. It would be wise for Jewish educators to communicate to children early on that they have this power, and that it will give true and lasting meaning to their Life. For example: every time a child brings a can of tuna fish, or a sweater, or a stuffed teddy bear to the synagogue, to later be taken to a food bank or soup kitchen — educators can tell that child: *You are doing life-saving Mitzvah work.* Then this young person will know from earliest childhood that she or he is capable of making an awesome difference in the lives of others.

7. The Great Paradox

Rabbi Yehuda Nesiah and the Rabbis had a disagreement.
One said:
According to the leader, so the generation.
The others said:
According to the generation, so the leader. — *Arachin* 17a

This dispute makes for a great discussion topic in leadership seminars. Which contention is true, or are they both true? Is one scenario more prevalent than the other, depending on the times and the leaders?

8. Difficult Enough Being a Jew; Harder Being a Jewish Leader

When the members of his community
wanted to appoint Rabbi Akiva their leader,
he said,
"Let me discuss it with my household."
They followed him home and overheard them saying,
"If you take the position,
know that they will curse you
and they will despise you." — Jerusalem Talmud, *Pe'ah* 8:6

Even though Rabbi Elazar ben Azariah assumed a position
of distinguished leadership in the community,

nevertheless,
he lived a long life. — Jerusalem Talmud, *Berachot* 1:6

In a generation of spiritual, Jewish, and human giants, Rabbi Akiva was the preeminent Sage, hero, and leader of his generation. How, then, could he be despised?

My students who have pondered the tale of Rabbi Akiva largely came to either one or the other of two conclusions:

A. It is the nature of the job. No matter how hard Jewish leaders try to be faithful to the task, they will be mistreated, abused, misinterpreted, and beaten down by criticism.
B. The story only relates to Rabbi Akiva and some, but not all, Jewish leaders. While such divisiveness frequently occurs, it doesn't *necessarily* have to happen. Surrounding oneself with caring colleagues whose ultimate concern is the dignity and wellbeing of others is one of many safeguards. It would be worthwhile to conduct leadership seminars covering this topic: how to respond to mistreatment and abuse, how to respond *Jewishly*.

The story of Rabbi Elazar ben Azariah (related, I believe, with a little Talmudic humor) would seem to indicate that one can manage not only to survive the trials of Jewish leadership but thrive, and live long and well.

9. Arrogance: Unacceptable

There are four kinds of people no one can stand: . . .
[One of them is]
a communal leader who is arrogant toward his people
for no good reason. — *Pesachim* 113b

Anything (or *nearly* anything) accomplished for the good of the Jewish people by arrogance and high-handedness can likely be achieved at least as effectively by kindness and humility. Arrogance implies a lack of *kavod* (respect) for human dignity and other human beings, all created in God's image. According to the Torah, Moses was the most humble person on earth (Numbers 12:3).

10. Torah and Leadership

When Rabbi Chaggai would appoint communal leaders,
he would teach them Torah,
explaining to them that all authority is given by virtue of its
    Torah-source—
"Through me [the Torah] rulers reign . . .
Through me, sovereigns rule . . ." (Prov. 8:15–16). —Jerusalem
    Talmud, *Pe'ah* 8:6

Rabbi Yehoshua ben Levi said,
I once learned eighty laws
concerning graves that had been plowed over
from Yehuda ben Pedaya,
but, because I was so involved in community affairs,
I forgot them all. —*Ecclesiastes Rabbah* 7:7

According to the first text, the very reason for Jewish leadership is to be a partner in working out God's plan for a decent, Menschlich world. Torah provides the source of Jewish values from which leaders can work to create a better world.

The second text reminds us that, sometimes under the stresses of leadership, and because of the demanding hours, the Torah that has already been studied is forgotten. So much the more do leaders need to concentrate their efforts on Torah study: to retain what was once learned and to continually gain new insights. Without the Jewish text/Jewish values element, there would be no difference between the director of a Jewish community agency and the president of a hospital or university.

11. Brains and Talent, Life and Privilege

Happy is the person who is מַשְׂכִּיל in relation
to the person in need. (Psalm 41:2)

Rabbinic literature records three variants of a statement by Rabbi
Yona on this verse, all of which play on the word "מַשְׂכִּיל — *maskil*," from
the familiar Hebrew/Yiddish root "שכל — *sechel*," meaning "insight,
common sense, intelligence." Each of the three texts offers specific
ideas about the way Jewish leaders should think.

> A. Rabbi Yona said, "Happy is the one who *gives* to the person in
> need" is not what the verse says, but rather, "Happy is the one
> who is ... *Maskil* in relation to the person in need," namely, one
> must examine the Tzedakah situation thoroughly in order to
> find the best way possible to perform the Mitzvah. —Jerusalem
> Talmud, *Pe'ah* 8:8

Since Jewish leadership is a matter of examining Tzedakah situations,
i.e., places where injustice and inequity exist and things need to be
returned to proper balance, this text is a reminder that the leader
must use heart, mind, hands, talents, creativity, personality—all of
God's gifts—to make this happen. Leaders are to determine *exactly*
what the person or situation requires, and then bring all these forces
to bear to meet those needs.

> B. Rabbi Yona said, "Happy is the one who is ... *Maskil*, i.e., using
> one's talents, [and discovering new talents in the Mitzvah process]
> when giving to those in need."
>
> What does *Maskil* mean in this case? That the person-doing-
> Tzedakah takes an intense look at the Mitzvah situation at hand
> and considers the best way to give the other person back his or
> her decent and dignified Life. —*Midrash on Psalms* 41:3

The Hebrew for "to revive" is *lehecheyoto*. It can mean "to give life
back to someone," "to revivify someone," "to bring one back to life."
All of these tell us that by using the power of Tzedakah, the Jewish

leader can give people who have lost their vitality and hope a chance to begin again.

Doing this effectively takes creativity, which is Rabbi Yona's point. I often consider: if all Jewish creative artists would take only 10% of their talent for painting or sculpture or poetry or music and apply it to Mitzvah creativity—how much closer would we be to Menschlich society?

> C. Rabbi Yona said, "Happy is the person who gives to the person in need" is not what the verse says, but rather, "Happy is the one who is . . . *Maskil* in relation to the person in need," meaning: Look at the situation carefully, and keep in mind how great a privilege it is to do the Mitzvah through that person. —*Leviticus Rabbah* 34:1; Margaliot 4:773

According to Rabbi Yona, doing the Mitzvah of Tzedakah is one of the glories of life. To use his term, it is a *zekhut*, a privilege, to be afforded this opportunity.

Thus, whatever the burdens and trials of being a Jewish leader, if the Jewish leader remembers that to spend one's days fixing what is broken in life (broken people and broken hearts among them) is one of the great opportunities we have been given—then the labors of leadership will become a treasured source of great meaning, joy, and peace.

DNA Analysts

Parashat Shemot (1996)

> "The average height of young Chileans has
> increased by 6 inches in the past thirty years."
> —Dr. Fernando Monckeberg[3]

> But Moses said to God,
> "Please, O God, I have never been a man of words,

either in times past or now that You have spoken to Your servant;
I am slow of speech and slow of tongue." (Exodus 4:10)

"They won't believe me; they won't listen to my voice. They will
say, 'God didn't appear to you.'" (Exodus 4:1)

Why, of all people, did Moses have a speech impediment? Several
possibilities have been posited for this:

1. It is a constant reminder to Moses and the people that no one
   is perfect. There is no danger of mistaking Moses for some
   supernatural or divine being.
2. By the same Midrashic line, it made Moses humble. Humility
   is an absolutely essential quality for leaders, as the Torah states
   later on, "Moses was very humble, more humble than any per-
   son on earth" (Numbers 12:3).
3. The people had to listen to Moses that much more carefully
   to catch the meaning of his words. (Someone once told me—
   though I can't say for sure it is true—that Chaim Weizmann
   always spoke very softly, so people would have to pay closer
   attention.)
4. No one could accuse the Jews of accepting the Torah because
   Moses was a dazzling speaker. To the contrary: As I learned
   from Professor Saul Lieberman, Moses's inarticulate mum-
   blings prove it was *the content* of the Torah, and not the mode
   of delivery, that moved them to say, "We will do and we will lis-
   ten" (Exodus 24:7).
5. It is living proof of the ability of people with disabilities to
   succeed.

Our Job in Life:

1. To question diagnoses.
2. To try *all* methods, *absolutely all* methods, to differentiate
   between genetically caused or trauma-induced limitations and

false or temporary disabilities that can be eliminated through (a) the Mitzvah of Tzedakah, i.e., what is just and right, (b) love and care, (c) creative therapeutic techniques, and (d) a constant reminder to ourselves that a certain percentage of the irreversible (17%?, 29%?, 68%?) is not irreversible.

A thirteen-year-old young man, president of his day school student body, told me about the students' visits to the local residence for Elders. They visit, they talk, they listen, they sing and entertain, but underlying it all, as he described it, is that most of the Elders are "gone," irrevocably condemned to a zombie-like state.

He is wrong. Until everyone involved in the lives of those Elders reassesses which ones are absolutely, irreparably *biologically* damaged, the thirteen-year-old's job, the day school students' job, is to discover and develop any and all methods to bring out the best, most glorious, and noble aspects of their beings back into the light of day.

We need to find out what is caused by weak or damaged genes, cellular degeneration, and poor nutrition, as well as depression, loneliness, or uselessness, so we can proceed accordingly with the appropriate acts of Tikkun Olam—fixing things.

That's our job, too, no less than the physician or psychologist, or the day school students.

Three Common Examples:

1. Helen Keller and Annie Sullivan.
2. The Special Olympics.
3. Wilma Rudolph, world record holder in the 1960s of the 100- and 200-meter dash . . . despite having a childhood reality that included polio, scarlet fever, double pneumonia, and a damaged leg supported by orthopedic braces.

We, the Teachers:

1. We would do well to apply the First Rule of Special Education to all education and human interrelationships, namely: Look

at the other person fairly and lovingly, discover by any and all methods what the person's abilities and talents are, and use any and all methods to actualize those abilities and talents, i.e., to always seek out the glorious soul within, the *gute neshamah*, the good, sweet divinely given soul from which all human grace and poetry spring.

2. We should buck the trend of complicating terminology. On résumés, on tax forms, on applications, and when referring to ourselves, we should write and say, "Teacher." There is really no need for the word "Educator" or "Pedagogic Specialist." Making it longer doesn't help. Think of the medical term PIE — pyrexia of indeterminate etiology, compared to FUO — fever of unknown origin. If it was good enough for Moses to be called *Rabbeynu*, Our Teacher, it should be good enough for us. Indeed, we would do well to consider that, of all the descriptives the Talmud and Midrash could have given Moses — Our Leader, Our Prophet, Our Liberator — they chose *Rabbeynu*, Our Teacher.

And so, it would seem that what we might want to be when we grow up is a Teacher, the one who reveals all that is hidden in the human soul, reveals the grandeur and the glory to the person himself or herself and to all others who would meet that human being in the course of a natural lifetime.

Why Young Chileans Are 6 Inches Taller Than Their Parents and Grandparents Were in the 1950s:

Suppose you and a friend are traveling through Scandinavia. At some point, perhaps while savoring the herring in Reykjavik or Oslo, you might remark on the striking height and build of the Icelanders or Norwegians. Finishing the meal with some unusually tasty flatbread, you might add, "What marvelous genes these folks have!"

Suppose you and a friend are on vacation, strolling around Santiago or Valparaiso or Antofagasta. You might never remark, "How short the children are compared to ours in America!"

... because Dr. Fernando Monckeberg set up infant nutrition centers throughout Chile.

... because Dr. Fernando Monckeberg established a system of intensive treatment centers for infants throughout the country.

And another statistic: Whereas in the 1950s more than two-thirds of Chile's children age 6 and younger were undernourished and mentally damaged, today, about 8% are undernourished, most of them to a mild degree.

And another statistic: In the 1950s the infant mortality rate in Chile was more than 130 deaths/1,000 live births. Today it is fewer than 16/1,000.

Let us, then, consider all those Chileans in their early and mid-childhood, teens, twenties, thirties, and forties who are bright, active, animated citizens, because of The Good Dr. Monckeberg.

Let us, then, consider all those Chileans in their early- and mid-childhood, teens, twenties, thirties, and forties who might not be alive today were it not for The Wise Dr. Monckeberg who suspected all along it wasn't in the genes at all.

And so, what we might want to be when we grow up is a Fernando Monckeberg.

Rachel:

According to those who knew her, Rachel died at age 100. Born in Kurdistan, she came to Jerusalem many years before, perhaps in the late 1940s or early 1950s.

In her old age, for reasons unknown to me, she became one of Jerusalem's street beggars. Into her eighties she sat there, hand extended, rattling her coins to get the attention of passers-by. And sometime in Rachel's eighties, Myriam Mendilow, God rest her awesome soul, came along and put her to work at Life Line for the Old. Rachel made ceramic beads that became beautiful jewelry. Hundreds, perhaps thousands, of Jerusalemites and tourists from around the world wear jewelry fashioned by her ancient hands.

This is what Mrs. Mendilow wrote me a number of years ago, "I regret to inform you that we lost Rachel, from Ceramics. She was one hundred years old when she died—she just lay down and fell asleep forever. For me, she represented the story of Life Line. I shall always remember her. From a beggar in the streets, we made of her an honourable and beautiful citizen."

She might have lived her last years as a beggar whose body was found one day in her room by some neighbor. No one would have noticed. No one would have missed her.

That is why, when we grow up, we might want to become a Myriam Mendilow.

Va-yishlach

Our Ancestor Jacob, the One with the
Bad Hip, and Other Tales (1999)

By way of introduction, a personal note:

As the old Yiddish saying goes, "Before I begin to speak, I wish to say a few words." People wonder why I, with a perfectly good Hebrew name—Daniel—have the Hebrew name Yaakov, Jacob.

The explanation is simple: my grandmother, Tzirel Devorah bat Binyamin, wanted an Avraham, a Yitzhak, and a Yaakov in the family (my father is Yitzhak, and my older brother, Stan, is Avraham).

All my life I have followed the story of Jacob, worried about him, and reviewed two passages in which he is featured again and again—the dreams with the ladder and with those angels going up and down (Gen. 28:10–22), and his wrestling match with the angel (Gen. 32:25–33). I have tried to make sense of them in the broadest sense, in the overall context of his life, but with little success. All I come up with are pieces here and there, fragments of some ancient shard of pottery, but not quite enough to see whether it is a simple water jug, a container for the winter grain, or one of those marvelous jars found decades ago in the Judean desert containing scrolls that will help make ultimate sense of God's world and what we, the People, must do to make it "the Best of All Possible Worlds."

The Wrestling Match vs. the Dream

Jacob wrestles with the angel, is told he has struggled with a Divine Being and a human being, emerges triumphant, is injured, has his name changed from Ya'akov to Yisrael, and then gets on with his life.

This commentary is not about how all of life is a struggle, how if you take on the mighty ones — corrupt corporations, evil forces, governments and councils who care not for their citizens and wards, classic family dysfunctionalities — you will have to fight mightily and will emerge exhausted and scarred for life. I never liked that approach, though it is certainly true some of the time. The message is too discouraging: Take on God's and humanity's injustices and you will be covered with dirt and grime, perhaps never to recover from the contest.

I prefer Jacob's earlier, more gentle, and more soothing encounter with the Divine: the silent dream. In this dream he followed the angels up the stairway to heaven, saw God's plan, returned to earth with the vision firmly implanted in his imagination, awoke, and set out to live his life as a Jew.

> He said, "How awesome is this place!
> This is none other than the abode of God,
> and that is the gateway to heaven." (Gen. 28:17)

He called the place "awesome," "God's House," "the Gate of Heaven," and, sure enough, wherever he will go until his last day will be awesome, God's House, and the Gate of Heaven. He then took an oath about Tzedakah:

> "I will give away a tenth of everything you give me." (Gen. 28:22)

As for myself, I would be a dreamer rather than a wrestler. Indeed I would. In my imagination, I can feel the smooth glide of the angels, going up and down the stairway to heaven, extending their hands, beckoning me to follow.

Our Ancestor Jacob, the One with the Bad Hip

As I write this *derash*, it is summertime in Jerusalem. I am making my annual rounds with my interns and the hundreds of United Synagogue Youth Israel pilgrims who will visit Tzedakah projects and meet mitzvah heroes here and throughout the country. Our conversations impel me to wonder if our ancestor Jacob, visiting our synagogues in our time for the bar or bat mitzvah of a grandchild, would be able to get up to the *bimah* for an *aliyah*. If there were no ramp, how would he do it?

He was limping on his hip. (Gen. 32:32)

All night Jacob struggled with the angel, and as dawn breaks by the Yabbok stream, he limps, the consequence of a nasty all-night struggle. Either he injured his sciatic nerve, he dislocated his hip, or he tore ligaments and joint-connectors. Maybe he limped in pain for a day or a few days or the rest of his life. Whatever the simple meaning of the text, he was not the man he had been the evening before.

For that matter, we might wonder if his father, Yitzchak, would be able to follow along in our *siddurim*. Yitzchak had severely impaired vision in his old age (Gen. 27:1). There is no large-print siddur for him to use.

Would we leave two of our ancestors out of our congregational life (and other communal activities) today for lack of access? Indeed, at least three out of seven of our direct ancestors might be said to be on the fringes of Jewish life:

Leah's eyes were weak. (Gen. 29:17)

It is summertime in Jerusalem, and I am making my rounds. Just last night, my friends and I visited Yoel Sharon and Nachum Prital, founders of Etgarim/Challenge. Etgarim provides sports, athletics, and wilderness survival opportunities throughout Israel for individuals with physical disabilities. We saw videos of people going down rocky hills backward, tied to a cable, rocking in their wheelchairs, tilting at serious angles, sometimes tipping over, emerging triumphant. We saw clips of a man doing his thing on water skis (it seemed irrelevant whether he had lost a leg by accident, disease, or genetic mishap), and another man, blind (by accident, disease, or genetic mishap) doing the same. We saw groups of Israelis on sitdown, single-ski contraptions enjoying their thrills in the Austrian Alps, wind- and sunburned at day's end, triumphant. One would hope that the descendants of Jacob and Isaac and Leah would meet the Etgarim people (who consider themselves neither Tzaddikim nor heroes) and—though perhaps discouraged at first, distraught at disability in the abstract and in their real lives—would come to have some fun, some sublime fun.

Just three weeks ago we met Yosef Lev, the master who teaches martial arts to many individuals with disabilities, physical and otherwise. He knows how to teach people the joys of karate, judo, and the other classical modes of self-defense. It is a wonder to behold, and according to my assistants (some of whom wound up on the floor after trying to attack individuals in wheelchairs), a greater wonder to experience. One would hope that the descendants of Jacob and Isaac and Leah would meet Yosef Lev (who considers himself neither a Tzaddik nor a hero) and—though perhaps discouraged at first, distraught at disability in the abstract and in their real lives—would come to have some fun, some sublime fun, and more peace of mind.

A Reexamination of My Grandma Tzirel's Wish

Ya'akov: It is a very uncomfortable name to have, to carry with you all your life. Everyone tells you it comes from the root *ayin-kuf-beit*, which means that Ya'akov is the Tricky One, the Sly One, the One-Who-Is-Willing-to-Take-Advantage—which is the point of the wrestling match with the angel. His life as trickster is finished. His new name is to be *Yisrael*: Jew, Yid, a person with *a Yiddishe neshamah*, a Jewish soul.

I am stuck with Ya'akov. No one ever renamed me Yisrael. Am I forever condemned to struggle, to overcome my name, to resist the urge to walk over people to get to things, to ideas, to goals that are phony gods?

When I was a student about twenty-five years ago, one of my Tanakh rebbis, the late Moshe Held, *menuchato shalom*, taught me that one of the meanings of the root *ayin-kuf-beit* is "to guard, to watch," as in Jeremiah 17:9: *Keep watch* ['akov], *guard your heart, protect it from all bad things.*

So the struggle is over: I, Ya'akov, and all others bearing the name are assured God's protection, as the verse states in Jeremiah 30:10:

"Be not afraid, My servant, Jacob," declares God.
"I will save you, even at times when I appear to be so far away you cannot sense My Presence."

As long as we can feel the touch of the angels, and keep a clear vision of what they showed us at the very top of the stairway to heaven, all of us will most assuredly be safe, under the glorious wings of the Shekhinah.

Teaching Jewish Texts Today (2020)

A Jewish library should have two types of books. In one category, there are standard, contemporary books on Jewish themes, such as the works of Elie Wiesel, a coffee-table volume of photographs of Jerusalem, biographies of Brandeis and Ben Gurion, and a history of the Jews of Eastern Europe. Alongside those are the classical Jewish texts—Bible, Talmud, midrash, and halakhic codes, all with their appropriate translations, commentaries, and updates.

This chapter is about the texts that have come down to us beginning with biblical times, through the Rabbinic and medieval periods, and centuries afterward. They are divided into two main categories: *halakhah*, legal material that relates to Jews' everyday practice; and *aggadah*, stories upon stories that are biographical, imaginary, fantastic, and mystical. Both types of classical literature express Jewish values and in many ways point to a life of Menschlichkeit.

I reject the idea that physical books are on their way to obsolescence. There is a familiarity, indeed an *intimacy* with a book— especially a sacred text that is studied, reflected upon, and returned to—that is irreplaceable. That said, the Internet age has provided new tools that have revolutionized Torah study. Just a few years ago I would remark upon how amazing the Bar-Ilan Judaic Library CD-ROM was, a substantial archive of Jewish texts on one slim disc—and yet now that technology seems so archaic! Sites and apps like Sefaria: A Living Library of Jewish Texts (www.sefaria.org) make a universe of Rabbinic literature available to anyone, anywhere—much of it also provided in translation. These tools don't *replace* the books, but rather *complement* them in a way that makes them more accessible than ever to students who seek them out.

In college, I was in the double-degree Joint Program of Columbia University's School of General Studies, majoring in comparative literature, and the Jewish Theological Seminary (JTS), with an emphasis in Bible and Talmud; upon graduating, I continued at JTS for another three years. Those seven years were filled with hours, days, weeks, and months of general literature and Jewish text study. Along the way, I began to realize that while Aristotle, Mann, Joyce, and Camus had much to say about living life deeply and well, there was a certain element they were not giving me.

What does the study of *halakhah* and *aggadah* provide that the classics of world literature do not? Jewish literature takes as its opening premises that life's value supersedes even the Law itself. It starts from a shared set of values, such as Tzedakah, *bracha* (blessing), the inherent spiritual value of Torah study, and *teshuvah* (the human capacity to grow, improve, and fix what has been broken). Most of all, *halakhah* and *aggadah* encompass the Jews' guidelines of living, by means of the Jews' stories. For this reason alone, they are worthy of our study, no less than a Hawaiian's appreciation of the stories of Pele (goddess of the volcano) and tales a Native American child is told by the tribal elders.

Learning *halakhah* is not restricted to explanations of Jewish practice, such as what Shabbat, holidays, and keeping kosher mean. We also ask value-laden questions and weigh their answers. When there is a conflict between Jewish practices and values, we ask which takes precedence. We may inquire, for instance, in what serious medical circumstances may a sick person be fed non-kosher food? In a similar vein, certain individuals—those who could be harmed by fasting—are not merely permitted to eat on Yom Kippur; they are *required* to eat. Fasting by those who may be impaired definitively contravenes the *halakhah*. Likewise, when it comes to saving lives, the *halakhah* says that even if it is not 100 percent clear that it is a life-and-death situation, many of the Shabbat laws are superseded. In fact, an Orthodox doctor who once treated me in Israel told me that during the Yom Kippur War he got in his car and drove to the war hospital zones, *with his* kippah *clearly visible*. Even though he appeared to be violating *halakhah* by driving on the holiest day of the year, it was indisputable that his life-saving work took precedence, and he did not need to mitigate anyone's false impressions by taking the *kippah* off his head.

From the values derived from *aggadah* stories—there are so many—I mention just two. The first describes Rabbi Akiva: When he visited a sick colleague, he swept and mopped the floor of the sick man's house, since that seemed to be what the situation called for. And when his colleague recovered, he declared that Akiva's act had contributed to his recovery (Babylonian Talmud, *Nedarim* 40a). In other words, no one should ever consider their Mitzvah-work insignificant or of little importance. Indeed, to another person it may make all the difference in the world, far more than we may have imagined.

The second story is one of my favorites. A certain Rabbi Broka met the Prophet Elijah one day in the market. He asked Elijah, "Who among all these people is destined to experience the rewards of Paradise in the Next World?" Pointing to a specific pair, Elijah told the rabbi that *they* qualified for eternal life. The rabbi approached them and asked, "What is it you two do?" They answered, "We are jokers. We make people laugh" (Babylonian Talmud, *Ta'anit* 22a). I really love this offbeat talmudic tale. Just think—of all the people scurrying about in a busy marketplace, the text singles out these two jesters as supremely righteous people! It reminds us of our task to employ every human talent available to us to bring more peace, kindness, and hope into the world . . . including our sense of humor.

As I was taught the value-laden meaning of these texts, I was also trained in the necessary tools to go deep within them. One such element, the linguistic usage of the words, has become my longest-lasting interest. I have dictionaries everywhere: biblical and modern Hebrew, talmudic Aramaic, Greek, and Latin; the standard French, German, Spanish, and Italian; the more exotic Dutch, Hawaiian, and cowboy colloquial; and specialized tomes like *Stedman's* for medicine and *Black's* for law. Before I myself began teaching from the texts, I needed these dictionaries to catch the many nuances of the words in front of me. Besides, as a poet attuned to flow, translation, and meaning of language, they often gave me a "feel" for the text others might understandably miss. They also kept me from wooden translations, outmoded English, and misunderstandings.

A classic case is in Psalm 23: "I shall not want." "Want" doesn't mean "desire," but rather "lack." Another example is whether to translate the Hebrew term *chacham* as "scholar" or "sage." The word "scholar" implies an impressive accumulation of knowledge. By contrast, the word "sage" is a value-laden term, applied to a person whose *knowledge* has made the crucial transition to *wisdom*, which includes perceptiveness, good sense, and human insight.

A third instance—and critical to my work—is that the common word "Tzaddik" in Jewish texts does not always mean "righteous person." It often means a "good person" or a "Mensch" ... which changes the nuance of some texts immensely. In these cases, the Tzaddik is no longer an unattainable, superlative example of human virtue. Rather, a Tzaddik (or its feminine construct, Tzaddeket) is a role model of certain behavior that we imperfect and all-too-flawed human beings can occasionally reach.

In sum, with the appropriate tools, a good quantity of texts (even the out-of-the-way, neglected, or "offbeat" ones) at one's disposal, and a Jewish sensitivity to their message, a person is equipped to teach authentic Jewish values, not the least of which are compassion, generosity, and Menschlichkeit.

That is the Siegel strategy for 2020 and beyond. It's an essentially educational plan. Namely: train pupils to centralize texts in their education, give them the tools to work with the texts, and if need be, help them to overcome the hurdle of merely thinking of themselves as students by telling them, "You can do it! You can teach Torah!"

3

Portraits of Mitzvah Heroes

The Giants of Jerusalem (1981)

The kids and I are sitting in rows in the courtyard. We are reviewing our morning tour. Inevitably, Mr. Wolf appears, howling, cracking bad (but not embarrassingly bad) puns. He asks the kids, "Do you want to hear a song I learned at camp?" They begin to cheer, and Mr. Wolf, our Hero of the Day, breaks into some ditty about a froggy and his girlfriend. He motions for us to sing the chorus with him, and the kids and I go at it with gusto. When he finishes, they cheer and applaud wildly and demand to take his picture, though they have already done so earlier that day. Some shake his hand and are surprised that someone in his mid-eighties still has a wrestler's grip. When Mr. Wolf leaves, it is difficult to hold their attention again—their minds are drifting. Neatly packaged chunks of myths they had acquired in their teen years are being thrown out. They have learned the meaning of "Elders," and many are surprised that they have fallen in love.

I have gone through this scene a hundred times—more than a hundred times. It has been a typical summer morning for me at Life Line for the Old in Jerusalem. Just me, a few friends perhaps, and most important of all, thirty or more teenagers from the United Synagogue Youth Israel Pilgrimage. Three thousand teenagers over the past five years.

And I love it.

And they love it.

When I lecture on Jerusalem and the Righteous of the Land of Israel, I tell everyone that more than half my friends in Jerusalem are in their sixties and seventies and eighties.

My personal salvation is there, somewhere in the courtyard and workshops of Life Line. There is a call, despite the drag and chaos of the Big World—a call to some shred of idealism, of a far-reaching vision. Of dreams I may have dreamed when I was younger but gave up because some uninspired, cynical human erroneously convinced me that life just doesn't work the way I want it to.

Let me describe the morning's program. The kids and I walk or ride to Life Line, which is housed in a part of Jerusalem that used to sit right on the border with Jordan. I give them a brief introduction right in the courtyard, in the thick of things, with Elders of every stature and origin passing by. Then, Myriam Mendilow, founder and director, prophet, hell raiser, and seventy-year-old miracle worker, comes out and speaks to them from a bench. (She stands on a bench because, even in thick-soled shoes, she is at best five feet tall.) After her blazing words (we are amazed at her energy—"What a giant!," we are thinking), we divide into two groups and walk through the thirteen workshops, then to the store to buy things, then back to the courtyard to discuss the guts of Tzedakah and to talk about the people we have met. We think about Old Age, make resolutions, search recesses of our hearts we had forgotten to look into. It is rather like the night before Passover. Life Line is the candle we use to examine the corners and nooks of ourselves, seeking out the *chometz*—the artificially leavened pieces of our minds that have spoiled our dreams.

That's where Mr. Wolf comes in—to tie things together in his own fashion. He reminds us not to forget the Persecution of Elderly Jews.

A few years back, Mr. Wolf told my aunt, "If I had stayed in New York, I'd be in an old age home. I'd be dead by now."

Life Line for the Old, or Yad LaKashish as it is known in the City of Cities, is *not* an old-age home. It is workshops. People come from their own homes, on foot, by bus, by two buses, to work Sunday through Thursday mornings. They complain of Shabbas and *yontif* because they can't come to work.

They are happy. Well, I can't lie about this. Some complain, but I also complain—and my life has been easy, very easy. Still, they are happy, and they more than impress us . . . they wow us (including an old-timer like me who has been there a hundred times and more).

They make wondrous things with their hands: tablecloths, sweaters, toys, wall-hangings, more toys, new bindings on schoolbooks, booties for infants, more toys. Each day there is something new.

Look, the formula is simple. A lady in her late forties, this Myriam Mendilow, quits her job of twenty-two years as a teacher because she is disgusted with taking her students to the streets and showing them decrepit, dying old people begging and sitting in misery and loneliness. She quits—just like that—begs for a teacher from the Ministry of Labor, and drags beggars and abandoned Elders to her first workshop: a bookbindery. She says, "Let the old rebind the books of the young, and let the young see who has done the job so well, so carefully and lovingly. Let them rediscover the meaning of Grandfather, Grandmother."

That's how simple it is. I have been over it again and again in my mind, trying to convince myself that there is some element, some complicating factor I have missed. But there are no hidden ingredients, no classified information. Everything is out in the open: a visionary, love and devotion, tenacity, a bullheaded will, and a Jeremiah-voice screaming at society.

Mr. Wolf tells the kids, "When I came to Jerusalem a few years ago, I went around looking for a job. No luck. I was told I was too old. Too old. Then I came here and they put me to work the same day I came."

Myriam Mendilow is a myth-breaker, an iconoclast of the first order. These are some of the myths that have been shattered before our eyes as we walk through the workshops:

Myth #1: You can't retrain most old people. "Lies!" Mrs. Mendilow would say. Almost everyone we saw is doing things they had not only never done before, but things they had never considered possible for them to do. As Myriam the Giant explains, "Some of them never had a tradition of work. We often start with nothing."

Myth #2: Laxatives, good denture glues, and Geritol (as the commercials would lead us to believe) are the true source of happiness for the elderly. Also in that vein: anti-hypertensives, bypasses, and tablets of every shape and color ease pain better than anything. Quite the contrary, we see that high expectations, caring, and love bring smiles and songs to the Elders at work.

Myth #3: Heart attacks and strokes kill most old people. Every kid sees that this is not so: In the reality of day-to-day living, loneliness and uselessness are greater killers of our Elders.

Myth #4: Begging in one form or another—welfare, handouts from all sorts of sources—will solve the problems of the elderly. Again—no! The old people work at Life Line for far less than they could make playing on heartstrings in the streets, with their trembling hands stretched out to Israeli and tourist alike. Myriam Mendilow shows us her photograph of the King of the Beggars (now deceased). She fought to get him to come to work, despite the very respectable sums he was bringing home from his street-corner perch with cup in hand. "But where was his self-respect, his sense of Kavod?" she shouts at us. This little lady, who is our Rebbi for that day and for long into the future, reminds us that dignity is the ultimate source of the will to live.

Mr. Wolf tells us his granddaughter in Maryland just had triplets. The kids take pictures, recite a mile-long string of mazel tovs. They wish him well, "Biz Hundert Und Tzvantzig . . . May you live to be a hundred and twenty!"

What strikes the kids right away, as soon as they walk into the courtyard, is No Stink! There is no stench of medicine, urine, or fecal matter. Now, I have to ask—with all the possibility of protests I will hear from This Great Nursing Home and That Grand Senior Citizens' Residence—where did these teenagers ever smell such smells? Somewhere they must have visited the old and been overpowered by it.

The smell of medicine is easy to answer. Almost to the last teenager, they have been inside a home or heard stories: the smell of antisepsis pervades each visit and tale. They make other associations, too: hyperkinetic children on Ritalin, mental patients, "One Flew Over the Cuckoo's Nest." And zombies.

"No zombies!" they say incredulously about Life Line. They know from zombies; they've entertained in old-age homes for Passover and Purim and Chanukah and Shabbat, leading seders and singing songs with their youth groups. They know that in many cases (not all cases; why should I exaggerate when the truth stands so well on its own?) staffers drug the old just to keep them under control. The kids are outraged. They would never let someone do that to them. They *know* what drugs can do to you. They have heard the sermons, read the notices of overdosing. They can recite every word for dope in the book. And yet they see how society condones drug abuse among the elderly, and they are shattered.

At Life Line for the Old, things are different. There are no white coats. No nurses, no doctors, no medical personnel of any kind circulate among the workshops. The cure-alls from the pharmacy are totally absent, and the teenagers are gloriously surprised. I share their joy. I feel their hearts take heart. "*Kol HaKavod!*" I want to say. "Well done, Myriam Mendilow!"

The kids are not stupid or blind. They have been great teachers to me over the past five years. They know. They see through things very quickly, and readily spill out their guts:

"My grandfather . . . ," one kid tell us his story. "I screamed at my parents: 'Take him out of the home!'" (This was a prominent old-age home at that. I, too, had visited there once.)

One young woman weeps near-hysterically after leaving a workshop. "Why is there nothing like this in the States? Why wasn't there one when my grandmother needed something like this?"

"Wonderful!"

"Incredible!"

"What can we do to start something like this back home?"

I reply, blind to rational thinking, stunned again by Mendilow's dream, "Start with the synagogue. Invite the Elders down one night a week. Begin with the needlecrafts—you don't need heavy equipment for that. Sell the products and give the money to Tzedakah. But don't start by storming the community old-age home. Some professionals have already told us they do not want you meddling in their schedules."

Later, as I compose this article, I admit to myself some doubt, even fear. I see the outcries, the letters of protest coming to my mailbox. "Who are you to criticize? You are naïve. Of course we welcome the teenagers' help." Perhaps Mendilow is wrong; perhaps she really doesn't understand how things really work out there. I am scared. . . . I begin to rewrite the article. Fear grows in me. I realize, and need to acknowledge, of course, that there are some wonderful old-age homes that do fabulous work of dignified caring for their people. Many do have workshops and programs that raise up the souls of the Elders in their care.

But I have to ask myself, "Where does all the kids' anger come from?" All those cries of Bingo, card playing, hours and hours of television, miles of endless walking around a track, second-rate borscht-belt comedians doing their bits. How is it that so many of these young people know that old people die sooner if they go into an old-age home (often against their wishes), than if they had stayed in their own homes, with outside care coming in when necessary?

By no means do the kids and I denigrate the skills of professionals in the field of gerontology. But I have to ask myself again, "Where do these kids come to be so amazed at a place where social workers and geriatric specialists are strikingly absent? How is it that the teenagers know that the jargon of 'group techniques, senior citizens' activities, and tranquilizers' is lethal if used as a euphemism for failing to care?"

We enter the carpentry shop. Avraham Ermosa, a seventy-five-year-old Sabra, begins his talk, sometimes in Spanish, sometimes in French or Hebrew—depending on which language the kids want to translate. He tells how he takes old, dead wood and brings it back to life. He is in the Resurrection Business.

He says he uses the sander for scratching his back—it is more efficient and effective. One minute and you'll never have to scratch again!

He explains that the buzz saw is for multiple brisses—2,000 boys at a time. The kids howl. (The males squirm a little.)

He shows us pictures of his family and tells us how he chases his wife around the house for a kiss. Then we step outside for pictures. Ermosa is still cracking jokes.

Back alone with our group, I ask questions: How many of you live 1,500 miles or more from your grandparents? Hands and more hands go up.

Ermosa explains he was sick last year. He has a bad heart . . . a bad physical heart, that is. He tells the kids, "They took me to the cemetery. I didn't like it. No sunshine, no air. So I came back to work."

I ask the kids more questions: "How many of you left for Israel afraid you would get a message that one of your grandparents died while you were gone?" Many hands. "How many of you are afraid your parents won't tell you until you get back?" More hands.

Ermosa recalls, from fifty years ago and more, a girlfriend who was mad at him. She called to say she wanted her picture back. But he couldn't remember which one she was. So he sent her his whole album of girlfriends' pictures and told her to pick out the right one.

I ask further questions: "How many of you have a grandparent in an old-age home? What about a great-uncle or great-aunt? A great-grandparent?" Many hands. Some teens tell good stories of their forebears' sojourn; others share sad stories. Some young people strike out at me for slandering all old-age homes. "What about Baycrest in Toronto?" they say. "What about the Shalom Home in the Twin

Cities?" I say, "You are right. I overdo it." But then I ask myself why only a handful of kids have this reaction.

The Old Yemenite in the wheelchair has died. God, I miss him. He married a Polish woman decades ago. She went back to Poland with the four children to visit her family. Then the War came, and he was alone.

The hunchback in the ceramics workshop has died. The one with one good eye.

Others I never got to know well enough also died, while I was in exile.

I ask another question: "How many of you have an older relative who was forced to retire because he or she reached mandatory retirement age?" Maybe four or five hands out of thirty. I follow up: "How many of you had an older relative who folded up and died shortly after being forced to retire?" Two or three hands. Then there is silence—a distinct, crushing silence.

I tell the kids about Miriam Itzkovitch, another half-mad woman in Jerusalem. They laugh at the name. (Itzkovitch laughs at "Lincoln" and "Washington"—she's Russian and speaks Hebrew with a thick Russian accent.) I tell them that among her far-reaching and varied Mitzvot are programs to take care of the old—more than three hundred Elders, seventy-five of whom live all alone. She brings them help and friends and visitors and people to clean and shop and talk and open windows. *Not a single one of them has had to move into an old-age home.*

The kids feel good about that. I feel good about that. Caring triumphs for the day! Jewish caring.

And then I confess to them that I do not know how I could manage caring for someone day in and day out, someone with multiple problems, physical and psychological. I tell them I just don't know, but I tell them I know more options now. I now know there are other options besides Death Row. In New York alone I know Project Ezra and Dorot and Hatzilu: visits, food packages for the Jewish holidays, shopping, a touch, a cup of coffee and conversation, a phone call in the middle of a long week.

One Hatzilu worker says to me, "When we brought the food for Rosh Hashanah, one woman kissed my hand." My God, I think. What have we done?

I am quick to blow holes in my self-righteousness. I remind the kids, and myself, that I, too, am slow to learn, and slower to act. I tell the kids, "You are our hope." Mrs. Mendilow loves them more than any millionaire who might walk in and throw stacks of big dollars on her desk. "Raise hell," she says to them. "Raise hell," I chime in, and hope they will be less insecure than I. I can only expose them to this Magic Kingdom of Life Line for the Old. They can't always count on me — I tell them that. But somewhere in the long stream of three thousand kids I have taken to Life Line over the years are new Myriam Mendilows, Miriam Itzkovitchs, Henrietta Szolds. My idealism is satisfied when I think of their potential. . . .

It is 8:30 in the morning in Jerusalem. I am standing on my bench in the courtyard of Life Line, the kids facing me in semi-circles. As usual, I ask the teenagers, "Who speaks French?" (They will want to use their broken, halting high-school French to speak to the Elders from French Morocco and Algeria.) "Who speaks Spanish?" (Among the Elders are Bulgarian Jews, South Americans, one from Hungary who moved to Argentina before coming to Israel.) "Hebrew? Hungarian?" (One teen speaks good Hungarian.) "German? Rumanian?" (No one chimes in for Rumanian.) And down the long list of languages Jews have had to learn to speak to survive in their wanderings.

This morning was different:

"Spanish?" Many hands.

"Russian?" Some hands, including one teenager who has just raised his hand for Spanish.

"Yiddish?" The same hand as for Spanish and Russian. All the other kids cheer. It's their boy—they call him "The Rabbi."

He speaks to all the Elders, fluently, and he sings Yiddish songs for them. God, you could have burst from the joy on their faces (and mine). Unabashedly standing there singing "Mein Shtetele Belz" while the Old Ones beat rhythms on the tables with their hands.

My hero.

It is the last day of the summer, the last group. After the tour and the buying and our discussion, some kids want to have their picture taken with Mrs. Mendilow. The last kid of all—he must have been six feet three or four—stands next to Mrs. Mendilow under the big Life Line sign. After the picture is taken, he turns to her and hugs and kisses her. I thought he would crush her— she barely reached his shoulder.

This is my greatest joy: the memory of those two giants, standing in the Jerusalem sunlight, embracing.

Trevor Ferrell (1988)

This is a story to feel good about:

I don't know whether or not it was a cold night in Philadelphia on December 8, 1983. I haven't checked the moon charts to see if it was dark, and I haven't dug up an old copy of the *Inquirer* to say whether or not it was snowing, but the local TV news had a story that night about the city's homeless people.

Out in the suburbs, in a large house with a pool in the back, an 11-year-old kid named Trevor Ferrell happened to see the news clip. It's been over three decades since I was eleven years old, and I can't remember very well what kinds of things I thought about at that age, but something moved Trevor to ask his father if they could go down and see the people who live on the street.

You may use big words like "revelation" or "epiphany" if you want to, but I would rather think Trevor was only mildly curious about the news report . . . perhaps a little more than "mildly curious," but still just curious. And surprised. That much I know, because I have met many suburban kids in the 1970s and 1980s who by Trevor's age have not had any contact with homeless people, and wouldn't suspect that they live near them. (This is a good human defense in the most positive sense: If human beings tried to absorb all the pain in the world—near and far—and felt it as if it were nearby and immediate, it might drive them over the edge. A teacher named Abba Binyamin said it centuries ago in the Talmud, "If the eye only had the power to see, human beings could not handle all the Evil Things, so overpowering is the weight and sum of it all" [*Berachot* 6a]).

So I prefer to think that Trevor was merely curious. And it appears he must have been very insistent. His father, Frank, agreed to take him down to see some of Philadelphia's homeless people, but when he agreed he meant "in a few days" or "next week." But Trevor pushed. Father and son went back and forth, maybe even arguing. Finally, Frank gave in, and Trevor, Frank, Janet (Trevor's mother), and one or two of the other Ferrell children got into the car to see the street people.

I am writing this before 7:00 a.m., when it's too early to call the Ferrells to get more details. So I can't say if, after a half-hour ride into Philadelphia's Center City, they spent ten minutes or forty-five minutes or twenty-eight minutes searching the streets before they found a "real-live" homeless person. And I don't know if—after finding the first one—they spent another five minutes or twenty-four minutes or an hour and a half driving around looking for others. There is one fact, though, that everyone who knows Trevor already knew: he had taken a blanket with him from back home.

The Ferrells locked the car doors when they got down to Center City. You do it, and I do it, and there is good reason to lock the doors, particularly when riding with children in certain places. But somewhere on their drive around the streets, they must have stopped the car for a moment, and before Frank or Janet knew what was happening, Trevor stepped out of the car with blanket in hand, walked up to one of the people, and handed it to him. Trevor was innocent (we'll come back to that) and unafraid.

As the Ferrells tell it, the man who received the blanket was very appreciative. They were very moved by the man's reaction, and on the ride back to their home they spoke about their experience.

The next night they went back to the streets again, this time with some food. The next night they went again, and then the night after, and the night after that . . . every night until at least last night, May 5, 1988. And I assume they will be back again tonight and tomorrow night and the night after that, too. Most of the time it's some member or two of the Ferrell family and a number of volunteers who have since joined Trevor's Campaign for the Homeless.

As of this writing, they have fed 180,000+ meals to homeless individuals. And regardless of rain, snow, sleet, whatever, Trevor's people have never missed a night on the streets.

In the interim, the media had gotten hold of this "hot story." Within six months, Trevor's name was appearing in headlines around the country and on the TV news. And someone wrote *Trevor's Place*, a must-read book about Trevor and his Gang. It was the Media at Its Best.

As a result of all the publicity, people came to help Trevor and the family. All kinds of people helped: rich people and poor people and people in between; old people and young people and people somewhere in the middle; suburban folks and people who worked and/or lived in Center City and people from towns an hour or more away; individuals who couldn't see and others who could; and people with problems and people without problems; fancy law firms (like Dechert Price and Rhoades) and builders; teachers with their schoolchildren; Christians and Jews; and, I would suspect, doubters and fanatics of every sort, too. Many came, and still come, because people who are hungry and cold would be without food and warmth without their efforts. Others probably came because they needed this moment of human connection as much as the people on the street, but once they rode with "Trevor's Gang," they grew, and now do it because of the needs of the people on the street.

I fell into some of those categories: a suburban writer, living 120 miles away from Philadelphia, Jewish and a sometimes religious skeptic, neither young nor particularly old, not particularly normal, not quite sure whether I had come totally for the benefit of the street people. In that last phrase is a tricky aspect of all Tzedakah work: are we (1) doing it for those who need it, (2) doing it for ourselves, or (3) doing it for other people, and, along the way, managing to reap many benefits because of the nature of Mitzvahs? In my case I think it's fair to say that I wanted to be with Trevor to see if I could recapture some of my own childhood innocence.

First Visit

After having read many articles about The Kid, I wanted to meet him and see him in action. As it happened, I had a speaking engagement one winter morning in Philadelphia, and I decided to take the train in the night before. I called the Ferrells and arranged to meet them at Trevor's Place, the shelter they had established. I also made sure that my old friend and host for the night, Marty Millison, would meet me down at the shelter, so I wouldn't be alone. I was, quite candidly, scared. Even though I had always talked a good game of doing this kind of Mitzvah work, I felt I was really putting myself on the line.

It was a ten-minute cab ride from 30th Street Station to the address Frank and Janet had given me. This *was* a snowy, cold night, and I was saying to myself in the cab, "I hope Trevor or Marty gets there before I do." I didn't know what I would do if I got there first and would have to walk inside the shelter alone among the people Trevor had taken in. I didn't really know how to talk to "them" and listen to "them" (it was still "them" and "me" back then).

I have to backtrack.

The shelter, Trevor's Place. In February 1984, only two months after they had begun their work, a woman named Mother Divine (widow of Father Divine) gave Trevor a run-down building they could use for a shelter. By March 18th—about the 100th day of Trevor's campaign—it was opened.

In those days Trevor's Place was a wreck. It violated so many building and health codes, I am not exactly sure why the city let them keep it open so long. A couple of years later it was closed for massive renovations, and then reopened, serving about fifty people at capacity. As of Spring 1988, Trevor and Co. had managed to find permanent housing for 84 percent of the people who had come into the shelter, and 80 percent of them had found jobs.

Returning now to the earlier, cold, snowy night when I went to see Trevor and the family—Trevor and Frank did, in fact, get there before me. When I stepped out of the cab, I looked into the window and saw Trevor standing in one of the big rooms hugging one of his friends, someone who otherwise would have been out on the streets. The scene was very moving. While it did not do away with all of my apprehensions, it certainly made things easier for me.

When I went inside, the first thing I noticed was the heat. It was inordinately hot, like the thermostat had been set at around 80 degrees. (Later on, I would theorize that if you were used to living on the cold streets and thus had very real fear of freezing to death, and then an alternative to the streets presented itself, you would want to make absolutely sure you were going to be warm. I also read a *Washington Post* article reporting that in the Winter of 1987–88, thirteen people froze to death in Washington, most of them on the DC streets. Then the issue of the heat made more sense to me.)

I said hello to Frank and met Trevor. I watched him too. I noticed that The Kid was quiet, even shy (except with His People). Somehow I had imagined he would be a high-powered dynamo shuffling schedules and contractors and meal plans and forms for getting government assistance. He seemed so quiet and low-key. And innocent.

Trevor was about thirteen at the time. He looked very cute in his "braces-years." There was something obviously surrealistic about the scene. This young kid in braces was hugging and talking to a bunch of people from the streets and playing with their kids and in a low-key manner introducing me to his friends and taking me on a tour of the building, and showing me the private room of one of the people he had taken in . . . like this was as natural and normal as it could be.

Within a few minutes, this innocence and naturalness had set me at ease. Later on, as I would think more about my time with Trevor and the family, I would begin to develop talks for my audiences about normalcy. Trevor had taught me — among many, many other things — that it *can be* perfectly normal to be a Kid and to feed, clothe, and house homeless people, and maybe it *should be* normal to do such things. Maybe kids of all ages who *don't* do this might not be "normal" . . . at least not yet.

Second Visit

I still hadn't ridden with Trevor and the volunteers on their nightly circuit.

It was one thing to go to the shelter and see the street people as former street people in the controlled setting of a shelter. These were mostly people who were working hard at getting into a real home, getting employment, getting on their feet. Some were starting all over again. They could stay as long as they needed to at Trevor's Place; it was their home. There, they were safe from the dangers of street life, protected by Trevor Ferrell and his volunteers.

It was something altogether different to go out on the streets to feed the homeless. Searching around dark corners of buildings and on heating grates . . . it felt like a risk.

Trevor wasn't afraid, though I believe there is reason to be afraid in many places. You just don't go out on the street in certain parts of town and go up to a stranger who might be down on his or her luck and give out blankets and food and juice or coffee.

In Philadelphia, though, it had been safe. Trevor had a protective shield around him. He was the friend of the people who lived on the streets. They respected him, loved him, would do anything to make sure he was safe and happy. One of Trevor's friends, Chico, put it this way, "Anybody try to hurt that boy, they gotta walk through me. And that's the truth."

And so, I went back to Philadelphia in September 1987 to do the night circuit, and I wasn't quite so afraid. First, I was under Trevor's protection, and second, he had helped dispel the myth that a very high percentage of the homeless are mentally ill. (A few months later, a *New York Times* article summarized a New York Psychiatric Institute survey of homeless people in the city's shelters. The researchers concluded that 37 percent of these shelter residents could live entirely on their own, another 37 percent could live independently with some support, and the remaining quarter needed various levels of supervision—but only 10 percent required twenty-four-hour-a-day supervision or psychiatric hospitalization.)

Frank picked me up in a "Trevor's Campaign" van (a local dealership leases one of the vans to them for $1.00/year), and we went back to the Ferrells' house for a while before beginning the nightly run. They have a nice house in a nice neighborhood, though it's clear the Ferrells have neglected it somewhat. The front door needs painting, the lawn needs better care, and other things are noticeable. For now, they're a little too tied up to worry about the door and the lawn.

I met Janet, Trevor's eleven-year-old sister, Jody, and later Trevor's older brother, Allen. (Trevor's other sister, Liza, was a junior in college in Boston.) We talked for a while, loaded the van with food, and then six of us—three Ferrells, two volunteers from a church about an hour up the road, and me—headed for Center City. It was warm and a little muggy, about 75 degrees outside.

By this point, Trevor's Campaign had two or three regular stops before Trevor et al. would start combing the streets for individuals. At the first stop, about forty people gathered around the van. All the Ferrells were recognized and greeted, and the friendly, dignified process of feeding casseroles and juice to the people in line began. Trevor asked if I wanted to dish out the food from the back, but I was still hesitant (though unafraid), so I said I'd do the juice from the side. The people would first go to Trevor for their food, then come to me. Some people were saying how hungry they were; I heard the recurring phrase Trevor's Gang hears night after night, "Can I have seconds?" I kept glancing back at Trevor and kept Janet close by, but I had loosened up. There were no fistfights, no tensions in the air, no pushing or shoving. I began to see just how natural and easy this Mitzvah was.

When we finished the first stop, Frank worried that we would run out of food. It happens now and again. We decided to go to the nearby Wendy's to see what could be arranged. At the counter, Frank asked for twenty-five orders of chili, taking the Wendy's employee a little by surprise. Frank asked to speak to the manager, and when he explained the situation, the young woman in charge of the restaurant responded with the same spirit that so many others have shown: she filled a big jug with lemonade for free and gave us about forty or fifty portions of chili, charging us for about twenty of them. She even loaned us the big chili pot.

It was a fine moment for all of us. Fewer people would go hungry tonight.

At the second stop, we fed many more people (and now I was serving the food, too). Then we started to comb the many streets the Ferrells knew so well. We spotted individuals in the alleys and in the open, on side streets and on main streets like Walnut and Spruce and Market where during the day "regular life" goes on. (The next morning, when I would go downtown, I would be struck to see all the businesses and offices and restaurants and travel agencies bustling where we'd been the night before. It had been such a different world.)

At one point Trevor showed me a slanted grate, angled such that people could not sleep on it and gain the benefit of the warm air coming up from the building's heating.

At another time Trevor asked, "Do you want to take care of that person?" I took a deep breath, decided to grow up a little, opened the van door, and walked out to the street where a young white woman, perhaps twenty years old, sat on some cloth bags that looked like carry-on luggage. I supposed she had all her worldly possessions in those bags. She seemed distant, spacey. I approached and asked if she was hungry. She said she wasn't. I asked if she wanted some lemonade and she said "Yes." I brought her over to the van, gave her some lemonade, walked her back to her bags, and then we drove off. The Ferrells took note of who she was. (They told me they had seen many, many young people—and little kids, of course. The Ferrells worked for two years with one young person who used to ride public transportation all night. She is now a pre-medical student at the University of Pennsylvania.)

A little later Trevor sent me out again, this time to an elderly black man who was sitting on a street corner. Next to him, lying on a grate, was a piece of white bread. I went up to him and put my hand on his shoulder (which astounded me, and still astounds me; I am still growing up; you feed the street people, you shelter them and give them blankets, but you don't *touch* them, or so I thought, until that moment). I told him who we were, and asked if he wanted something to eat. He turned his head toward me and said "Yes," and I saw that he was blind. I brought over some chili and lemonade, said what Trevor always says, "God bless you," and went back to the van to continue the circuit.

At various times people would approach the van and ask if there were any blankets. It was September and very warm, and I thought Winter was a long way off. Our seasonal timeclock is much different than that of the people who live on the streets.

I did not find the work depressing in the least. There was a certain joy in it—something immediate was being done: hungry people were being fed and their spirits were being raised at every turn. There was also a lot of joking around, which eased some of the tension. Trevor's good at joking around—not because it's good therapy, but because that's the way he is. I kept asking the Ferrells more and more questions. Enthusiasm and an incredible sense of caring pervaded our conversations.

Occasionally, as we drove around, people would honk their horns. At first I thought it was because Frank was such a bad driver, which *is* a fact, but the Ferrells explained that other people driving around the streets recognize Trevor's van and want to make contact. Sometimes they honk; sometimes they pull up at a traffic light and hand them a contribution. Frank says a cop pulled them over once. He was sure he was going to get a ticket, but the policeman only wanted to give them a contribution.

Later, we went out for pizza, and back at the house Trevor gave up his room for me. It was a nice room, though a little too teenagey, with too many glaring posters of teenager-type heroes on the walls.

Scattered Additional Facts about Trevor and His Family

Trevor has been showered with honors throughout the United States. But he's not a publicity-seeker. No one in the family is out there to become famous.

Trevor's been to Calcutta twice to see and work with Mother Teresa.

His record for largest audience addressed: six thousand people, kids out in Colorado.

In the beginning, as Trevor started to get national publicity for feeding homeless people, some of his friends at school made fun of him. Perhaps they thought he was a bit of a freak. Soon, though, they joined him.

Trevor failed public speaking in school. He talks quietly and, compared to some fiery speakers on the lecture circuit, he can be very boring. He usually speaks for a few minutes and then invites questions. But no one is bored, and his style of delivery doesn't matter very much. *It's who Trevor is* that counts. No matter how deadpan the presentation is, people want to listen.

Trevor is learning-disabled, dyslexic. So is his brother, Allen, as is Frank. In fact, Trevor is now in a very small special school in Massachusetts doing fabulously well in his studies. (His brother has a fistful of acceptances at fine colleges.) When he's home from school he's back on the streets, and while he's away, the family and the large company of volunteers carry on the work. Trevor-just-being-Trevor has made me rethink what the authentic achievements in life really are.

The Kid knows failure from his academic record in school, from the people who occasionally refuse the food he offers them, from the ones he helps get off the street and who later slide back out into homelessness. He's not naive about the harsh realities — not having enough funding to feed all the people, to pay all the resident counselors at Trevor's Place, to purchase the needed supplies for a well-functioning thrift shop. . . . The family is not particularly good at fundraising. But at the end of one of the videotapes Trevor says, "I am only one, but still I am one. I cannot do everything, but still I can do something. And because I can't do everything, I will not refuse to do something I can do." It sounds like it's right out of an ancient Jewish text, *Sayings of Our Ancestors* (*Pirke Avot*). Had someone else said it, it might ring false. But it is Trevor speaking, and it makes sense.

Here's a nice note from Trevor's Spring 1985 newsletter, written when he was thirteen years old:

> I would like to thank you for your help and I hope you will continue. This past month has been exciting. I met the President in Washington, Brother Joe Ranieri who helps the homeless in Florida and Darrell Gilliam who helps the homeless in Oklahoma.
>
> A lot of people have been concerned about my school grades. Well, things are going fine. I have been trying harder and I am getting all A's and B's. On Spring break I went to Disney World and had a great good time.
>
> I am glad that winter is over. One night my dad and I tried to sleep on the street, but it was so cold we couldn't do it. We lasted only 3 hours. I don't know how my friends on the street do it.

Four years after Trevor started this work, he grew to six feet tall. He's no longer cute, just gorgeous. Proud Mother Janet tells me that when he goes on the road to speak they practically need to call the police to keep the drooling teenage girls off him.

What hasn't changed is this: Trevor is still Trevor. Many people feared that all of this work and subsequent fame would warp him, scar him: "Where does he go from here, famous so young?" But my friend Joel Grishaver in LA said that when Trevor was out in Los Angeles, after they (naturally) worked the streets, Joel, Trevor, and Frank wanted to go to a movie—Trevor's choice. He wanted to see *The Fly*, a rather gross movie I might have liked when I his age, but not really to my taste at this stage of life. *The Fly* it was.

Another time, when Frank, Trevor, and Janet came out to one of my programs in Philadelphia, someone asked him how all this had affected him. There he was, nearly six feet tall, into his fifteenth year of life, answering, "I'm still the same kid."

The Ferrells are churchgoing people. They go to a Presbyterian church in their community. They're not fanatics, and not evangelical. They don't try to impose Christianity on you, but I have seen from them what Christian can mean in its highest sense.

Frank explained that they used to hear and talk about charity on Sunday mornings, and now they were doing what they had talked about for so long. In our many talks about the Jewish idea of Tzedek and Tzedakah as Justice and Righteousness, it is apparent that the love element merges comfortably with Tzedek and Tzedakah. They are—to whatever extent they are able—setting aright some things that are just plain wrong in this world.

Frank closed up his electronics store a while back and they live off some grants from the foundation. It's hardly an enormous salary. They were better off financially before.

And I won't lie to you that there aren't family tensions, normal ones and ones that have become worse because of Trevor's Campaign. There are strains, tensions, personal needs that get overridden because a van breaks down or a volunteer can't make it one night or the cost of fixing up Trevor's Place is so overwhelming. It's a rosy picture, but not all rosy.

But the videos and news clips and articles that tell Trevor's story are all true. Don't doubt them for a minute.

Something that Recently Shook Me

I was doing a talk about Tzedakah with a group of teenagers. One of them remarked something to the effect that there will always be the same number of hungry and homeless people out there. I was taken aback, and I realized I had lost perspective because of my age. Many teenagers see life differently because they were born at a certain time in American history.

I had talked to my parents about the bread lines and soup kitchens and unemployment in the Great Depression. I know Dorothea Lange's and Margaret Bourke-White's and Walker Evans's famous photographs from that period of American history, the sharecroppers and Dust Bowl victims and the migrants Woody Guthrie sang about. That was more than fifty years ago, in my parents' growing-up years. My own parallel years, the 1950s and 1960s, never experienced such an all-pervading calamity. Now, the 1980s have been much worse than when I was a teenager and in my early twenties.

I know it won't *always* be that way; I just *know* it.

Trevor assures us simply that it won't always be the way it is now.

If you want to see the world differently, if you want to be sure about things like this, meet Trevor, his family, and the rest of the Gang, and ride the Van.

Yossi Samuels and Shoshana Weinstock (1997)

Of course, Yossi is going to be the center of attention. My friends and I have come to meet him: Yossi Samuels, the Helen Keller of Israel. He is the one who has to live with the reality that he was going to be blind and deaf all his life; he is the amazing person we have heard so much about from his parents, Kalman and Malky; and he is the one we want to learn from this evening. Through his marvelous interpreter, Shoshana Weinstock (pronounced "Veinshtock"), we will come to understand more about him: his struggles and triumphs, pain and pleasures, what Life itself is for him. We expect somehow to be touched more deeply in our souls than we have ever been touched before.

Some of us have expressed concern that he will be on display, like some sort of freak in a circus sideshow who comes out from behind a curtain with a third arm (real or fake is not the matter) for gawkers to gawk at for lack of anything better to do with their time. Kalman, though, has assured us that this is not even remotely the case. Yossi loves walking into a room and taking over, orchestrating the people as he sees fit, teasing them, giving and taking with them, putting *them* on the spot if he feels like it, enjoying the tumult he creates just by being Yossi.

But Yossi is late. His parents had forgotten to remind him of this evening's meeting at Shoshana's. Not knowing he was expected, he has gone out for coffee or ice cream with a group of the young women who volunteer at the Samuels' great Mitzvah project, Shalva.

In the meantime, we start asking Shoshana about herself. How did you come to be the Annie Sullivan of Israel—the interpreter, the break-through person who brought Yossi's dark and silent inner world together with the musical and noisy and bright and shimmering world outside of himself?

Shoshana begins to answer us in Hebrew in a loud voice. Because she is deaf, she can't know how resoundingly she is speaking. (She also often signs to us simultaneously, even though we don't know Hebrew sign language.) Throughout her explanations and tales of Yossi, I worry: are the neighbors going to call or knock on the door and tell her to please keep it down?

Since she is articulating her words moderately-to-extremely clearly, I can make out most of what she is saying. Occasionally, though, when there are communication difficulties, her daughter Yael signs to her to repeat what she has just said. Yael is also translating our questions into sign language for her mother to answer.

Soon it becomes clear that it is Shoshana's own story that we need to hear. She became deaf from meningitis at age five. Once she met and began to work with Yossi in his difficult, hyperactive states, she would sometimes lead him around the neighborhood and the kids would throw stones at him. (They also threw stones at *her* when she was a child.) We're appalled, but she tells us with words and emphatically shows us with her hands that Yossi was a very *proud* boy and whatever they threw at him couldn't hurt him. (Shoshana pulls herself up to full height, draws her hand up with intense muscular motion, holds her head and chin high. *Proud!*)

She tells us about her family and about the Samuels family and how she loves them and couldn't have possibly accomplished what she did without their support. She is intense. Her face glows with a holiness whose source is her humility. She explains to us that she has become who she is because God has been good to her and has placed her in Life exactly where she ought to be. No crisis or sadness can bring her to despair.

And still no Yossi, even though Kalman has called everywhere to try to locate him. We tell him, "It's all right, we're doing just fine with Shoshana." Not that we won't be disappointed if Yossi doesn't show up. But we're so absorbed in Shoshana's stories that in her presence, we are in awe.

More Yossi stories follow: about how bright and inquisitive he is, how there is nothing in the world he doesn't want to know about, how he has grown physically, intellectually, spiritually, and emotionally. How at nineteen he is a man, different from other men only in that he cannot see or hear. . . .

After listening to Shoshana, this doesn't seem like such an absurd thought. Nothing is freakish any more: neither her stories nor her (initially) unsettling voice patterns.

But . . . the evening isn't only a string of high moments. Despite the exhilaration, there is a very real concern: what will Yossi do, now that he is a man? How will he make a living? Where will he live, since he cannot live completely independently? This evening has a tenor I have come to know well: a combination of the mundane and the sublime.

Now it is almost 9:00 p.m. and still there is no sign of Yossi. Finally, sometime after that, after more conversation with Shoshana, Yossi saunters in. (Barges in? Storms in? Roars in?) From the moment he comes in and sits down, there is no doubt about who is in charge.

Yossi

He's having a wonderful time. I'm not sure if he has apologized for being late, since it really wasn't his fault, but he starts in right away with Shoshana, talking back and forth in their finger-spelling way of communicating, just as you would expect if you saw the Helen Keller plays or movies . . . except that Yossi and Shoshana are talking *with both hands* at the same time, back and forth, back and forth, fingers of Shoshana's hands in Yossi's palms, Yossi's fingers moving in hers at a spelling speed (which includes custom-made abbreviations) decidedly quicker than any of us could type. It takes us a while to get used to this, but we have to, because there's no other option: Yossi has jumped right in.

Sitting next to me, with Shoshana on the other side, he hammers away at me with questions: How long have I had a beard? (Hint to his father: how about me?) Do I always wear shorts? (Hint to his father: he should sometimes be allowed to wear shorts, even though they are religious and live in a religious neighborhood.) Do I smoke? (Yossi does; Kalman is not at all happy about it.) More questions, until he switches to someone else, eventually getting to my friend Arnie Draiman. Arnie (through Shoshana) explains that he and his wife Smadar were in Columbus, Ohio, for three years while his wife served as a community Shaliach-Israeli representative for cultural programs. Yossi knows that means Arnie had to buy a new car when he came back.

Yossi: What kind of car?
Arnie: A Subaru.
Yossi: A piece of junk! You should have gotten a Volvo!

On and on it went. All of us were completely caught off guard, laughing so hard at a dozen unexpected moments. Considering Yossi's heavy life story, we hadn't expected to laugh at all.

Later on, after we've conversed with Shoshana and Yael for a while, when it's finally time to leave, my friends and I thank the two women and suddenly realize we can't find Yossi or Arnie. We *do* find them, in the parking lot. Gripping Arnie, in total control of the situation, Yossi is taking him on a tour of the lot. Yossi is playing his favorite game: showing Arnie how he can tell any make of car by the shape of the door handle. We've been told he uses this particular expertise to engage the neighborhood kids, so they won't be afraid of him. Yossi also makes Arnie run his arms through the spray of the water sprinkler on the way out, to feel what he feels.

When we are finally allowed to leave, we are exhausted.

The next day, when we call Kalman to tell him how extraordinary it was to spend time with Shoshana, and later with Yossi, he can't understand why we are so high from the experience. I suppose there are sermons and essays to be written about Kalman's reaction: how, over time, things that are very much out of the ordinary become accepted and understood as Normal Life for some people . . . how, if we open ourselves up to more profound experiences, we find that we can make them at once awesome *and* normal.

A thought flashes through my mind: God gave human beings hands for many purposes — to make tools, to eat, to build fires and circuits and musical instruments and toy ducks for children to play with. Anthropologists have written about hands — our thumbs and the human ability to grip. And poets — there must be hundreds of great poems in the literature of the world about the touch of love. And painters — has anyone created more magnificent hands than the ones Michelangelo painted? Genesis according to Michelangelo is this: God gave life to Adam (and to all human beings) by the Divine Touch.

Finally, I understand. . . . *That* is what it is like to watch Yossi's and Shoshana's hands.

It is all so mysterious and beautiful.

Shoshana

What must it feel like to be Shoshana Weinstock to have been intimately involved in bringing out the great human being that had been locked so deeply inside of the deaf and blind Yossi Samuels? What goes on in her mind as she reviews the breakthrough that he would know "cloud" in finger-language and "cloud" in the real sky, even if he couldn't see one? Or "honey" or "biochemical" or "green"?

Even among the few who have met or read about Yossi, even fewer know about Shoshana. In the store or crossing the street in Jerusalem, she's just another deaf woman, nobody really special. Besides, her humility won't allow her to see herself as anything out of the ordinary. According to her, God just happened to put her in the right place at the right time, giving her meningitis and making her deaf along the way, in preparation for her work with Yossi and the many other students she has inspired over the years.

We should respect her humble view of herself, though I think she would allow us to consider her our teacher, too. And if she will graciously concede this point to us, then I think we ought to learn from her that *all of us* are potentially Shoshana Weinstocks to some degree. *All of us* are capable of finding the very best that is deep inside of others, and working with them to bring it out into the world. Is this not why we were put on this Earth to begin with?

Spend an evening with Shoshana and Yossi. Have her spell your name in the palm of your hand.

Words cannot tell us who we are. Only touch, the Divine Touch, can. The Divine Touch that is ours.

The Rabbanit Bracha Kapach (1988)

It's the Rabbanit Kapach's faith that throws you off balance. Whenever you sit with the Rabbanit in her living room and talk about her Mitzvah work, she will always say things like, "HaShem Ya'azor — God will help" or "Be'Ezrat HaShem — With God's help."

But she is not a religious fanatic.

I met her in one of my usual ways. More than a decade ago, Yitzchak Jacobsen, who coordinates my summer programs with United Synagogue Youth in Israel, said (read: *insisted*) I should meet her. He was absolutely right: she personified everything I was looking for in my search for Mitzvah heroes.

Now I visit her every year, often in June, shortly after I arrive in Israel. The Rabbanit welcomes my friends and me and starts laying out the fruit and baked goods and something cold to drink. If it is a Friday morning, she will give me some home-baked pita bread for the Sabbath a few hours away. She will add some *s'chug*, a green, fiery Yemenite condiment—her special dip for the pita. (Fiery is an understatement. It opens the pores, the sinuses, and just about everything else.)

Each year she tells us about how she helps provide Passover food for about 2,000 families. She is still in debt from this Mitzvah project... more in debt than the worst credit card abuser's nightmare in America. As an annual ritual, I ask her how much she still owes for the Matzahs and flour and oil and other things she provided. Each year she quotes an ever-larger figure. Continuing the ritual, I ask, "How are you going to pay off the debt?" Her annual reply is, "HaShem Ya'azor—God will help."

Early on in our relationship I used to be troubled, even angry at her for expressing such naive faith in God. I am hardly a person of such faith. I was raised in American surroundings, with a better-than-average Jewish upbringing... but nothing like this. I couldn't see how anyone could be so confident about God's gracious relationship with human beings. Yet she believed this so gently, so inoffensively... and lived life so meaningfully by that faith.

Now when I listen to her say it with her inimitable sincerity, I think, *She may very well be right.* She may have convinced me that this is the way God *really* works in the world. She's no peasant in some remote steppe in Russia or some primitive outback or bush where you might hear such phrases as an expression of the Simple

Faith of the Simple People. No, the Rabbanit is very well educated, *very* bright, very knowledgeable in Torah (she teaches it regularly at an old-age home, within women's groups, in yet other places)— and she is more aware of the pain and suffering and very nature of human beings than I could possibly be. Through the Rabbanit, the words of our Jewish tradition are turned into a way of life filled with insight, warmth, and joy. Her knowledge has become wisdom; she is *very* wise. I always go away from a morning with her thinking she knows something I don't know about God and the Universe and Life.

At first all this had been difficult for me to comprehend.

Biographical Notes

The Rabbanit was born in Yemen about sixty years ago. When she was eleven she married Yosef Kapach, who is now one of Israel's preeminent Torah scholars. If you take two steps into his library downstairs you will get a hint of that—bookshelves so high you need not just ladders, but *high* ladders to get to some of the books.

She married Yosef Kapach at age eleven because he was an orphan and in those days in Yemen, the government grabbed Jewish orphans and forced them to convert to Islam. The Rabbanit knows about the problems of teenage marriage, so we joke that she married so young so she wouldn't have to be a teenage bride. (I have frequently wondered how I can sit there just joking around with someone who has been honored as a "Distinguished Citizen of Jerusalem." When you meet her, you will immediately sense her easygoing, unassuming nature, her humility.)

She gave birth to her first child at fourteen, and then had two more. She was a grandmother in her thirties.

She and her husband came to Israel years ago, by donkey and then by boat. Here, too, we share some humor. I tell the Rabbanit she is probably making this all up. Knowing that sometime in the future I'll write up her story, she's flavoring her background with romance, like journeying from Yemen by donkey through broiling desert days and freezing nights. But that *really* is how she came to Israel.

She is—among many other things—a seamstress of rare skill.

And she is called "Rabbanit," which means "the Rabbi's Wife" (equivalent to "Rebbetzin" in Yiddish), but she is much more than just "someone-defined-by-being-married-to-someone-else."

The Wonder Woman of Nachla'ot

I think it is safe to say that part of my own late growing-up took place in Nachla'ot, the Rabbanit's neighborhood in Jerusalem.

Nachla'ot is a poor neighborhood, though you can clearly see some of the fanciest apartment buildings in Jerusalem from the Rabbanit's apartment. Out her back window, beyond the Valley of the Cross and the ancient monastery, is the Knesset (Israeli parliament building) and part of the Hebrew University campus on Givat Ram. Next door, or down the block, or around the corner, though, are families—a multitude of families—in distress, who need small or large or medium-sized Mitzvah efforts to keep them going.

Any hour of the day that I am with her, the phone or the doorbell rings. Some person or family has come up short and they need Bracha's help. (They call her "Bracha," though I never do. To me, she is always "the Rabbanit.") Hushed conversations take place by the door, out of earshot. You could pick a thousand or ten thousand or a million human problems—the Rabbanit has heard and worked to solve them all. She is the equivalent of an entire social service agency.

And beyond all this, she is a pleasure to be with, to work with, to listen to. You can rely on her to work out both simple and incredibly complex human problems with great compassion and understanding. *No one* is embarrassed to come to her with whatever difficulties they are experiencing at that moment. No man or woman or child who comes to her need feel ashamed that something has gone wrong, that there is not enough food for the Sabbath, that the children are having trouble in school, that work doesn't pay enough to provide a fair and decent mode of existence.

This point calls for some additional emphasis. As an American involved in many local Tzedakah projects, I hear over and over again that one of the problems in North American Tzedakah work is that people are too embarrassed to ask for help when they need it . . . even if they are in the most desperate of circumstances. They don't want to take charity. In that sentence, "charity" has a negative connotation. It means "a hand-out" and it suggests debasement, a lack of worth on the part of the one in need, i.e., for some reason the person-who-asks-for-assistance is viewed as not enough of a person to provide for himself or herself. Something has gone terribly wrong, and the victim ends up blaming him- or herself.

"Tzedakah" carries none of that weight. "Tzedakah," meaning "Justice" or "the Right Thing," simply signifies that something has, indeed, gone wrong, but no one is casting aspersions on the integrity of the person who needs an act of Tzedakah to set things right. The situation is not defined as one of "helper" and "helpee." Rather, someone "needs," someone else "has," and the one who "has" sets the imbalance aright by sharing. Moreover, "Tzedakah" means that the person-in-need is *entitled* to a response, and other people are instructed to respond. The Tzedakah-actor is not doing the other person a favor. According to Jewish tradition, it is an *obligation* to respond to the person in need.

The Rabbanit Kapach responds because—as she understands her Judaism—God has instructed people to respond. In her worldview, *everyone* is entitled to the good things in life, and if something has gone awry she—and anyone else she can teach and mobilize in her Mitzvah legions—will put out whatever time, energy, effort, and money that can be found to reestablish the person's balance.

She expects no less of the people who come to her with their problems. They, too, are expected to do Tzedakah, to reestablish this balance of a decent life for others. No person who calls or comes to the door or opens the door when she comes to visit is exclusively a recipient; each must be a giver, too. With the Rabbanit there is no one-way flow of Mitzvahs. It is always bidirectional. Otherwise, where is the dignity of the situation; where is the grandeur of being human?

(I keep thinking of movies about crime bosses—how they always say to someone for whom they have just promised or done a favor, "Sometime in the future I may need a favor from you." When the Godfather says it, there's always some heavy, ominous music in the background. What a contrast to the Rabbanit's two-way exchange!)

One article about the Rabbanit calls her the "the Angel of Nachla'ot." I'll temporarily demote her to Mitzvah Wonder Woman.

The Range of the Rabbanit's Mitzvah Activities

Besides the throngs she manages for Passover, the Rabbanit has great numbers of families that enjoy a better Purim holiday because of her. Purim, celebrating the Jews' historic victory over the evil Haman, must be a joyous day, so the Rabbanit is also in the Joy Business.

Plus providing many families with their weekly needs for the Sabbath.

Plus setting up a summer day camp for neighborhood kids who would otherwise just hang out and possibly get into trouble.

Plus managing every imaginable domestic problem: fighting, physical and verbal abuse, alcoholism, unemployment, in-law interference, catastrophic illnesses, deaths of spouses and parents and children, war injuries, orphans, psychological scarrings, difficult pregnancies and difficult births, physical and mental exhaustion, personality aberrations, heating and electric and phone bills.

Plus maintaining a small warehouse of used clothes in a big room underneath her apartment. Clothes and sheets and towels and blankets . . . lots of things.

Plus the swimming class. Here's where the Rabbanit's Mitzvah range comes into full play. When we hear "Tzedakah," we tend to think of food, clothing, shelter, medicine, and the like. The Rabbanit goes beyond that. Take a harried mother with many children. Take the daily pressures of managing a household of that size with little reasonable opportunity for substantial financial improvement. Imagine the tension, the potential for feeling trapped. Thus, the swimming class for mothers. Mothers in this situation have to get out, enjoy themselves, feel refreshed. The Rabbanit arranged the class, but the mothers wouldn't go unless "Bracha" swam with them too. So she does. (Did I mention that "Bracha" means "a blessing"?)

Plus the exercise class that she coordinates for neighborhood mothers who need a break. One day my friend David Morris and I are sitting in the Rabbanit's living room, just sharing a few majestic moments with her as usual, when the doorbell rings. The woman at the door insists that Bracha come with her down the block to the school building. The school year is over, so we have no idea what is going on. The Rabbanit takes us with her, and when we get inside, we see there's a party going on in the gymnasium. About twenty women are there, and plates and plates of fine Oriental Jewish food are laid out in front of them: hummus, baba ganoush, salads, pita, fruits, nuts. It's the end-of-the-year celebration. Having concluded a season of the Rabbanit's exercise class, these harried women (who at this moment hardly look harried) are having a party, and apparently blowing all the calories they burned off all year. They feel terrific, and from the moment the Rabbanit comes into the gym, you can see how much they love her. (Now that I think of it, besides admiring the Rabbanit, you find it very easy to love her.)

Plus the weddings. The Rabbanit is involved in many aspects of the Mitzvah of *hachnassat kallah* — providing for brides and young couples just getting married. She and her husband are pillars of Yemenite culture in Jerusalem and far out into the Hills of Judaea. On a chosen evening before the wedding day, she makes certain that the Yemenite bride is adorned in the traditional Yemenite dress, a very exotic piece of clothing with chains of gold and bright colors and other things I can't begin to describe (I leave this to you to see for yourselves). This *halbashat hakallah* ("the dressing of the bride") is a lively celebration, and she organizes such events throughout the year. Her presence is essential to any such celebration.

Indeed, a traditional Yemenite wedding dress is on display at the Israel Museum in Jerusalem. *The Rabbanit made it.* (I mentioned she was an excellent seamstress.) And whenever there is a Jews from Many Lands exhibition, it seems that the Rabbanit is the one putting together the Yemenite display. She's also travelled to different countries, with trunks and suitcases brimming with that dress and the rest of the Travelling Yemenite Cultural Display.

That's only a small part of the Rabbanit's wedding projects, though. More important is taking care of brides and young couples who are starting out with nothing or nearly nothing. She is a Wedding-Dress Wonder Woman. She has racks of wedding dresses that people have donated. She gets them from everywhere. People going to Israel pack their wedding dresses and deliver them to her. Teenagers coming on United Synagogue Youth Israel Pilgrimages bring wedding dresses. I personally feel proud that I've managed to help gather a few. And that is how brides who would not have been able to buy one of their own (or even to rent one) can come to her, pick out one they *really* like, get fitted, wear it, clean it, and then return it to her for the next bride to use—all with the requisite lack of embarrassment.

But she does much more. If the couple can't afford a dress, sometimes they might not be having a decent wedding. Once, the Rabbanit took a friend and me to a room a few blocks away. There, a small wedding was being held for a young couple who did not have material possessions and whose parents had come all the way from India. Perhaps forty or fifty people were there. There had been family feuds and little support from either side, so few family members were attending.

Now, the Rabbanit doesn't go around helping people marry who ought not to get married. But she knew this particular couple well and saw this marriage would be a good thing, so, without much familial support, she arranged for a photographer, good food, a rabbi, *and guests*. Most of the people there were neighborhood people (plus a couple of us American tourists). How sad it otherwise might have been had this bride and groom gotten married with only a half-dozen people witnessing this pivotal moment-of-change in their lives.

The Rabbanit was there to make merry, to provide the all-holy element of *simcha*, of Joy.

The dress, too, made all the difference. I tried to imagine what this bride would have looked like standing with her soon-to-be husband in an everyday dress in front of a rabbi and a couple of witnesses. Clothed in the magnificent gown that "someone, somewhere" had donated, you could see she had dignity. Married life would begin just right because of the Rabbanit.

And, as with so many of these couples, there was need for more: sheets, towels, dishes, furniture, a set of silverware. *Nice* furnishings — things they would be proud to own and use. In Hebrew, the word for "pride," *kavod*, also means "self-image" and "dignity."

The Essence of the Rabbanit Kapach

My subtitle is misleading. No one can capture the essence of the Rabbanit. Words are one step removed, as are photographs. She's short, she's lovely, she's gentle and humble, she's awesome while being gentle and humble, she's easy to admire and love, she's as normal and natural as can be, she's scholarly, wise, and playful. She's even what teenagers in the fifties would have called "cool." And although she only speaks Hebrew, everyone is able to communicate with her because of her unique personality.

The Rabbanit is on close terms with Teddy Kollek, the mayor of Jerusalem. Presidents and prime ministers and Knesset members know her well. She has her awards and prizes, which she doesn't need in and of themselves, though they are a tool for more Mitzvah power.

The best way to capture the so-called "Essence of the Rabbanit" is to see her and to see her again. Take some stretch of time to be with her. "Hang out" with her through a day that begins at 4:30 or 5:00 a.m., listen to her and joke with her, study Torah with her and see her faith in action. Keep watching as she interacts with hundreds of people day-by-day, week-by-week. There is much to be gained: a softening of the soul, a certain holy energy, faith.

In sum: Apprentice yourself to her. Just call or write and set things up.

Update: In 1999, the Rabbanit Kapach was awarded the Israel Prize, the country's highest honor, for her contributions to Israeli society. To date she and the Rav Kapach are the only married couple who have each been awarded the prize. In November 2013, the Rabbanit Kapach passed away at age 90, leaving behind an extraordinary legacy of transformed lives. Today her granddaughter and others carry on much of her good work.

Samantha Abeel
The Kid Who Got It All Wrong in Class (1998)

Samantha Abeel, age seventeen, is sitting at a table in a bookstore autographing her book of poetry, *Reach for the Moon*. Sometime during the afternoon, a man comes in, takes a copy of the book off the table, and moves to a corner of the store to read it. He sits there for a half hour or 45 minutes reading the book, then comes back to the table. He gets on his knees in front of Samantha, and tears begin to form in his eyes. He says to her, "I am a surgeon. Every morning I have to take out a map and review the route to show myself how I can get from my house to the hospital. I thought there was something terribly wrong with me, something bad. You changed my life."

What Samantha Is Like

Samantha (or, as she lets me call her, "Sam") is very real.
    She is unpretentious.
    She is unassuming.
    She is very funny.
    She is fun. Samantha is definitely fun.
    I want to spend more time with her not only because she has become a great teacher of mine—one of the best I have ever had—but, even more, because she is fun to hang out with.

She's *very* lively. The biochemist who can discover which chemical gives her all that energy could win a *very* big award for his or her research. (When it finally hits the drugstore shelves, I will buy a gallon of it for myself.)

What Samantha Is Good At

Poetry. Public speaking. Inspiring people.

What Samantha Is No Good At

Anything having to do with mathematics, time, numbers, or languages.

How I Met Samantha

My friend Naomi sent me a review of an illustrated book of poetry called *Reach for the Moon*, written by a teenager. I wouldn't have been interested, except that the review included one of her poems, "Self Portrait."

I don't generally like to read reviews of other people's poetry books, for two reasons: (1) if their poetry (in my opinion) is not as good as mine, I get angry that this poet got a real, big-time publisher while I've been stuck for years doing book publishing and marketing on my own; or (2) if the poetry is much better than mine, I get frustrated and jealous that someone writes much better than I do . . . though I have mellowed on point number two in the past few years.

But I read the review and the poem anyway, and was stunned. The images in "Self Portrait" were so striking, I reacted as so many other admirers have: "How could a kid come up with such incredible images, so many perfectly accurate phrases, so many ideas and feelings in exactly the precise and economical words needed to express her thoughts?" It was so moving for me, I almost forgot that the reviewer had explained that this poem had been composed by a person with learning disabilities.

This is the poem, "Self Portrait":

To show you who I am
I crawled inside a tree, became its roots, bark and leaves,
listened to its whispers in the wind.
When fall came and painted the leaves red and gold
I wanted to shake them across your lawn
to transform the grass into a quilt, a gift spread at your feet,
but their numbers eluded me,
so I turned a piece of paper into my soul
to send to you so that you might see
how easily it can be crumpled and flattened out again.
I wanted you to see my resilience,
but I wasn't sure how to arrange the numbers in your address,
so I danced with the Indians in the forest
and collected the feathers that fell from the eagle's wings,
each one a wish for my future,
but I lost track of their numbers, gathered too many,
and was unable to carry them home
so I reaped the wind with my hair,
relived its journey through my senses, and
felt its whispered loneliness, like lakes in winter,
but it was too far and you could not follow me.

Now I've written out their shadows
like the wind collects its secrets
to whisper into receptive ears, and I
will leave them at your doorstep,
a reminder of what others cannot see,
a reminder of what I can and cannot be.[1]

I was "hooked" on Samantha.

Next, I ordered the book, read every poem and all the explanations and commentaries from Samantha, her mother, and her teacher.

Then I called directory assistance to get Samantha's phone number.

I called the house, spoke to her mother, then spoke to Samantha and told her how much I loved the book and how I would send her a book or two of mine and how I desperately hoped we would get to meet some time, though in some part of my mind I knew it was unlikely for a long time because she lived in Traverse City, Michigan, far away from the normal geographical range of my speaking engagements.

I just put it out of mind, on a mental list for "Later On, Maybe."

Then I got an invitation to speak in Grand Rapids. The *Rand McNally Road Atlas* showed me that Traverse City was three hours away.

I called, I pleaded with the Abeels. Could they come down to Grand Rapids for a day? I *really* wanted to meet Samantha.

The Abeels came to meet me, we walked and talked and talked some more, and the rest is belated history.

What This Is and Isn't All About

This story *isn't* about people as symbols.

Once you meet Samantha, you feel that she is so immediate and present, you would never think of her as a symbol. From the moment you meet her, it is Real and True Life happening.

And this story isn't about the abstract topic "People with Disabilities Who Have Overcome Their Disabilities." Not everyone is victorious in this struggle. For every triumphant story about someone with a disability, there are three or four or twenty-five more about frustration and failure, loneliness, missed opportunities, loss and a sense of loss.

And it is definitely not about heroes, because Samantha doesn't see herself as a hero, though she *is* aware of how she has inspired thousands of people. She'll have nothing of heroes and heroism. (Her father, David, says, "Huh, no Saint Samantha status?")

Samantha is about human beings and what makes them human. She is about all of us.

What Samantha "Has"

It's called dyscalculia, the inability to work with numbers, math, quantities. I particularly liked the confused and amused look on her face when she told me, "And then I went to junior high school and they told me there would be six minutes between classes. How was I supposed to know what six minutes means?"

She's lousy at spelling, too. And punctuation.

Samantha's "case" is quite severe.

Tales of Samantha: The Post Office

One day when Sam was in the ninth grade, her mother sent her to the post office to get the mail. Elizabeth had written down the post office box number on a piece of paper and given it to her most exceptional child. Samantha stood there for ten or fifteen minutes, trying to match the number on the piece of paper with the number on the right box, one among many other numbers all in neat rows.

Samantha couldn't do it. She just couldn't find the right mailbox. As Sam tells it, while she was standing there, little kids came in, got the mail for *their* families, and left, probably wondering why this teenager was just standing there staring at the mail boxes.

So she went home, and her mother had to go back and get the mail herself.

What I Have

I, Danny Siegel, have mild dyslexia. Sometimes when I am reading, I randomly switch around the order of the letters. On top of this I have a perceptual problem which causes me to read letters in certain words incorrectly. It has nothing to do with my eyesight; my prescription glasses give me 20-20 vision.

This is the way I read: "Ocean rafting" is "organ grafting," a "cheeseburger" is a "Chinese burger," "Cold War" is "Gold War," and "failing levees" might become "falling leaves."

Other typical examples:

1. I saw the sign "George and Rental Cars" which, on second or third reading, was really "Garage and Rental Cars."
2. Running to catch a train, I read "Metroliner" instead of "Montrealer" on the big board at New York's Penn Station. I also

wondered what a "fancard" was when I needed to board a Metro in Washington. (It was a "farecard.")

3. The Hobart Parker company became "Parker Hobart."

4. Junk mail in my mailbox advertised a Roy Rogers special for what I thought was 88¢. It was actually 99¢, and while I wasn't going to get one of these specials (since the hamburgers don't comply with the kosher standards recorded in extended passages in Leviticus 11 and Deuteronomy 14), you can imagine what this kind of problem can do to my finances when it comes time to calculate my taxes.

5. "Windflowers" are really "wildflowers." (The Spellcheck on my computer insisted the correct spelling was "wildflowers" ... but what does a Mac know, anyway?)

Some of the mistakes are quite amusing:

6. I was in Harrod's in London, that grand, vast store that sells almost anything (except perhaps a set of the Talmud), when I noticed a sign that really said, "South Lift." I thought it was a "South Left" and wondered, "For the life of me, what is a 'South Left,' and which way am I supposed to go to get an elevator up to the 4th floor?"

7. A new free medical service in Boston described how the staff would be determining the patients' needs. Instead of "determining" I read "undermining the needs"—not a great way to cure people.

8. I read a splashy, enticing advertisement to go skiing out West. Afterward I wondered what a "life ticket" ("lift ticket") was.

9. There was the movie I considered renting, *The Walking Deed* (*Walking Dead*). It's a good thing I didn't rent it. I'd have spent a long night trying to figure out the connection between zombies and things-we-do-that-have-legs.

10. And my favorite one: another advertisement, this one for a vacation in Jamaica, "You can dirty all night." Re-reading it, I saw that the Jamaica Tourist Board really wanted people to *party* all night,

and that if people want to come to Montego Bay to dirty things, perhaps they should stay home in Buffalo and Detroit, thank you sir and ma'am, and freeze without bothering the native Jamaicans.

Don't misunderstand. My life goes well. My learning problem is bothersome and often inconvenient, but not much more than that. I shy away from reading long articles or books unless I have a long flight somewhere or get to a vacation spot where I have nothing to do. If someone hands me a book to look at, I never start from Page One. I'll open it anywhere, scan a few lines or paragraphs, skip to another page then another and another, and eventually decide if I will read an entire chapter or the whole thing. (Looking back, I wonder how I ever majored in comparative literature in college. Then I didn't know why it was taking me so long to get through Joyce's *Dubliners*, a mere 224 pages, and Hemingway's *The Old Man and the Sea*, 127 pages.)

I read articles in *Newsweek* backward, last paragraph first, then the one before that. Sometimes, if I have the patience, I'll reach the title.

There is one other thing. I call it The Iron Bar. Sometimes when I am reading something—it could be a book or an essay or even the text of a comic strip—it feels like someone has placed an iron bar right behind my eyes, blocking the content of what I was just reading from entering my brain. There's no fighting it while it's going on. The hazy spaciness in my mind will just remain . . . until it disappears, sometimes so well I can return to the Old Days of high school when I could easily read and memorize fifty words for a Spanish exam in no time at all. I have kept very close track of this quirk. It has nothing to do with fatigue, emotional upset, or intake of aspirin or caffeine or the occasional antacid. It just happens, and I never know when it will happen, and just lasts, and I have no idea how long it will last. The special education specialists I have gone to *really* enjoy this one.

There is, however, one educational advantage to my learning disabilities: I never switch letters when I read Hebrew or Aramaic right to left.

Tales of Samantha 1: Sam in Grand Rapids, Michigan

I was in Grand Rapids, Michigan, serving as a scholar-in-residence that weekend at a local synagogue. Samantha and her family had just driven three hours to meet me there.

Though I had never seen her speak in public, I called her up to the bimah to address the audience for a few moments. She began to tell her story . . . and the atmosphere in the chapel changed immediately. Samantha was captivating.

They loved her.

Afterward, people came up to her, people with children with learning disabilities and other disabilities, people who themselves had learning disabilities and other disabilities, as well as "normal" people with "normal" children. They couldn't get enough of her.

She handled herself with great sensitivity and maturity (but not so much that you couldn't tell she was still a teenager). She listened. (She *really* knows how to listen.) She responded to these people, and they were touched.

Tales of Samantha 2: Language Exams

When Sam was a first-year student at Mount Holyoke College, she had to take the Modern Language Aptitude Test which "is used as a screening instrument to investigate a student's ability to learn a foreign language" (to quote the summary Samantha received from one of the college administrators). Anywhere from the 30th to 70th percentile is considered average; 71st and higher is above average. Sam came in at a ripping 5th percentile. To quote again from the paragraph Sam e-mailed to me, "below 20% is an indication of significant difficulty."

She knew that. She might be a student with learning disabilities, but, as she says in one of her lectures, she is not stupid. Her parents and elementary and high school teachers knew ahead of time how she would do on the exam, and by now, even *I* had guessed it, and while it is no laughing matter, we laughed. Her father says she tried really hard, buckled down to do really well, but it didn't work. Her brain can't do it. But she can handle it. That's why we all laugh when we tell the story.

Samantha's Long Road, or to Quote the Kid, "LD Doesn't Mean Lazy and Dumb"

Samantha's parents, Elizabeth and David, went through the twisted paths and painful troubles of parents of children with special needs. Some of the details are very interesting and have an element of humor to them, though probably only in retrospect.

Starting before second grade and through fourth grade, Elizabeth and David became increasingly aware that their daughter wasn't doing well with math flash cards.

In the fifth and sixth grades they started asking if she was learning disabled.

For many reasons, the school was reluctant to give her the label. The stigma is hard for any kid to take, and, besides, there exists a major bureaucratic system that has to kick in once a student is officially designated a special needs child.

In seventh grade they got her tested, and sure enough she had a learning disability. At that time, though, they still had to enroll her in a regular math class so the school would have a year of documented disability in the files. Sam had to be a guinea pig, as it were, and the teacher, Dee Massaroni, was on her side. Finally, by the beginning of eighth grade, after her parents' persistent efforts, Sam got her label and was placed on a special education track.

And it was in seventh grade, also, that another teacher, Roberta Williams, began to notice the other side of Samantha: her incredibly fine gift for imagery and writing.

The rest, as they say, is Sam's ever-unfolding and increasingly dazzling biography.

Samantha and her parents spent two years visiting at least a dozen colleges and universities to find the one best suited to her special needs. Before they even started their journey, they had read through an impressive pile of college catalogues. Sam's father told me that when they arrived at many of the schools, Sam didn't even want to get out of the car. She felt the "chemistry" just wasn't right. She did take the tours, though, and went through the motions.

Ultimately convinced that Mount Holyoke was the place for her, The Special Sam, she applied for early decision, got in, and is doing well there.

Things Samantha Says on the Video Her Publisher Produced

She says, "It's not my fault." Those four words alone should be made into a poster and given to every parent with a child who has some difficulty learning the A-B-C's, the Three R's, and anything else in school. Maybe two posters per parents: one for the kitchen and one for the bedroom, more if necessary to get the message across.

I have always wondered why so many people in my audiences raise their hands when I ask, "Who is terrible in math? Who is a First Class Incompetent in chemistry or foreign languages?" So quickly the hands go up! And you can hear the chuckles. How quickly they recall their struggles with "Yo soy, tu eres, el/la es, nosotros estamos," or having to solve the sum of the squares of the two short sides of a right-angle triangle. I frequently ask the question, "How many of you who are parents have said to your children when they come home with a 96 on an exam, 'What did you get wrong?,'" and all too often these same adults will raise their hands. (There is some buzz of laughter; at least they are squirming a little.) I hope they will reconsider what they are doing to their children.

Most of all, when you have kids with real live learning disabilities, the organic ones in particular, coming down hard on the kids is like blaming the person with muscular dystrophy for having muscular dystrophy or a person who is recovering from a stroke for dropping a spoon from a limp hand or not speaking clearly. It doesn't make sense. Organic is organic. Parents who assume their little genius will blossom once he or she buckles down and works harder (and, besides, they want to teach their child that Life is Tough), or tell themselves their child will simply "snap out of it" like a groggy person after the second or third alarm bell or Dad's shouting "Wake up you sleepy head!" make things so much more difficult for their child.

Which leads us to Samantha's second striking statement.

She says, "Special education is the best thing that ever happened to me."

Once Samantha got her rightful and critically needed label, once anyone in her type of situation knows the real situation, then everyone—the child, the parent, the grandparents and aunts and friends and teachers and specialists—can begin to work with it. Samantha, for one, used to have panic attacks, but they went away as soon as she knew what the problem in school was all about.

Which brings us to the third wonderful thing Samantha says in the video.

With some paraphrasing, Samantha says, "Some people think my learning disability goes away at 3:00 when school is over." It doesn't go away like the flu running its course or like a parent kissing a baby's boo-boo and then the infant stops crying. It's there twenty-four hours a day, all your life.

Nowadays you hear people grumble, "Everyone is claiming he or she is learning disabled, and *they* [the professionals, researchers, authorities on the subject] just keep coming up with more and more names for these things." Let us hope that as time goes on and the researchers and the mental health practitioners and the teachers and the parents continue to do their jobs, we will come up with seventeen types of learning disabilities, and consequently be able to see things even more accurately. And whatever that research will show, let us proceed from that knowledge to do what is best for people like Samantha, who is trying to emerge as the best human being she can be. Applying the best teaching methods or drugs or their combination—synthesized with the all-important elements of specialized teaching, caring, and love—will give us more Samantha Abeels. Everyone will benefit, not just the Samanthas in our society . . . even if every individual with learning disabilities doesn't develop into someone with Samantha's gifts.

In the video Samantha also makes it absolutely clear that she would have preferred not to be learning disabled. For all her stamina and courage, it is still very wearing for her to have to negotiate her way through reality day in and day out, to compensate and work around living situations that others take for granted. It takes its toll on her, even though she is so far ahead of where she was as a second grader and no one really knew what to do for her, other than the fact that her parents *just knew* that something had to be done.

Some of the Awards for *Reach for the Moon* (through December 1996)

The 1994 Margot Marek Award from the Orton Dyslexia Society, New York Branch.
The International Reading Association's 1995 Distinguished Book Award.
A 1995 Best Book for Young Adults Nominee by the American Library Association.

Things Samantha Said in Her Keynote at a Dyslexia Experts Convention

1. How am I supposed to use a calculator?
2. How am I supposed to dial a phone?
3. I once had a teacher who said, "You can't be learning disabled. You don't *look* learning disabled."
4. Having my learning disability is like having a minor case of Alzheimer's Disease.
5. My brother likes to play card games with me, like Black Jack. (Laughs in the audience.)
6. I was a Mouse Child in class. (As in "mousey" — quiet, hanging back, never participating, afraid she was too stupid to

contribute anything to the class. She didn't get it. "Mouse Child" . . . what a wonderful Samantha-term.)

7. If you are going to write a poem about a tree, you have to *become* that tree.

8. Everyone is learning disabled and everyone is gifted.

(I asked her mother if people buy her book at these talks. She said that at one of the lectures, it was the nearest thing to a riot she had ever seen.)

One Statistic

USA Today (March 26, 1996) reported the results of an interesting poll taken by the National Organization on Disabilities. They hired the famous Harris pollsters to discover the effects of certain movies on people's attitudes toward individuals with disabilities. It turned out that 48 percent of the people who saw *My Left Foot*—that marvelous movie in which Daniel Day-Lewis plays a physically disabled man growing up in Ireland—changed their perception of people with disabilities for the better. After Dustin Hoffman starred in *Rain Man*, 41 percent of the audience understood better and reacted more positively to people with autism.

I would think that after audiences watch the video of Samantha talking to kids, viewers will understand the constant challenges of living with a learning disability more clearly.

Some of the Things I Have Learned from Samantha

I learned that it wasn't my fault. I knew that already. Some close friends had told me that, reinforced it in me, but after meeting Samantha, I *really* knew it.

I learned that the real issue is not that some people learn better or worse than others. They just learn *differently*.

I remember sitting in many Talmud classes in the sixties and not being able to lock into the flow of the text. I could recite back the right answers for some of the elementary texts and even for a few of the intermediate ones. But it was like geometry class: I just didn't *get* it. One class in particular comes to mind: six of us sitting in our professor's study and studying Talmud together two or three times a week. The other five students were graduates of yeshivas, intensive Jewish day schools where they had studied Talmud since fourth or fifth grade. They were comfortable there, and I was tense; they did well with the usual effort associated with preparing for a Talmud class. I only did "all right," but with twice or three times the preparation and review. Only after meeting Samantha did I see my difficulty wasn't fundamentally an issue of background, training, or accumulated knowledge. Their minds were made for the classical method of Talmud study, and mine was not. While they were better at classical Talmud study than I was, they weren't necessarily *better people* than I was. And the fact is, whenever my own unique style came into play, I far exceeded them. I could understand the written words laid out on the page better than they could, though I didn't do that very much in those days. I suppose I was a Talmudic Mouse Child.

Now that I know what was happening back then in my classes, I can prepare and present and write about Talmud in the classical way whenever it's necessary to do so. But I do it even more frequently *my own way*—with complete deference to Jewish tradition—when others and I need it *my* way: with a touch of poetry or lyricism, or with some disjointed imagery that *they* couldn't have seen because their minds have a chemistry and circuitry that's different than mine.

I even tell close friends that I once read through the entire Talmud. Since at the rate of one page a day it takes seven years to cover all five-thousand-plus pages even on the most elementary level, they wonder how I could have done it. When I describe my method, not one person who knows the Standard Way says he or she would ever try it my way.

Samantha, this gifted poet who couldn't even find the right post office box, taught me that not only is that all right, *it's what I should be doing.*

And she taught me the dangers of self-absorption—the perils of perceiving that I'm a bad person just because of my brain's unusual, unique design. Her perspective is: I have this problem. Now that we know what it is, we can work with it on its own terms, but I shouldn't be spending my life working on Me, thinking about Me, getting Myself together. This Thing shouldn't interrupt my Real Work of making the lives of other people better, richer, stronger.

From Samantha, I learned that it's tough living with this Thing, but not nearly as difficult as the daily, hourly, or minute-by-minute struggles of other people who have different or more severe learning disabilities. And beyond that, there are countless refugees everywhere fleeing danger, and people who can't afford a warm coat in winter to shield them from the bone-chilling wind, and still others for whom a plate of rice and beans would be a blessing beyond imagining. They demand more of our attention than wondering what "George and Rental Cars" means.

Most of all, Samantha taught me that I am free. I am free of whatever it was that was making me subconsciously feel that I was a damaged person in comparison to others.

I have some difficulty finding the right comparison to describe this feeling of freedom. Sometimes it feels like that moment when a kite suddenly catches the wind and seems to hang effortlessly in the sky, free of the pull of gravity. At other times, it feels like the moment of lift-off on an airplane. Even that comparison needs to be refined: at times it is like a 747, so big, so heavy, lumbering down the runway so slowly I think it just won't ever have enough power to get off the ground, but it does, and in a minute, the wheels will be up because they aren't needed any more and the long June flight to the Promised Land will be smooth and easy. At other times it's like being in the smaller 737. When the pilot shoves the handles forward and jams the engines up to full throttle, the plane races so quickly along the tarmac, I am thrown against my seat with a surprising and exhilarating force. We are in the air so quickly, I don't even need to count off the seconds. Passover and the Exodus from slavery in Egypt also come to mind, of course.

Free.

A Curious, But Not Depressing, Question about Myself

I keep wondering: had there been some time warp, and Samantha and I were the same age, and I had lived in Traverse City, Michigan, as she was growing up, and my family and her family were friends, and my mother and her mother had sat in the kitchen or den over coffee and talked about their kids . . . I keep wondering, how different my life would have been.

I'm not angry or jealous of Samantha. I was fortunate that my very wise mother saw early on that I learned differently than other kids. She always emphasized my specific talents. But she, and my teachers, and all the counselors along the way didn't see what was wrong with the other parts of my learning style. In many cases they couldn't have known. No one knew. Mom made sure I went to a special private high school in Washington for creative people. She even pushed to send me to Bard College in New York, though I resisted and went elsewhere. She was on the right track, but who knew back then, in the early Fifties, what to call it, what to do with it, what was really best for me?

I wonder too who I would be now had I had met Sam when I was thirty-nine or forty-two instead of last year when I was fifty-one, or even more important, had I seen and listened to her years before I started writing poetry when I was twenty-six. She would have taught me so much about how my learning disability was really the source of my poetry, and that it was a single phenomenon, not two separate things. *She would have known that my disconnecting brain was the same place my lyricism came from.* She might have listened to me talk about how I could be having a light conversation with someone and find myself suddenly hanging on to a single word or phrase and then fading out into my own world. She would have understood, as she would have understood why so many Good Thoughts come to me out of nowhere while I am taking a casual stroll, or at 4:30 a.m., or swimming, or driving to nowhere in particular.

It is a curious and rewarding train of thought. My anger is a thing of the past; the frustration is long gone from my emotional life. I can move on, returning to these thoughts whenever I need them or whenever they just happen to come to mind.

Tales of Samantha 4: Getting Home Over Winter Break

I talked to Samantha's mother Elizabeth this morning. Here's the latest problem: how is Samantha going to get from Mount Holyoke in South Hadley, Massachusetts, to Traverse City, Michigan, for winter break? By plane, naturally. When *we* were in college, We, Regular People, we would buy a ticket, pack our bags, go to the airport, check in, go to the gate, get on the plane, fly home, get off the plane, and be met by someone who welcomed us and mercifully let us sleep late most mornings, waking us only to feed us delicious home-cooked food.

Not Samantha. First, Mom had to push her to go across the street to a travel agent. Sam did manage to buy the ticket, but afterward, when her Mom asked, "What time does your flight arrive?," even though Sam was holding the piece of paper in her hands, *right in front of her eyes*, she insisted that the flights times weren't on the printout. She got all worked up, time and numbers haunting her once again. And then there was the problem of finding the right gate . . .

She'll make it. Mom is sure she'll get home, though I said, "If you don't hear from her within twenty-four hours of when she should be in Michigan, call me. I have a friend who is a State Trooper, and he'll get out an All Points Bulletin for her."

We laugh, no longer worried. We feel bad that Sam has to go through this day in and day out, but every day she manages her world with greater success.

Maybe Elizabeth will send me a picture of Sam getting off the plane, beaming with pride that she found the right gate.

Samantha is about human beings and what makes them human. She is about all of us.

I used to read "Self Portrait" to my audiences. Only half of the time can I get through it now without getting choked with emotion. About a month ago I showed Sam's video to one of my audiences, but about halfway through, I stopped it. I was overcome. Perhaps I should have stepped outside until it was over so I wouldn't have deprived others of the experience. Perhaps my own needs and memories and life's wanderings interfere with teaching about Sam and I distort her importance because of my own learning problems. But this story really isn't about me. It's really about human beings in their entirety, and what makes them human.

Samantha is about all of us.

Mitzvah Heroes Are Everywhere—We Just Have to Know How to Look (2020)

Looking back, I believe one of my most significant contributions to the practice of doing greater Tikkun Olam has been to teach the *centrality* of Mitzvah heroes—the imperative to integrate them, their work, their absolute commitment to repairing the world, and their Menschlichkeit into our consciousness and lives. These Teachers-in-Life are our true Heroes to admire and imitate and turn to in order to guide us in implementing ever-greater and more effective Mitzvahs.

To make Mitzvah heroes central to our giving-lives, we need to disabuse ourselves of the thought that people just *automatically* know how to do Tikkun Olam actions. There is really nothing genetic or innate about giving to others. We go to doctors and other health care professionals, lawyers, computer techies, car mechanics, plumbers, electricians, investment counselors, etc., for their knowledge, experience, and guidance. So, too, going to Mitzvah heroes should bring us the desire and the skills to do the work of Tikkun Olam.

The urgency of the situation struck me a few years back, when I discovered how few university students could name a professor about whom they could say, "I want to be like that kind of *person*." I realized that in the rarified world of academia, students are not expected or trained to seek out Menschen and Mitzvah heroes. Furthermore, there is little expectation upon a professor to do anything besides share his or her specific expertise. Brilliance becomes a thing to admire, in and of itself. It's almost as if there is a bifurcation of personhood: the intellect is the essence, and other elements of the human being are of lesser—if any—importance.

An exception that sadly proves the rule is a story my late, dear friend Allan Gould told me about a huge class he attended with the distinguished literary critic Northrop Frye. At one point, a student asked a question that was superficial, even stupid. Professor Frye carefully considered how to reply without humiliating the student. Kindly he responded by saying, "Perhaps you meant to ask your question this way . . . ?" I suppose there were more lessons being learned in the classroom that day than simply the subject matter at hand.

We need to remember that there are more Mitzvah heroes around us than we might have imagined. This is true in the twenty-first century as it was in any real or mythical past. For someone experienced in being on the lookout for them, they often appear unexpectedly. Some would call it by accident, or chance, or luck, but others would insist, as they say in Yiddish, that it's *bashert*—in some way divinely planned.

A significant encounter happened to me a few years ago after I delivered a talk in Chicago. I was shmoozing with my friend Kate Kinser when, by chance, she turned her head and I saw she was wearing a beautiful multicolored crocheted *kippah*. When I asked where it was from and who made it, she told me about Mayan women artisans in Guatemala who make a living crocheting them, and that the organization, MayaWorks, was based in Chicago. The office—really the home of the executive director, Jeannie Balanda—organizes the marketing, website, and annual trips to Guatemala for an encounter with the women.

The story was so off the beaten path I suspected I would be hooked. Indeed, I have now been to the Central American hinterland villages five times to meet the craftswomen and see this for myself. Some fifty to sixty indigenous Mayan women are crocheting *kippot*, plus a couple are weaving *tallitot*, and others are making challah covers. The labor conditions are the diametric opposite of the classic images of a sweatshop. These women work individually, in their own homes, on their own schedules, so they can simultaneously raise their children; otherwise, they would probably have to move far away to find work as a housekeeper or nanny. The employment conditions meet Fair Trade standards, which means in part that they are asked for and receive an appropriate price for their product, they are paid half up front, and there is no child labor.

How did it transpire that these women in a remote part of Central America are producing exquisite Judaica? In brief, it began in 1990 with an American volunteer named Patricia Krause who was doing work with Behrhorst Partners for Development, a Central American development and aid service. She brought a suitcase full of weavings by Mayan women in rural Guatemala back to the United States to sell on their behalf—and soon established a significant niche with buyers who were struck by the beauty of the products and the opportunity to make a difference in these women's lives. In 1996 MayaWorks was formed as a nonprofit 501(c)3 tax-exempt entity.

On one MayaWorks trip to Guatemala, a Jewish woman, the late Becky Berman, saw that the women were making colorful, crocheted hacky sacks. In her mind, she made the tremendous leap and thought, "Maybe they can make *kippot*, too." Becky arranged for the Maya-Works to try their hand at Judaica items and for a cadre of American volunteers to come and teach the women how to make them—and it was a resounding success. The Mayans are deeply spiritual people, so the women were pleased to learn that *kippot* (and, later, *tallitot* and challah covers) are Jewish religious items.

The key to the beauty of the *kippot* is especially obvious when you encounter the women in person. They all wear multicolored hand-embroidered *huipiles* (blouses), with unique, creative designs; they are, to be truthful, absolutely dazzling.

The Judaica project took off, and MayaWorks began marketing these items with their other products. Soon Jewish families in the United States were buying scores of Guatemalan *kippot* at a time for their B'nai Mitzvah celebrations and weddings.

The essence of MayaWorks is so Jewish—that is, Maimonides's highest level of Tzedakah in action, creating a situation where the individual can be self-sustaining. Not only are the women doing dignified work and earning respectable salaries to support their families, but they also are enabling their daughters to get educations that otherwise would have been denied to them. Public education in Guatemala is generally limited and difficult to access, especially for girls. Since education there is primarily vocationally based, girls are often denied basic educations, since it is assumed that boys will be the future breadwinners for their families. Furthermore, while public school is free, the not-so-incidental costs—books, transportation, uniforms, and school supplies—can be substantial; indeed, these costs can be the difference between impoverished children attending or not attending.

Not only do the women's salaries make education for their daughters possible, but MayaWorks also provides scholarships for girls to attend elementary, junior high, and senior high school. And more: MayaWorks also offers literacy classes for their artisans and extends microloans for them to create their own small businesses. All this works toward the very essence of human dignity: empowering the women to create lives of self-sufficiency for themselves and their children.

On my most recent visit, one of the women proudly told us someone had taught her how to sign her name. This, of course, was a profound first step toward empowerment. Yet when we asked their daughters what they wanted to become, common answers included "nurse," "social worker," "teacher," even "doctor" and "lawyer." In this kind of way, every encounter with the women and their daughters was personal, powerful, and somewhat surreal. What a contrast to my homelife in Rockville, Maryland, with its Trader Joe's and Baja Fresh and seven sushi restaurants within a mile! And yet, in the remote villages of Central America, it all seemed so natural.

While Jeannie Balanda, the boss, has the official title of executive director, along the way it dawned on me that her essential description is *Tzaddeket*, Mitzvah hero. She has a full-time job separate from her Mitzvah-work; at MayaWorks, she serves fully as a volunteer. That in and of itself, however, is not why she is a Mitzvah hero. She qualifies because of her absolute devotion to the women and their children. She knows what her lengthy hours of compassion-put-into-action achieve: whenever MayaWorks sells a *kippah*, a *tallit*, or a challah cover, it raises the self-dignity of the worker, stabilizes the family, and offers a future to her daughters. And Jeannie does her work with great humility. Unassuming by nature, she is no less humbled and awed by the result of her organizational skills and tireless efforts.

Jeannie is just one of more than one hundred Mitzvah heroes I have met in my fifty-year involvement in Tikkun Olam. This may sound overly lyrical, but to me connecting with these heroes allows me/us to encounter an intimate view of deep reality and may bring us closer to the true meaning of Life. Once we train ourselves in the art of seeking them out, we discover that they are everywhere—from our local neighborhoods to the Central Highlands of Guatemala. When we know how to do that, the world can seem tremendously more exciting, pregnant with potential for healing and world repair.

4

Living a Life of Menschlichkeit

My Father's Personal Passover Ritual (1978)

Passover in my father's household has always been a celebration of freedom and equality. Two nights a year, twenty to thirty people would sit around our table and join my father in the recitation of the tale of the Jews leaving their bondage in the Land of Egypt.

From the first seder nights I can recall, our guests were our closest friends, plus soldiers (there was World War II, and Korea, and they were far away from home), and students at universities in the area who could not afford to go back to Missouri or Illinois or California for the holiday . . . and a special element, as if Chagall or Dali or Kafka designed the scenery and script: about a month before the onset of Passover, my mother would call local institutions for brain-damaged children. She would ask to come down to acquaint herself with six or seven of the Jewish children, talk with them, bring them things, and tell them Passover was coming. And then, the afternoon before the first seder, my brother and sister and I would set the tables as my parents took both cars to the institutions, to bring the children back in preparation for the evening in our home.

Besides the regular guests, there were always some new faces—a rotation of doctors, a new patient of my father's who had not seen a seder-ritual in years, perhaps the parents of a child my father, the physician, had delivered in their home long ago. My grandfather was there, of course, and my grandmother (until she died when I was a teenager), and an aunt and some cousins, a friend or two of mine, and the six or seven children.

You will say their noises disturbed the recitations. That is true.

You will say my mother was burdened enough, cleaning house and cooking the week through for fifty or sixty people. That is true.

You will say the children needed watching every minute: they would spill things, throw up, start to shout. That, too, is true.

But next to each member of my family and in between other couples was one of these children, and each of us was charged with caring for the child, watching over all of them and treating them as best as Moses might have treated them among the masses being taken from Pharaoh's slavery—for we must assume that there were palsied and polioed children three or four thousand years ago, too. Each of us was to bring the message, however differently perceived, to these children.

And when it came time to eat the meal itself, my father would rise in his white robe and go from seat to seat, cutting the lamb or roast beef, spoon-feeding whoever needed to be fed in such fashion, and joking with each.

The meals would last long past midnight. The mishaps were many, and the fulfillment of the dictum "Let all who are hungry come and eat" went slowly, for each had his or her own needs and peculiarities. Yet each was fed with the utmost care.

In our household on Passover nights, everyone felt comfortably at home. No one winced, sat in silence, ignored, or paid extra attention to what was taking place. Our guests-of-many-years knew what was to happen, and the newcomers soon learned, became momentarily uneasy, then leaned back against their pillows (as free people must have pillows on Passover night) and partook of the wonders of freedom.

The following afternoons, each disease was explained to me. The names were impressive in their Latin and Greek configurations, but the symptoms and the sufferings were terrors to conceive. Nevertheless, these children—some of whom had been cast off by their families—were an integral part of our People, of our Greater Family. They were no more or less normal for their chromosomal defects and their birth-traumas, the disorders of their nervous systems and their Down syndrome features, than the doctor who fed them.

Those nights, the feeding done, the thanks recited, the singing would begin. It was a dissonant chorus resembling (in my early imagination) a choir of Heavenly Host, but with flesh and blood instead of halos; twisted words and sounds of human beings in place of the perfect harmonies of angels who needed neither food nor drink nor my father's affection.

That is why it is better to be a human being than an angel.

A Tribute to My Friends in the Rabbinate (1981)

All too often I am criticized for writing about people who are larger than life. The people I describe are strong-willed, energetic visionaries who move mountains and bureaucrats and slow-to-shift societal currents into some prophetical program grander than the status quo would believe possible. Others conclude that because I am so impressed by their accomplishments, I am advocating similar lifestyles for all Jews. The Romantic Poet, as it were, wishes to bring people with ostensibly limited capacities into more expansive, breathtaking realms.

It is true that I believe, more than most people, that more of these "unbelievable" people live in our own communities. And I believe they can be "discovered," much as one young woman, a certain Rachel, "discovered" the great Rabbi Akiva in the clothing of a crudely clad shepherd one day in the fall sometime in the first century. Underneath his coarse appearance, she knew: here was a Jewish Leader personified, someone at once noble and humble . . . and if he was offered the opportunity to study with the Great Teachers, he would reveal himself to himself and his people. Indeed, though he was already 40 years old, their combined wills produced the classic metamorphosis: a Jewish peasant assumed his place as the greatest Talmud teacher in Jewish history.

But Akiva—a thinker, Mensch, embodiment of the best of Jewish values, molder of a new Jewish vision—appears larger than life as well. So it is unfair to analogize from his biography, just as it is unfair to expect a randomly selected woman from Dallas or man from New Orleans to suddenly throw away his or her former lifestyle and turn to other, greater things. A new life—with newfound energy and spiritual resources, concomitant with less sleep and less time for shopping, business, and the full array of errands needed for survival—that is not a realistic expectation. . . . That, I believe, is why the Talmud tells us there are only thirty-six Righteous Ones in the world. This figure might not be absolutely accurate—other opinions surface in the Talmud—but clearly the number is limited.

On the other hand, if I did not believe that the so-called "average Jew" could not broaden his or her vistas—accommodating to the larger considerations of Life-through-Tzedakah—I would not spend as much time as I do thinking, writing, and teaching about that Mitzvah. And, furthermore, beyond the stories I hear of local Tzaddikim, people who wholeheartedly give to others beyond the expectations of the "norm," more frequently I am told of individuals whose small patterns of giving are truly impressive. In scattered sectors of the Jewish world, generous gestures abound, kindnesses are freely offered, devotion is ingrained in the givers' personalities.

This is the model I seek—rather than the lives of the Thirty-Six.

An Overview of Some of My Friends

Because of the direction my thinking has taken, I have recently begun to consider my many friends in the rabbinate. They occupy pulpits in Massachusetts, Florida, New Jersey, New York, Minnesota, Louisiana—in most of the states in the union, and in various locales throughout Canada.

Having visited some four hundred synagogues in the last three decades, I have been very impressed with many great personalities in the pulpit. Some are wonderful teachers or preachers. Some have packaged powerful Soviet Jewry programs that would be the envy of any impresario on Broadway. Some have developed moving and memorable Torah study and Mitzvah programs that bring the message of Judaism deeply into the minds and hearts of their people, our people. Some are great figures.

Even the greatest of rabbis, however, have their weak points—just as we all have our own faults. All the while, their basic humanity is obvious, both in their strengths and failings.

It is a thankless job. Meetings, contract hagglings, and the rampant ignorance, apathy, and insensitivity of select congregants are only a few of the tensions that plague my friends. Many is the time I have heard congregants complain that their rabbi is paid too much, though those same congregants do not apply the same criterion to their stockbrokers or accountants or dry cleaners. "The rabbi is never around when you need the rabbi" is ritually recited over and over again, as if it were wrong for a rabbi to take a Tuesday or Wednesday off each week to read, study Torah, and be with family.

Of all my friends in the congregational rabbinate, I cannot think of a single one who could be labeled as "lazy." If anything, they are overburdened in their official duties. I recall a rabbi's daughter telling me how rarely she and her father would go to the movies or circus or ballgame or county fair—there was always a call for a funeral, a last-minute phone conversation in low tones after which her father-rabbi would disappear into some congregant's house to console and comfort a Jew overwhelmed by a great sadness. Parties—we all have them, and count on our friends' being there. Rabbis, too, are entitled to the same—a bash, a blowout, or a small dinner get-together with friends. But the phone rings. Vacations—we are all entitled to vacations, and yet, even then, sometimes, a week in Florida or the Great Smoky Mountains is broken up because the phone rings.

Rabbis are even more exhausted in subtle ways, through hidden responsibilities they have undertaken by assuming the title of rabbi. While their devotion may be praised on occasion, more often it is trampled in the dust by unappreciative individuals who spread gossip about this or that shortcoming. In addition, many American Jews have collectively defined the rabbi as "their Jew"—the one who has to do all the Mitzvot, for themselves and for their congregations. This frees these congregants from the need for personal commitment. In their eyes, their three-day-a-year visit to the synagogue has fulfilled their Jewish obligations; their rabbi can take care of the rest of the year.

By this I do not mean to malign congregational Jews per se (who, as is well known, constitute only a small portion of all Jews in North America). Nevertheless, any pollster who spends two days in a synagogue can easily note all the phenomena I have mentioned. In some cases this has led to my friends' abandoning the rabbinate for other fields of endeavor: chaplaincy, counseling, business, professorships of Judaic and secular subjects.

Seeing them leave, I realize I am neither angry nor frustrated nor disappointed. I generally feel a sense of relief for my friends. They are now home with their families more often, and free of the immense pressures they once knew every day throughout the year. For the younger ex-rabbis, this sometimes means the end of job insecurity, that underlying fear of no-contract, along with the shift of neighborhoods, cities, and friends every two or three years. Leaving the rabbinate means a new stability and a chance to begin life again, hopefully without an insurmountable measure of despair and cynicism. They will remain good Jews, as they always were, but now it will be on their own terms.

I believe it is time for the Jewish community here to take note of this crisis. It is time for a warning: Jews—be gentle with your rabbis.

The Rabbi as Pastor

After that overlong introduction, I wish to address the unsung heroics of the rabbinate—the deeds of the rabbi as pastor. For centuries, a rabbi was essentially a teacher. That is no longer true. The pastoral demands—the duties of a shepherd tending his flock—have taken precedence. Whenever I am with a friend who is a rabbi, I ask, "How many funerals and shivas do you do a year? How many weddings, conversions, and visits to the hospitals and homes of congregants who are sick?" The sheer numbers are staggering, and each experience is an emotionally charged event that would turn many nonprofessionals into manic-depressives.

How many people can one person bury in a year without a great strain on the rabbi's emotional energies? How many breaking marriages with the parents fighting over their children can the rabbi counsel? How many times can the rabbi enter a medical center to see a sixteen-year-old with leukemia balding in a laminar-flow room? And even with weddings—the ostensible joy is often darkened by inter-family and intra-family strains. For a wedding or bar or bat mitzvah, the seating arrangements alone can present problems: Do the natural mother and father sit together, or is the father seated with his second wife and the mother with her second husband?

My friends the rabbis talk of how thick-skinned you have to be to be in the rabbinate: how often and how many people do not say "Thank you, Rabbi," just once in a while . . . how they wish people would treat rabbis at least as fairly as they will treat their law clients or customers.

I do not envy them.

But I do admire them . . . I admire the accumulated human-sensitive Mitzvot they have performed: holding the hand of the patient in the ICU, speaking words of Torah wisdom at a shiva-minyan, delivering eulogies that do honor to the dead and to the living.

Rabbis are not superstars. However, if I were to write a book about them, I would change James Agee's title *Let Us Now Praise Famous Men* slightly, to *Let Us Now Praise Famous Jews*. By this I mean famous in small ways: in gentleness, in comfort, in caring, in mastery of wise words in moments of high and low emotion.

Rabbis are heroes in the true Jewish sense of the word.

An Addendum: The Discretionary Fund

Nearly every rabbi I know has a discretionary fund: a bank account with money from various sources used for Tzedakah purposes. Some discretionary funds contain a few hundred dollars a year; others run into the thousands. The money comes in through individual contributions for a variety of occasions. Frequently the rabbis deposit in it all the fees they receive from weddings, funerals, bar and bat mitzvahs, and other occasions. If a grateful family wishes to thank the rabbi for having performed a Menschlich, sensitive life event, the rabbi often insists, "Make a contribution to the Discretionary Fund."

There are thousands of these funds in North America, each in its own way helping to sustain members of the Jewish community who might be ignored. Discretionary funds provide matzah and other necessities for poor Jews on Pesach, free loans, scholarships for Jewish educational programs, books for Jews who very much want to read Jewish books. Frequently discretionary funds assist down-and-out Jews whom we rarely see: authentic vagabonds and ne'er-do-wells who travel from town to town, often making ends meet only through the kindness of the local rabbi.

Let us assume that from funerals and weddings and bar and bat mitzvahs a rabbi could gain three thousand to five thousand dollars in additional income each year. Does it not strike us, the congregants, that most rabbis could make good personal use of the money? They have families to support, day school tuitions to pay, book bills higher than most of us—perhaps even a need to support an older relative trapped in the confines of a fixed income. And yet, they have set their standards: these dollars are for the discretionary fund. To them, it is Mitzvah-money, to be used only for Tzedakah . . . this besides their own personal contributions to Tzedakah. (After all, they, as all Jews, are required to give of their own incomes.)

Not every rabbi has the same policy, but I have been deeply impressed over the years by just how many of my friends do this.

I, as one Jew, wish them a *yasher koach*—more strength, more wisdom, more powers of insight in this work. Though the cynics and iconoclasts damn the organized Jewish community, screaming of crudeness and ugliness, I stand at the side of my friends the rabbis, who are bringing warmth and hope to Jews who come to know them, changing lives, carrying on Jewish life in the highest sense: with dignity, devotion, and love.

A Story I Once Heard from a Medical Resident (1981)

For my friend Dr. Jay Masserman, who told me this story

How much should one give to the poor?
Whatever it is that the person might need.
How is this to be understood?
If he is hungry, he should be fed.
If he needs clothes, he should be provided with clothes.
If he has no household furniture or utensils, furniture and uten-
sils should be provided. . . .
If he needs to be spoonfed, then we must spoonfeed him.
— Shulchan Aruch, *Yoreh De'ah* 250:1

An eminent physician is taking his students on morning rounds. Here
and there he explains to his entourage some fine point of the art of
healing, adding to their store of insight and knowledge so that when
they assume their positions as Healers, they, too, will demonstrate
the requisite skill and wisdom needed to ease suffering and pain.

As they go from room to room, the professor and students encoun-
ter an older woman recently arrived as a "social admission." She is not
desperately ill, but her complex of ailments makes it impossible for
her neighbors and friends to take care of her. The professor sees she
is depressed, withdrawn. She refuses to eat. There is nothing here to
be revealed in the way of book-knowledge or advanced scholarship.

The professor stops, and for twenty minutes feeds the woman.

She is capable of feeding herself, but she refuses. So, with delib-
erate and gentle care, the teacher teaches a lesson in kindness. He
does not do it as a demonstration to the students. No . . . he spoon-
feeds this old woman because that is the demand of the hour. If, as
a result of this long delay, the students will have missed some detail
of prescription or diagnosis, it matters little to the professor.

Human beings must be served with a touch of humanity.

The Lamed Vavniks (1988)

The Talmud teaches us that there are thirty-six Righteous Ones in the world. They are known in Hebrew as Lamed Vavniks. These thirty-six are Hidden Ones, unknown to other human beings, known only to God. With all the Evil and evils that exist in life, these thirty-six people give God the patience to let our world endure. Their work, their being, sustains all humanity.

We mortals can only seek out other, visible Righteous Ones who somehow resemble the Thirty-Six. By working with the Visible Ones, we can stretch our imaginations to speculate about the nature of the Hidden Ones . . . perhaps.

One thing is certain: there are many, many more Second Level Righteous Ones. They are everywhere for us to see and work with, if we but open our eyes to seek them out . . .

Yet there is another mystery about the Thirty-Six: we have no teaching as to how a new Lamed Vavnik is selected when one of the existing Thirty-Six passes on to Paradise. Are some of the replacements chosen from the pool of the ones we know? Are they here already, living unassumingly . . . then eased into their new positions by Divine Word?

In either event, is it our responsibility as Students of the Righteous to make certain potential replacements are ready to assume their roles in the Grand Scheme of Things? Is that our job, to raise up a generation of *possible* Lamed Vavniks?

And if we fall short, and there is no thirty-sixth One to fill the gap, what will happen to the world?

The College Interview (1988)

A certain seventeen-year-old from the New York area named Stephen Katz started a Mitzvah project called G.I.F.T., which stands for Generous Intentions Feel Terrific. He and his friend Mike Gerber gathered some two thousand items and delivered them to various shelters in Manhattan.

Then something went wrong.

He applied to a number of colleges, and showed a particular interest in getting into Vassar. What went wrong was his interview.

The interviewer was a college senior, who (as the article I read says) "either gave Stephen a taste of how the cold, cruel world really sees people like Stephen Katz, or gave him his first taste of the gamesmanship that passes for intellectual debate in academia."

The interviewer asked Stephen what he was up to. Stephen, naturally enough, told him about G.I.F.T.

Then all hell broke loose. As Stephen recalls the conversation, the interviewer said, "Do you think that's really practical? Aren't you just prolonging their suffering?" Then the college senior (with more than three years of wisdom under his belt) began to talk about Social Darwinism and other such theories.

An argument ensued.

Stephen felt disappointed. He thought he might have wrecked his chances for Vassar. "I don't think I did too well," he concluded.

The fact is, he did wonderfully well.

The Vassar genius blew it.

Li'at in the Park (1988)

1. Shabbas in Jerusalem

Shabbas in Jerusalem, Summertime.

Saturday morning, an early morning walk before going to a synagogue.

It is so quiet.

After synagogue, a lunch with friends, a nap, and another walk.

Jerusalem is quiet, and people are strolling. Hundreds, perhaps thousands, are out for their *Shabbas shpatzier*, the walk which is like no other walk, because you are free, because you are in a Shabbas mood, because it is summertime and the sun is out and the day is cooling down. And because you will always run into someone you know, either people you didn't get to during the week because you were too busy, or someone you haven't seen in fifteen or twenty years who isn't out looking for you either, but both of you expect to bump into *someone* from fifteen or twenty years ago.

It is prime time for Revelation. It *is* Jerusalem, after all, and it *is* Shabbas. I would suspect that a higher percentage of sublime encounters in the lives of Jews take place on Shabbas afternoons in Jerusalem than anywhere else at any other time, but I don't know that for sure. I only know that the odds change radically. And the radical odds stay the same whether you are walking somewhere-in-particular or just leaving your apartment and wandering to nowhere-in-specific. In both situations, something is going to happen. The odds are always in your favor.

The pattern is easy to detect. Just review the computer printouts of tours to Israel. See how many eight-day, nine-day, and ten-day tours include two Shabbases in Jerusalem. Any smart tour operator knows that it's good business: two Shabbases, more inspiration and Revelations, more joy in the memories, more cravings to return, more business. Simple.

Shabbas afternoon in Jerusalem. Summertime. Someone has overfed you, and, despite the nap, it takes a while to hit your stride. Waking up, *really* waking up, may take ten minutes or a half hour, but the after-nap haze is a pleasant haze. I believe it sets the tone and prepares the soul for Revelation.

2. A Certain Shabbas in Jerusalem

There is a park down in the German Colony, near the building called Beit Elisheva. It's not a particularly beautiful park, but there are benches to sit on, and things for little and middle-sized kids to climb on, so people are always there, chatting with each other, enjoying the kids at play.

On one particular Shabbas afternoon I happened to *shpatzier* down that way. Well, "happened" isn't really the appropriate term. These things just don't "happen." Let's just say instead that I got there, as I was supposed to get there for whatever reason, though I had not made arrangements to meet anyone in that particular park on that particular summer Shabbas afternoon.

As I sat on the bench, pulling out of my nap, I noticed one of the kids climbing on the climbing-thing. (It's actually a bunch of painted-over old tires made into a kind of sculpture-for-climbing.) Her name was Li'at, which means "You are mine." A lovely name. I knew her name right away because it was written on the back of her T-shirt.

A lovely name.

She climbed up and down and around and up and down again as kids do, and she was having a fine time of it, as kids do. On a nearby bench were two women who obviously knew Li'at, one of them probably her mother.

In her climbing and turning and jumping, she would occasionally turn my way, and I could see from her face that she had Down syndrome. She wasn't fat, her tongue didn't hang out, her eyes didn't roll, but her features gave a hint of an extra chromosome in her genes. Okay, so she had Down syndrome, and it was Shabbas afternoon in Jerusalem, and she was climbing up and down and around a climbing-thing, enjoying herself immensely, as kids do.

Other kids were playing, too, and other adults were passing by or strolling through the park, and I stopped focusing on Li'at's climbing. I noticed some stares, though I am not sure Li'at noticed them. She was busy, after all, climbing and having fun. But then, one of the other kids, maybe six or seven years old, noticed Li'at, ran down the climbing-thing and over to the other climbing-thing nearby, and explained rather excitedly to his little sister not to be afraid.

He said, "She won't hurt you."

But he said it afraid. He said it with warning in his voice and a hint of "Stay away from her." He had that tone in his voice that indicated that Something Different was around. Indeed, when Li'at started climbing near them, they moved away, though I cannot recall now whether or not they left the park completely or whether or not the parents took them away to a "safer distance."

It was and it wasn't a surprise to me. I wasn't surprised because I had heard about this kind of thing, read about it, seen it in movies and made-for-TV movies. But I was taken aback because I was seeing it with my own eyes.

I went over to the two women on the bench. They were in their late fifties or early sixties, and I could tell they were religious people since they wore long dresses, long sleeves, and *shaytelach*, the wigs some Orthodox women wear. I introduced myself, and we began to talk about Li'at, and Li'at's mother told me they had found out about her from someone when she was an infant, an infant all alone, and they adopted her. She spoke with such deep passion and love and warmth and naturalness, I knew a Revelation was happening. Li'at's mother was a survivor, and I recognized her accent, Hungarian most likely.

She had other children she had given birth to.

But Li'at, who happened to be slower than others, had no home, so she and her husband took her in and she became their daughter.

Now Li'at was fourteen or fifteen (though she looked a little younger), and this woman and her husband were older and couldn't give her quite as much as they used to, so Li'at was living in a group home setting. I knew the place she spoke about, a fine place near Tel Aviv. Li'at was home for the weekend, and this was Shabbas afternoon in Jerusalem and time for a walk and a chance to play in the park.

We talked about the stares, about kids keeping their distance, about other moments of lack of understanding Li'at had encountered, but Li'at's mother assured me her daughter could manage. (She was managing very well that Shabbas afternoon.)

And then it was time to go. I wanted to spend more time with them some other time, but I have such a bad memory for figures, I knew that I would forget their phone number if I tried to remember it all the way up to the time when three stars would come out.

We said good-bye. Before I left, Li'at had come over for a while, and her mother had put her arm around her so she could put her head on her mother's shoulder. It was a lovely mother-and-daughter scene, but I had to go, and we had to say good-bye.

I came back the following Shabbas, hoping just maybe they would be there again, but they weren't. Next summer I will try again.

3. The Daydream

I am taking a Shabbas walk in Jerusalem. It is summertime, and the late afternoon becomes cooler from around 4:30 on.

I leave my apartment with no-place-in-particular to get to and wind up somehow in a small park in the German Colony, near Beit Elisheva. There are painted tires arranged in a kind of climbing-sculpture and kids are playing on it, climbing up and down and all around.

I see that one of the kids is wearing a T-shirt that says "Li'at" on it, and she and the other kids are racing up and down the climbing-thing together, laughing.

Klal Yisrael—All Jews (1989)

Klal Yisrael means all Jews—everyone: Jewish prisoners, IQ-deficient Jews, battered Jews, Jews who are old-time Yiddish-speaking Socialists, alcoholic Jews and Jewish drug abusers, rich and poor Jews and middle-income Jews, Orthodox Jews, simple and fancy-schmancy Jews, downtrodden and lonely Jews, burned Jews and scarred Jews (by accident or by defense of the Homeland), deformed Jews and ugly Jews as well as gorgeous ones, Jews with AIDS and nowhere to go in some Jewish communities, elderly Jews (Moses told Pharaoh that they would leave Egypt with old and young alike), Reform Jews, hungry Jews and poor Jews—the ones who cannot afford a decent Passover or Purim, or any Passover or Purim at all, or have no family in the whole world to eat Shabbas dinner with, Reconstructionist Jews, homeless Jews, unemployed Jews, displaced Jews, suicidal

Jews, *imglicklich* Jews, i.e., Jews who have never had any luck in life, sad Jews, mean-spirited, *momzerish*-and-arrogant Jews, humble-and-decent Jews, Conservative Jews, caring and callous Jews, Jews who are hot shots and Jews who are *shleppers*, crooked and honest Jews, Soviet Jews who would be free and who would be free and involved and Soviet Jews who would be free and uninvolved, Jews living in terror and Jews unaware of the blessings of life, liberty, and the pursuit of happiness or unable to attain those blessings, Jews who used to be non-Jews, insightful and dull and boring Jews, scholarly and ignorant Jews, wise and foolish Jews, active and committed and assimilated Jews, Jews who are hypocrites and Jews who are sincere, insensitive Jews, and those who can't sleep at night for the suffering of Klal Yisrael.

And that is just some small portion of the Jewish People.

And as my friend Mark Stadler has pointed out to me, when the Torah states that God spoke to all the Children of Israel, it means *all* of them.

Tzedakah and *Tzedek* (2020)

When I reflect upon everything I have taught to date about repairing the world, I realize there is a great need to include an additional critical element: *Tzedek*. Etymologically, *Tzedek* and *Tzedakah* are from the same root, and in different biblical verses they may alternate meanings, though both essentially mean "justice," "fairness," and "what is right."

Throughout this book, I often use "Tzedakah" as a synonym for an individual act of Tikkun Olam. In contrast, I use *Tzedek* to mean societal change through voting, demonstrations, legislation, fair trade practice, and demands for good government and governance. Bold acts of *Tzedek* have dramatically transformed the world we inhabit: just consider how Social Security, Medicare and Medicaid, the Voting Rights Act, the Americans with Disabilities Act, the Pure Food and Drug Act, and similar laws have transformed innumerable people's lives.

I personally have a special interest in the federal Bill Emerson Good Samaritan Food Donation Act, signed by President Bill Clinton in 1996. The law is a response to studies and reports that have shown there is theoretically enough food in the United States to feed every hungry and food-insecure person in the nation's borders. This law provides protection from civil and criminal liability to food establishments that donate to nonprofit food banks and soup kitchens, provided the appropriate foods are chosen, packaged, and delivered in a proper manner. Thus the Bill Emerson Act has made it possible to provide hungry people with ample food that would otherwise have been discarded. Now the problem has largely become one of logistics: how to get leftover, perfectly edible food to the people who need it. Food rescue programs nationwide are a key part of the system of making sure that leftover food from community events, restaurants, hotels, summer camps, business meetings, and everywhere else gets packaged and delivered.

How do you create a system of getting leftovers to hungry people in need? First, identify the institution that will rescue its extra food. For instance, you may determine that your synagogue will no longer dump its leftovers from large-scale events (*Oneg Shabbat* celebrations, Bar/Bat Mitzvah parties) or smaller gatherings (committee meetings where food is served, lunchtime classes, or staff gatherings). Ensure a commitment from the community that after a gathering where food is served, any leftovers will be packed and wrapped in containers or aluminum foil. Be sure to have a copy of the Bill Emerson law handy, to counteract the naysayers! If you live in an area that already has an efficient food rescue service that will come to where you are—such as City Harvest in New York City and Philabundance in Philadelphia—then 90 percent of the work is already done. Several apps and websites will also help locate local food rescue programs throughout the country.[1] If not, creating a network of volunteers to transport leftover food from events and functions could be a fine undertaking for a Tzedakah committee or youth group. The hosts are responsible for packaging the edible leftover food neatly and securely; the volunteers are responsible for identifying local partners (soup kitchens, shelters, food pantries) and delivering the food within a reasonable time frame. That's really most of the work. In the meantime, we are fulfilling two crucial Mitzvot: *ha'achalat r'ayvim* (feeding hungry people) and *bal tashchit* (not wasting or destroying items that could be valuable to others).

A favorite example of this Mitzvah in action is Syd Mandelbaum's Rock and Wrap It Up!, which started with collecting leftovers and uneaten food backstage at rock concerts and sporting events on Long Island. From there, musical acts like the Allman Brothers Band, Tom Petty and the Heartbreakers, the Rolling Stones, and Bruce Hornsby added to their professional riders that the backstage food at their concerts would be harvested by groups like Syd's and delivered to local organizations that feed hungry people. Eventually Rock and Wrap It Up! grew into one of the major, and most innovative, food harvesters in the country. Today they are not just a food rescue service, but a serious antipoverty think tank whose motto is "Feeding People, Not Landfills."[2]

Thanks to the interaction of Tzedakah (the networks of volunteers who deliver the food) and *Tzedek* (the passage of the Bill Emerson Act), never again can one can protest against doing this Mitzvah with the excuse of "liability," arguing that the givers are at risk if something should go wrong. When the food to be shared is the caterer's leftovers, it simply isn't true.

To expand on these two concepts as I use them—*Tzedek* efforts such as legislating, organizing, or mounting campaigns have often led to vast societal change. Some such reforms that were considered radical in their time and now Americans accept as just "as the way things are" include lowering the voting age and raising the drinking age, speed limits, special parking spaces for persons with disabilities, and curb cuts for individuals who use wheelchairs. More recently, the United States Postal Service has requested that on such-and-such-a day, citizens leave an item of food by the mailbox for others who are living with food insecurity. Tzedakah, again as I use the term, refers to a person's individual acts of generosity. With the sheer enormity of the problems in the world, an individual might feel absolutely helpless to change anything. Tzedakah teaches us that personal acts *do* make a difference, sometimes much greater than expected.

So it is that the combination of the two — Tzedakah and *Tzedek* — allows a person to see both the more human side and also the vast societal and global aspect of Tikkun Olam.

Here are some crucial points about the necessity to work on both *Tzedek* and Tzedakah in tandem. *Tzedek* advocates tend to devote themselves to finding the root cause of society's problems and then trying to eliminate the source, say of hunger or violence. The most radical of these individuals sometimes views acts of Tzedakah as mere "band-aids." However, Jews have been taught that whoever saves a single life, it is as if that person had saved an entire world. In keeping with this is what I call the "In-the-Meantime Principle." If a person's only activity is societal change through legislation and other means — more often than not a lengthy process — *in the meantime*, who is going to take care of the woman down on the next block being battered by her ex-boyfriend? And who *in the meantime* will feed the children and parents in a family that has become homeless because of a flood or tornado? A person's individual acts of Tzedakah are meant to solve this very human and compassionate part of Tikkun Olam. And this macro-view stems directly from the personalized commitment on a micro-scale by individual acts of kindness, simple goodness, and thus *world* repair.

Let us always remember, too, Tzedakah's deep *personal* effect on the Mitzvah-actor. As my teacher, the late Rabbi Abraham Joshua Heschel, succinctly and eloquently stated, "I am convinced that the sense of meaning grows not by spectacular acts, but by quiet deeds day by day."

The relationship between Tzedakah and *Tzedek*, then, should be a dynamic flow in both directions. For instance, spending a night volunteering in a shelter for homeless people is a worthy and meaningful Mitzvah, and the proliferation of temporary shelters in synagogues and churches says a great deal about a community's willingness to live by the principles of, say, Isaiah 58:7: "to share your bread with the hungry, and to take the desperate poor into your home." However, a visit to a shelter shouldn't be considered a "finished" Mitzvah until one asks larger, systemic questions: Why are there still people without a safe place to sleep in the wealthiest society the world has ever known? What is the threshold of a livable wage today, and what factors are inhibiting affordable housing in my area? And, how might I help be part of the solution? Tackling these fundamentally political questions falls into the realm of *Tzedek*. At the same time, the policymakers and social justice advocates need to know firsthand the lives and the trials of the people who need support *today*. That is the realm of Tzedakah. The interplay between the two realms is dynamic; each should inform the other.

Thus, looking ahead, my recommendation is that both the "*Tzedek* people" and the "Tzedakah people" make a concerted effort to learn about and engage in their complementary aspect of Tikkun Olam. I believe both will be pleased—even at times a bit surprised—at how both approaches in partnership bring greater benefit.

To all this, I would add one more crucial factor: the connection of Tzedakah/*Tzedek* and life-lived-as-a-Mensch. Note how the words Tzedakah and *chayim*/life appear together in three separate verses in the Book of Proverbs:

> Righteousness [Hebrew: Tzedakah] is a prop of life. (11:19)
> The road of righteousness [Tzedakah] leads to life. (12:28)
> He who strives to do good [Tzedakah] and kind deeds attains life, success, and honor. (21:21)

Again and again the wisdom teacher of Proverbs affirms the intimate connection between doing acts of justice and kindness and connecting to a deeper sense of purpose. Even in ancient times it was understood that being immersed in the work of Tzedakah and

Mitzvahs is a conduit to our ultimate Source of Meaning—the realization of just what, exactly, the art of living is all about. Exploring this interrelationship—what greater imperative could there be for a Jewish educational agenda in the twenty-first century?

5

How and Why to Give
Tzedakah Money Away

The First Tzedakah Report (1975)

To: Those who gave me charitable (Tzedakah) funds for my trip to Israel, and others interested in encountering some of the people and projects I discovered during my stay.

From: Danny Siegel, your Shaliach-Messenger

I would like to report on my activities on your behalf in three parts: (1) a summary of where, when, and how much I contributed; (2) follow-up notes and addresses for your future reference; and (3) general comments I have to make, having just recently returned to the States.

At my disposal was a total of $955, or 5730 Israeli pounds (6 pounds = $1), which were distributed in 1975 in the following manner:

DONATION	ISRAELI POUNDS (DATE OF DISTRIBUTION)
Flowers distributed to Yad LaKashish for Shabbas	60 (1/9)
Flowers for soldiers at Hadassah Hospital	40 (1/10)
To Chayah Pe'er for a sweater for "Batya"	150 (1/12)
To Mrs. Michaelis—Magen	250 (1/12)
8 trees in the Peace Forest	144 (1/13)
To Chayah Pe'er for additional clothes for "Batya"	50 (1/14)
More flowers for a soldier at Hadassah Hospital	5 (1/14)
Rabbi Wolk for needy children	500 (1/16)
Yitzchak Almagor for Russian Immigrants	450 (1/16)
Flowers for Shaare Zedek and Bikur Cholim Hospitals	500 (1/17)
To Hadassah Levi for Me'on HaYeled children	600 (1/19)

To Mickey Shur for refreshments at a bris	50 (1/23)
Flowers for Hadassah Hospital patients	69 (1/24)
Rachel Zafrani for poor families	450 (1/26)
To Aharon Langermann for a private fund at the Welfare Dept.	350 (1/26)
Dr. Pesach Schindler — private charitable fund	200 (1/26)
Rabbi Simcha Kling for the Central Library for the Blind	250 (1/26)
Aviva Goldberg for the Mesillah girls	250 (1/27)
Lisa Schwartz for Mossad Ahavah (as instructed)	90 (1/27)
HaRabbanit Bracha Kapach for poor families	600 (1/28)
Sara Pearl for soldiers	150 (1/29)
Adina Geller for Mitzvot in Tzefat	150 (1/30)
Yeshivat HaKotel (as instructed)	60 (1/30)
Flowers for distribution by HaRabbanit Kapach	44 (1/31)
A beggar in Jerusalem (as instructed)	6 (1/31)
HaRabbanit Kapach for shoes for children	150 (1/31)
Amy Eilberg for a widow (a loan)	175 (2/2)
Boris Fiman for gasoline to drive HaRabbanit Kapach around	100 (2/3)
Ya'akov Maimon for essentials in poverty areas	150 (2/4)
Marc Goldman — books for tutoring	25 (2/4)
Bennet Spungin for an orphanage	100 (2/4)

General Remarks

This entire Mitzvah-month was a privilege for me, and I wish all those who contributed a *yasher koach* — continued strength to carry out similar work on their own.

The month was also very difficult, in that most of the people pointed out in part 2 [see "Gym Shoes and Irises" in chapter 1] were very high-powered, devoted people who, when you sit in their presence and watch their work, cause an emotional drain in the observer. Somehow in the presence of suffering or "unfortunateness" they are capable of rising to sublime heights, day in and day out. For someone not used to such intense contact, it is particularly difficult to adjust, though ultimately rewarding. My thanks to you for entrusting me with the responsibility-turned-pleasure of discovering these people, for myself and for you when you go to meet them.

I found that there are two distinct psychologies in distributing funds: Big-giving and Small-giving, neither being easier than the other—just different ways of thinking. While I may have misevaluated on some of the contributions, each person and place was carefully considered on the merits of the absolute directness to people and the reliability and devotedness of the person doing the work. While I would not advocate withholding funds from Israel Bonds and UJA, I am firmly convinced that we should all set aside some money from our normal Tzedakah funds for these types of work, which guarantee Menschlichkeit-Humanity with a minimum-to-zero of red-tape and woe that we associate with institutions and government. I am also convinced that to some extent, everyone's future trips to Israel should include visits to these people. These are, indeed, the people who make the Land holy.

I am exhausted and evangelical: exhausted after being your representative to works which I believe move Heaven and Earth, and evangelical about spreading the stories of these people.

If you want more information or want to comment to me, do write.

Perhaps this is the essence of Chevra-Friendship: sharing a month such as this and making something of ourselves through the grandeur and splendor of other people.

Na'aleh V'Natzliach—may we continue to do more of the same in the future.

Theology and Tzedakah: Two Points (1982)

#1—Origins

It has been years since I have taken a course in philosophy or theology. Even when I was in college, I took only the minimum requirements, perhaps one or two semesters of each. I felt uncomfortable in the rigorous framework of building systems from premises, piecing many building blocks into distinct shimmering palaces of thought, wonders for the mind. I was never much good at that, making things. In junior high school we had to take a class in industrial arts, and now looking back, I see that the ashtray and bookends I made were embarrassingly crude. Somehow this lack of manual skill must have carried over into the college courses—intellectual structural skills— and even years later I lost patience when trying to follow an argument that builds from too many logical axioms. My lectures lack coherence; free association carries me from one point to another, and the audiences often struggle to find the connections. I concentrate on single points, pausing to examine from many angles a specific idea that excites my imagination: What does it mean, a curved universe? How much of an uncertainty factor is there in physics, in life? What is the Nothingness out in space, in between atoms and molecules stationed at incomprehensible distances from each other? One at a time, at different times, I would put haphazard energies to wandering through these problems, unsystematically . . . and, as to be expected, often without any productive results. Still, the few rewarding breakthroughs have encouraged me, and I continue to work with this flexible method from time to time.

For the present, I am concentrating on aspects of origins and birth: the Creation story of Genesis, Adam and Eve, the birth of children. . . .

Birth—the amazement a parent must feel as the baby breathes through lungs for the first time, no longer dependent on nourishment through the umbilicus. Birth—a passage from slavery inside another body to freedom on the outside. A paradigm for Passover, a birth of our people, forever having to struggle with the new constraints of freedom. Birth and death — their proximity, the utter contradiction of their realities, the multiplicity of Talmudic and Midrashic tales linking the two. I even discovered an ancient custom of burying the placenta shortly after birth . . . a guarantee to the Earth (from which we were taken) that some day we shall return to it.

Even now, in the midst of considering the broader meanings of Tzedakah, I see connections. I call to mind a critical passage in *Pirkei Avot*:

Against your will you were created;
Against your will you were born. (4:22)

It is such an obvious fact: we were not consulted as to whether or not we wished to be conceived or born. Our most basic existence as human beings began before — long before — we were capable of evaluating the implications of such an event. We were conceived and born encompassed by an aura of surprise, and as the late Professor Abraham Joshua Heschel warned us again and again, we must retain this sense of surprise throughout our lifetimes. It is essential to our humanity.

As the first light strikes our eyes as a seconds-old infant, we are filled with wonder. Were we able to express this feeling at that time, I am certain our parents would join us in reaffirming that emotion. We are, in those moments, a gift. Later on (so the Talmud tells us), two becomes three: we are old and weak, our two legs can no longer carry us, so we are left to walk with a cane. It is all so mysterious. One moment we do not exist, and another we are alive. Then, for days and weeks, months and years, we move along, unaware, shielded from that other mystery, the presence of the Angel of Death.

We did not ask to have eyes to delight in the springtime, nor vocal cords to pronounce blessings at seeing the trees' first blooming. Unsolicited, too, we were given tongues to taste Shabbas wine, hands to make *fraylach* music on the clarinet, hands even to burst chains, feet with which to dance, so much to make even the most discouraged creature's heart beat to enlivened rhythms. Everything about us is a gift. That is, perhaps, more poetry than theology, but in the world of Tzedakah, it leads to a logical conclusion:

For those of us who are blessed to share that common origin, that first dazzle of light in our eyes, that first warmth of body touching body, mother and child, grateful for waking each morning and seeing our fingers move, the machine of our body restored to new vigor . . . the least we can do is give to others some portion of these gifts.

Jewish tradition offers us two ways to do this: donating 10 to 20 percent of our incomes, and giving a comparable portion of our time and energies, for the benefit of others. When the larger context of life is considered, these are modest gestures of gratitude. God does not demand back *all* of our possessions. God does not ask that we give others *all* of our time and energies. Just a specified portion.

We do not usually think in these terms. On most days the mythical Person in the Street is called to wrestle with much more mundane struggles. Perhaps only the theologians and philosophers (and the poets) — perhaps the obstetricians and midwives, too — can treat themselves to the luxury of basking in such high-sounding lyricism.

And yet, at some point, the element of birth must be considered: on Rosh Hashanah we consider the world's birthday; on Passover we take note of freedom and slavery, rebirth; on Shabbat or on a vacation, when our mind is free to roam the horizon or admire the sunset, we ought to say to ourselves, "I am indeed alive. Therefore, . . ." It is a logical "therefore," though we may be embarrassed that we have risen to such heights. From that single insight, the many acts of Tzedakah may flow more easily . . . even if we but consider it from time to time, once or twice a year.

#2 — Jewish History and Tzedakah, from a
Broad Theological Viewpoint

If my grandparents did not actually see pogroms, then their parents or grandparents certainly did. They may have been awakened at dawn, shaken, terrified to think that their town, too, was being struck by the hordes. My not-so-distant cousins never left Europe, and when the War came, though my father's mother's mother died before the rise of Hitler, other members of her extended family lived to die at the hands of the Nazis.

I am confused.

"Tzedakah saves from death," the Book of Proverbs proclaims. It is not enough that King Solomon records it once (in Chapter 10) . . . he repeats it again in the following chapter. How many sermons have been delivered based on this statement! How many eulogies!

One rabbi says, "Tzedakah-money saves the despairing from their ultimate despair—suicide."

Another announces, "Your money prevents starvation in so many places. It helps others escape oppression and death at the hands of warring enemies. It buys freedom."

And another, "Tzedakah saves the living from a living death. There are many who plod through life, reamed clean of their enthusiasm, their joy . . . they can be revived through Tzedakah."

And yet another declares, "The good acts of Tzedakah live on after you. They are a memorial to your upright manner; they shall be remembered long after you have passed away."

To some extent, all these sermons are true. And they are comforting. But they do not explain why so many were not saved from the storm of the Holocaust, or from the other catastrophes of Jewish history. They do not answer why, during the Inquisition, so many good people were burned at the stake, as the Holy Church sat in judgment and gloated about their victories over the unbelievers. They do not tell me why Cossacks could pillage and murder and then go home to their families and drink their vodka with roaring gusto, and no hint of regret.

I wonder why life is so cheap. I wonder—perhaps too often for my own good—about all the senseless killings in the United States today—the random Americans old and young who become victims of wild maniacs or cool-headed killers.

How dare I say, "Tzedakah solves all this. It makes Life not a Hell, but an opportunity to rediscover the wonders of Eden"?

How dare I say, "Nevertheless, let us proceed with the Tzedakah-work at hand"?

This is the life of the poet—the singing one day, the depression on another. I ask a friend, a psychiatrist, "What is the nature of the manic-depressive patient?"—wondering if I, too, am a textbook case. I sing—exalt—in the onset of fall in Virginia, the reds and browns and rust colors that charge my senses. And then I grumble to myself, "The deaths, the nice kids."

It would appear that to proceed with Tzedakah, we must have blinders or be naïve or bullheaded to an incredible degree. Tzedakah must demand a faith, an affirmation that rides high over bodies strewn everywhere at every time. What a bizarre kind of faith!

I am not so simple-minded as to say, "Yes, despite it all, we must." I have no pat answers. I am enraged that I have discovered so important a question, only to be taught by my teachers that the questions are more important than the answers. I find no comfort in that.

I will let the matter rest with a story of some illumination. In the midst of my dark moments, I am speaking to one of my teachers, Rabbi Jack Riemer, in a synagogue parking lot on the way to an afternoon service. He is a Rabbi in the greatest sense of the word. I confess to him that I do not understand "Tzedakah saves from death." I say, "And what if, God forbid, we are set upon by the Enemy?"

The Rabbi, quoting in turn from his Rabbi, Abraham Joshua Heschel, *alav ha-shalom*, says, "It may be that we will not be saved, but at least we will be worthy of being saved."

Profound as this is, something is still wrong. It is comforting, but troubling. It answers, and yet not completely answers. It soothes, but is insufficient to soften the blows.

What a bizarre kind of faith.

The Second Rule of Tzedakah
There's No Such Thing as a Small Mitzvah (1982)

Make sure you count.

Even if your job is frustrating and you feel locked in a rut.

Even if you're underpaid and overtrained.

Even if your bosses show no appreciation whatsoever for the hours of effort you put in.

Even with all that, there is still a chance for personal reappraisal. If you pick a place where you can send part of your Tzedakah money, where you know it will make a difference, there is that chance that you may restore your self-image to its proper place. As the Book of Genesis informs us, self-image is really a reflection of God's image.

Let us assume you are a lawyer, and you're being taken away from your family week after week for long-distance trips, working on a mammoth case that doesn't interest you in the least. Let us further assume that the case will drag on for another few months, and you feel that—other than the fact that you are earning a living—you are wasting your time. An opportunity presents itself to you (perhaps on the plane trips back and forth to the trial-site): you can allocate some of your Tzedakah funds to fund a university scholarship for a graduating senior who is similarly locked in: tough family, tough neighborhood, stagnating influences stabbing from all sides. Someone has discovered a specific lead for you: a Russian immigrant by the name of Bronovich. He lives in Tel Aviv, has finished the army, hopes for a college education. Bronovich has never met you (and will never meet you). He doesn't even know someone is thinking about him. And you, seven thousand miles away in Kansas City, gather some friends and put the money together, transfer the funds quietly and anonymously to an organization that will inform Bronovich that the door is open to him.

This will not get you off the case. It won't prevent your law partners from overworking you. But it will remind you who you are—a person who is ultimately in control of his or her own life, capable of rising above the immediate whirling activities and projects to bring about changes, immediate, striking changes.

You have made you count.

This Tzedakah work is refreshing, encouraging. And it does not have to interfere with your other Tzedakah work. You may still continue to contribute to UJA, ORT, Hadassah, and/or other large organizations, where your $100 as part of a multimillion will play its important role in Tzedakah schemes on a larger scale. But, by this additional act somewhere in your overall Tzedakah budget, you will have made a *specific* difference. Even if you have asked your "contact" not to tell you the recipient's name—you wish to keep the anonymity solid on both sides—and thus there will be no formal thank-you's, you will still know: somewhere, in the midst of three million Jews in Israel, you will have done just that much more to make the reborn country live, and live well.

Here is another variation on the theme. Say you have just graduated from law school. You are in that six-month interim period where you don't have a job (you didn't go to Harvard, Yale, Columbia). Your funds are limited and you can't by any means buy a year's worth of college education for anyone Over There. You have only $50 to work with.

The solution is still the same: pick something where what you have *will* be useful, direct, of immediate consequence.

Fifty dollars, properly placed, will bring five Rosh Hashanah meals to Jews who wouldn't have a decent *yontif* dinner—were it not for you.

Fifty dollars, properly placed, will buy enough cloth and materials for five elderly Jews to get back to work, needlepointing, crocheting, knitting, crewel-working, embroidering wonderful pieces of craft-art that will adorn other people's homes. They can begin again to use their hands, sell their products, regain their own sense of usefulness . . . all this while you are still out of work, searching for a job. The right people can get this project rolling, or, because of you, expand an already successfully functioning project. (Try reaching out to Life Line for the Old, 14 Shivtei Yisrael St., Jerusalem.)

What if you have only $10 to spare—the rest having been pledged to other Tzedakot, or because you are only fifteen and have only $10 to give? Exchange that $10 for some refreshment and flowers; go to the local hospital, or wherever the lonely lie in bed or sit in wheelchairs; and sit for an hour and ease a little pain. My mother used to speak of the Gray Ladies—the hospital volunteers who would fill in where doctors might not go, with conversation, with patience, with a touch. You can be a Gray Lady, even if on only one occasion. You are entitled to the satisfaction of having made a difference, of coming home with the memory of the flowers' fragrance and saying to yourself, "It was good." (The phrase echoes back to Creation.)

How much does it count?

An example: the cantorial students at the Jewish Theological Seminary go to the Montefiore Hospital cancer wards a few times a week. They sing, entertain, talk, teach, relax with the patients. It might seem like the most unpleasant place on the face of the Earth, the place any right-minded person would least likely want to go with time of his or her own to manage. But the stories are more than just heartwarming. I will retell one I have heard, in brief . . . A woman says, "They have tried every kind of drug and therapy on me, and nothing helps. I am always in pain. But after the cantors come, I feel no pain for a couple of hours."

That is how much it can count.

The same can be done with money, or time. Money can be so versatile; you can make things happen. You can give the Cantor's Institute a small sum and tell them to buy cantorial records, to set up a record library in the bowels of the cancer ward, so that in between the visits the melodies will always be on hand. The tunes bring soothing moments of respite from agony; let the patients have more access to them.

The variations are infinite, with just a few dollars.

And with time—though there was an outcry a while back that Volunteerism is Dead, I do not see it as being so absolutely true. So many people still offer one afternoon a week, or an evening, or a Sunday morning, tutoring a learning-disabled child in Hebrew, walking an old Lower East Side resident to the store, to the park, to the pharmacy, to a minyan. See what the dentists do . . . an ever-growing group of them have committed themselves to an unpaid summer in Israel, volunteering on kibbutzim up and down the country. And from what they tell me, the simple dentistry they are doing has saved many a painful, complicated mess in future years.

Think of the thousands of Pioneer Women, Brotherhood Men, the Shriners, the Knights of This and That Order, extending themselves to some limited time-commitment, making sure there are enough eyeglasses and hearing aids for whoever needs them, overseeing tons of rice shipments to distant lands where starvation is omnipresent, raising not only funds, but spirits. . . . Not full-time, and not encompassing all their Tzedakah money, but still, in their own lives, this giving is a most significant aspect of their self-definition. If some part of them cannot be free to be of service to others, then, they ask themselves, just what are they, who are they?

Let us leave the complex overall problems of Tzedakah to the experts. They can usually predict trends and cost-analyses better than we, and consequently formulate reasonable plans of attack. We, then, can carve out our small part of the Larger Picture. We can work within the Larger Picture energetically, with our own personalities, our own unique elements of individuality. This is how the Small Ones complement the Experts in their work.

Thus we can be useful, even in the face of staggering statistics.

Set your own pace. Select your own money-and-time budget. Only make some portion of that money and time useful. Making it count for the beneficiaries of these gestures can only make it count for us, too.

From my few years of contact with the Gray Ladies, I have noticed a brightened countenance, a vigorous speech pattern, a certain radiance that surrounds their presence. Even social workers, who should, by all rights, be overwhelmed with despair, privy as they are to uncountable chronicles of aches and troubles — even they, on the forefront of the battle to make life decent and full of hope — demonstrate a lively affirmation. This is realized by giving of themselves *outside their jobs*.

I know this because I listen to them unravel their stories. Their wisely distributed Tzedakah money, the extra Tzedakah time outside of their jobs, restores their vision to a renewed clarity.

A quote from Dante comes to mind: over the Gates of Hell is this inscription, "All hope abandon, ye who enter here!" I think of the Montefiore cancer wards, the hell of our modern society, and then I think of the cantorial students, engraving instead some less august, less foreboding phrase. Something modest like, "By all means, be useful."

Singing Yiddish melodies and Hebrew folksongs, they are making even Hell itself a livable place.

Does Tzedakah Money Really Belong to You? (2006)

> [If a farmer says,] "I vow that the *Kohanim*/Priests and *Levi'im*/Levites should have no benefit of anything that is mine, they may still take, even against the farmer's will.
> — Mishnah, *Nedarim* 11:3

In biblical times, farmers had certain obligations to use a portion of their crops for Tzedakah. Among the types of Mitzvah-produce designated for poor people were *Leket* (gleanings), *Pe'ah* (the corners of the field), and *Shikhecha* (areas the farmer forgot to reap). In addition, special portions of the sacrificial offerings were set aside for the Priests and Levites: *Terumah* for the Priests and *Ma'aser* for the Levites.

These are some of the rules of distribution and their underlying principles:

> Even if the farmer solemnly vows not to give *Terumah* and *Ma'aser*, the *Kohanim* and *Levi'im* can still take the *Terumah* and *Ma'aser*, because these *rightfully* belong to them. This is clearly stated in the Mishnah above.
> This means that *Terumah* and *Ma'aser* never really belonged to the farmer.

Consequently, the farmer cannot *not* give them to the *Kohanim* and *Levi'im*.

In certain situations, the farmer may designate *which Kohanim* and *Levi'im* may receive the *Terumah* and *Ma'aser.*

No matter which specific *Kohanim* or *Levi'im* the farmer designates, the *Terumah* and *Ma'aser* still must be set aside.

The farmer is not even allowed to use the rest of the crop for personal needs until the *Terumah* and *Ma'aser* have been set aside.

Other Jewish texts support this position concerning what you really do and do not own. Tzedakah money doesn't belong to you to begin with. Therefore, rather than viewing yourself as sharing what you own, you are asked to understand that you are a trustee — God's trustee — over this percentage of your money. As a trustee, agent, and partner-with-God, you therefore have the *sacred duty* to live up to your obligation to distribute your Tzedakah money wisely.

On the one hand, it is an awesome, perhaps overpowering thought to be God's partner. It is certainly very humbling. But on the other hand, it is very empowering to know that there is a distinctly Divine element in the act of Tzedakah.

Thus, in Jewish life, there really are two kinds of money — money for your own personal use, and Tzedakah money, to be used for the good of other people.

Many questions that apply to your own money also apply to Tzedakah. The two most crucial questions are:

1. "Yours" — How much money do you require for *your* personal needs?
2. "Theirs" — How much Tzedakah money do *they* need?

The more you think of "yours" and "theirs," the more you will observe different categories of people and how they relate to money.

"Yours" — In the extreme, some people live as if there is never enough money in their account and always crave more. They may consider a 10-room house on five acres of land insufficient for a two-person household. A friend of mine once called this "living large."

"Theirs"—At the other end of the people-and-money scale, some people never stop wanting more Tzedakah money to accomplish that much more Tikkun Olam. Instead of having X dollars to distribute, they wish that they had X to the 10th power of Tzedakah dollars at their disposal. They "live large" through their insistence on doing the Mitzvah with an extra-generous touch. This is known as *Hiddur Mitzvah*, Doing a Mitzvah Beautifully.

"Yours and Theirs"—Another one of my friends said it succinctly and eloquently, "If you *live* large, *give* large."

The distance between the two extremes is very great. Most people are somewhere in the middle.

You may know a few people who are so successful that they have a winter beachfront mansion on Maui and a ski chalet in Utah and still want more and more and always more. Most likely, they are not your "main crowd." There is even a slight chance that you, yourself, are one of the "never enough" people.

You may be fortunate to know several people who have a private jet, $3,000 suits, and a landscape architect on retainer to redesign their grounds at their slightest whim—but who are generous-to-the-extreme (in the most positive sense) with their Tzedakah money. They *live* large and *give* large. You may be one yourself. You are *living* large and *giving* large.

You may be one of those who *doesn't* happen to book the penthouse suite at the Plaza Hotel in New York or have umpteen thousands of shares of stock in your portfolio. You may be just plain old upper or middle or lower middle class, living well within your means while worrying about meeting the next college tuition payment for your daughter. *But* you consciously and frequently let your mind wander to thoughts like, "If I only had $10,000,000 for Tzedakah." Good. That's a very healthy approach to "yours" and "theirs" money.

In conclusion, I would add two practical items:

Find some useful short quote you can memorize that will allow you to be constantly aware of the "yours" and "theirs" of money. I personally think that Winston Churchill's quote is one of the best: "We make a living by what we get, but we make a life by what we give." Also excellent is Maurice Sendak's, "There must be more to life than having everything."
Calculate where you are at present on this "yours" and "theirs" scale, and every so often review the results. Make a note of all the changes that have occurred over time.

Most of all, whatever you do — do as much of "theirs" as you can.

What Does It Mean "To Do Tzedakah Jewishly"? (2006)

Judaism offers many ways to do Tzedakah. Several of the principles, values, techniques, and strategies are unique to Jewish tradition. In addition, while some of the fundamental concepts include elements common to other systems of giving, Judaism places a different emphasis on those concepts. Furthermore, the organic and dynamic interplay of these Jewish concepts with acts of Tikkun Olam provides a distinct approach to fulfilling the real needs of others. The *Jewish* way of giving becomes most evident when you examine *exactly* how these needs are to be met.

"Doing Tzedakah *Jewishly*" involves two essential elements:

1. Giving your money away according to distinctly Jewish values and guidelines, and
2. Determining your actual Tzedakah allocations, i.e., how much you give to Jewish programs and how much to general programs.[1]

Jewish guidelines for proper Tzedakah giving are as necessary to a civilized, ordered society as traffic laws, fire codes, and fair rental contracts. Tzedakah directives are established to allow you, the giver, to be more efficient in your desire to benefit others. You should be able to easily integrate traditional Jewish practices into contemporary life. Most important, once you are familiar with Judaism's procedures and rules, you will find there is vast room for individuality and creativity in your own giving.

Jewish tradition does not provide a simplistic or absolute way to establish Tzedakah priorities. Some texts teach that Tzedakah's first priority is saving lives. Other passages give primacy to local needs in contrast to those far away. Still others stress the priority of the people Israel's needs: redeeming captives, supporting Torah study, and more. All of these texts indicate that *their* recipients should be the most important beneficiaries of Tzedakah. No clear text ties all of these positions together and gives an authoritative list of "first priorities."

Furthermore, Jewish tradition certainly allows and, indeed, encourages contributing to causes and needs beyond the Jewish community—most strikingly exemplified by the outpouring of funds for victims of the September 11th attacks, or any time after a natural disaster occurs somewhere in the world.

With these considerations in mind, it would be important to learn:

1. How much money do *non-Jewish* organizations and individuals give to support *Jewish* needs?
2. How much money do today's descendants of wealthy Jews contribute to Jewish causes? Studies show these Jewish children and grandchildren are giving the same *absolute* amount of Tzedakah dollars as their parents or grandparents, but giving significantly smaller percentages to Jewish causes—which may adversely affect the sustenance of the Jewish community.
3. What are the specific needs of the various organizations benefiting the Jewish community, and how efficiently do they accomplish their goals?
4. What are the uniquely crucial needs of Israel and its people?
5. How much will your own support make a difference?

Your Jewish Identity

Most likely, your own sense of Jewish identity will largely determine both to what degree you give Jewishly and how much you give to Jewish Tzedakah programs. However you identify with your Jewishness, it is important to remember that *there is no need to feel defensive about giving to Jewish needs*. Being Jewish, it is natural for you to care about your own, and to act to assure the wellbeing of your own. Native Americans are not defensive about supporting the needs of Native Americans. The same is true for African Americans and other ethnic, racial, or religious groups. While there are advocates of strictly universalistic giving, every group still donates to programs with which they have common ties. "Particularistic" Tzedakah is perfectly acceptable.

The following three quotes may help you articulate the suitability of your "particularistic" choices:

> Solomon Schechter, one of the great Jewish scholars of the early 20th century, wrote, "We can no more have Jews without Judaism, than Judaism without Jews. We Jews have proven that we can survive difference, but not indifference."
>
> My teacher Rabbi Saul Teplitz wrote, "Often, one finds a phrase on theater tickets that reads: 'Void if detached.' So, too, Jewish life becomes void when it is detached from the practices and principles of Judaism, from synagogue and prayer, from Torah and study." Rabbi Teplitz later concurred with me that his list should include "and doing Tzedakah as Jews and for Jews."
>
> Finally, Hillel's famous words (here printed with the order changed) come to mind: "If I am only for myself, what am I? / But if I am not for myself as well, who will be for me?" (Pirkei Avot 1:14).

Ultimately, "Doing Tzedakah *Jewishly*" encompasses two important elements:

> Absorbing the unique Jewish material on Tzedakah by whatever study method you do best.

Exploring how your own Jewish identity displays itself in the practices and emphases of your own Tzedakah giving.

Should You Always Do Your Tzedakah Giving Anonymously? (2006)

Background: Maimonides' Principles of Tzedakah and the Issue of Secret and Anonymous Giving:

> The highest degree [of Tzedakah] is to strengthen the hand of a Jew who is poor, giving that person a gift, or a loan, or becoming a partner, or finding a job for that person—to strengthen the person's hand, so that the person can become self-supporting and will not have to be dependent on others. . . .
> One degree lower is a person who gives Tzedakah to poor people and is unaware of the recipient, who in turn is unaware of the giver. This is indeed a religious act achieved for its own sake. . . . (Maimonides, Mishneh Torah, *Hilchot Matnot Ani'im*, Laws of Gifts to Poor People, 10:7–8)

At my lectures, I frequently ask, "What is Maimonides' *highest* level of Tzedakah?" Quite often the answer given is, "When the recipient doesn't know the donor, and when the donor doesn't know the recipient." Reading the actual source, though, we see that they are really responding to Maimonides' *second* level. The highest level includes finding someone a job so she or he can become self-sufficient.

To meet this level, you have to know enough about the person. You might even conduct an interview with this individual in order to make the appropriate employment match.

Three organizational examples provide a broader understanding of Maimonides' highest level of Tzedakah. While each requires "non-anonymity," you can donate to the cause while preserving your own anonymous relationship to the actual recipient.

1. Pa'amonim is an Israeli organization that works specifi-
   cally with a certain well-defined category of people who have
   fallen between the cracks of the government social service
   system. These are individuals and families who are *definitely*
   close to being able to reestablish their financial stability—
   provided they receive the proper guidance. Some of the
   issues Pa'amonim addresses are credit card debt, temporary
   or long-term job loss, unexpected illness, and similar extraor-
   dinary circumstances. Pa'amonim could not do its work
   without knowing all the necessary details (including bank
   statements and similar documents) of the people with whom
   they are working. See https://www.paamonim.org/en/ for
   more details.

2. Jewish free-loan societies offer interest-free loans. They also
   require certain knowledge about the borrower.

3. "Microloans," loans of as little as $50 or less, have enabled
   millions of individuals and families to break out of the cycle
   of poverty. A single individual, Muhammad Yunus, invented
   this approach, which grew into a worldwide microloan
   movement—truly one of the great Tzedakah stories of the
   modern age. Yunus and the Grameen Bank—the poor per-
   sons' bank in Bangladesh he founded—were awarded the
   2006 Nobel Peace Prize for their lifesaving work. The incredi-
   bly wise *theory* of microloans, coupled with the most remark-
   ably well thought out *practical* process of distribution, can
   leave you stunned, sometimes breathless, and occasionally
   saying to yourself, "Why didn't someone think of this hun-
   dreds of years ago?"

On the Absolute Need to Talk About Your Tzedakah Work

Unfortunately, I believe that many people have extended Maimonides'
second level to mean that they should *never* tell anyone what they are
doing with their Tzedakah money. Yet there is an operative Jewish
principle which supersedes the secrecy principle: *keday lechincho*

beMitzvot, for the sake of Mitzvah education. In Talmudic literature this principle is mentioned in several different contexts, and would most certainly apply to many areas of Tzedakah.

Thus, in my opinion there is a desperate need for us to share our Tzedakah knowledge and experiences with others, so they will not only be encouraged to do more of their own giving, but become more skilled at *how* they give Tzedakah.

When you are sharing about your own Tzedakah work, you should, of course, protect the anonymity of recipients. You will also need to decide whether or not to tell others *how much* you have given in each situation. But neither of these prevents you from telling others, "I have discovered these incredibly fine Mitzvah heroes (or Tzedakah organizations), done all my due diligence, checked them out 100 percent, and given them some of my Tzedakah money to show that I believe in what they are doing."

If you choose to do this, you may accomplish two things:

1. gain additional support for the people doing fine Tikkun Olam, and
2. prevent others from misdirecting funds to inefficient or unworthy individuals or organizations

However you do this, you will be changing the direction of the trend that says, "What I do with my Tzedakah money is my own business."

When Secrecy and Anonymity Is a "Must"

You are also likely to encounter many situations in which you *absolutely* want to keep your identity secret. A classic circumstance is when a relative, friend, or acquaintance is in need and you want to offer financial support. Anyone who knows you might be embarrassed to find out you had contributed. In this situation, your best option is a third party, such as a Tzedakah fund or Rabbi's Discretionary Fund, both of which can route the money to the recipient without disclosing your contribution.

One extreme end of the scale is the joke about a Jewish institution's building that was constructed *entirely* out of donor plaques. Not so far removed are places you have been where the walls are covered with names and categories of giving such as "Angel," "President's Circle," "Builder," "Patron," and "Benefactor." Then there are the organizations that restrict plaques to one small corner of the building. Finally, there are the institutions that do not display a single plaque or certificate of donor recognition anywhere.

There is a similar scale for a related phenomenon, "naming opportunities"—from "none" to "as many as required to bring in the funds we need." Undoubtedly you have your own view regarding what kinds of recognition are appropriate and in good taste. Despite your general opinion one way or another, it's prudent to allow for specific exceptions. If, for example, you find the naming practice overdone, keep in mind that the plaque syndrome is not 100 percent about the ego-needs of the donor. Frequently donors will allow their names to be posted so that others who know them will be encouraged to join in the giving.

Since Jewish tradition *does* allow for public recognition of this kind, ultimately you yourself will need to decide if this is to be part of your own way of giving.

Will You Find "The Meaning of Life"
by Doing Tzedakah? (2006)

> I am convinced that the sense of meaning grows not
> by spectacular acts but by quiet deeds day by day.
> —Rabbi Abraham Joshua Heschel

You might.
Many people have.

What is certain, however, is that you will know there *is* meaning in your life when you have fed a hungry person that very day or for a week or a month into the future.

This person—for any one of a number of reasons—cannot afford to feed himself or herself. Your act of Tzedakah will have given vital sustenance to a human being who might otherwise have wasted away.

That Mitzvah should also shift your own sense of what it means to be a human being into some higher realm. *You*, an "anybody" on the Earth, used your money and saved a life. *That* is amazing, awesome. By changing the life of one individual, *You* changed the world.

Now you have become more than just #2,476,551 in a census, or a tax-paying resident of Cook County, Illinois, or the sister of Jacob Levinson. You are *really* someone.

It is also possible that you will build on these individual acts. Because of what you have done, you may find yourself seeing things in a new light. What may happen is bi-directional, namely:

1. If you are now thinking constantly about Tzedakah, you may find yourself looking for new opportunities to do Good Things, and

2. As you gauge your daily—even mundane—activities, you will notice how many more of them can be tied into acts of Tzedakah.

What happens may be a gradual process, or it may come in a sudden flash of insight. The end result *could* lead you to a general sense of spiritual serenity and wellbeing.

Consider, for a moment, the search for The Meaning of Life, a most worthwhile human endeavor. Engaging in Tzedakah *during* the search may appreciably ease the restlessness and anxiety of the entire process.

Human beings want to feel that this gift called Life has depth, breadth, and a "feel" of awe-inspiring value. Jewish tradition teaches that money *can* become the ideal instrument for finding true, deep meaning. This is particularly curious, since money is so commonly maligned as the tool of greed and egocentricity.

Yes, you might possibly find The Meaning of Life through your Tzedakah. At the very least, you are likely to find more Meaning in Your Own Life.

How Do You Evaluate Financial Information from a Tzedakah Program So You Can Decide to Whom to Give or Not to Give? (2006)

Giving Tzedakah wisely means evaluating many facts. It is not enough simply that "they" are doing good things. *Trustworthiness* must be our ultimate concern when we donate our money.

If you are giving to an organization, you are entitled to see a copy of its financial report and a detailed summary of the organization's activities. The Jewish reasoning is relatively simple: Tzedakah money is never "owned" by the donor. Rather, God entrusts that portion of our income intended for Tzedakah to us for reaching appropriate recipients. If we are trustees, Jewish tradition teaches we should certainly be *responsible* trustees.

In a situation where you know the organization 100 pecent top-to-bottom and backward-and-forward, you may want to get copies of the budget and program as a simple formality and point of reference. This is one of the wonderful advantages I have enjoyed in my many decades of working with Mitzvah heroes. Since the Mitzvah heroes are absolutely trustworthy, examining the finances is relatively easy.

If, however, you do not know the organization, or you know it for its work but not its finances, ask for the "numbers." If the staff hesitates to send you documentation, Judaism frees you from any obligation to give to them.

In addition to the information the organization provides, you have other tools at your disposal. The most reliable resource is somebody you trust who knows the organization well and can tell you whether or not it is responsible. Can your source verify that the group does its work honestly, efficiently, and with integrity?

Likewise, online tools are available to help with your investigation—and information may be out there that you need to know. Check the Internet for the backgrounds of the organization's supervisors and board members. A site like charitynavigator.org may be useful for accessing data about a particular Tzedakah organization, as well as offering counsel about giving intelligently and avoiding scams.

A few words of caution apply, however. Charitynavigator.org, among others, may define "charity" differently than the Jewish definition of Tzedakah, and their staff may not take all the factors outlined here into consideration. The Internet is a valuable tool in your toolbox, but it is not the final decider.

When you *do* get a copy of an organization's finances, assess the numbers by asking these questions:

1. How much is the overhead (costs of running the operation, salaries, fundraising expenses, publicity, office expenses, and the like)? It's not enough that the Tzedakah program is simply doing good. Ultimately, *you* need to use your own sense of what is an appropriate amount and/or percentage of overhead before you contribute to the specific project you are considering.

2. Is the financial sheet clear and easily understandable, without detours or obfuscating terminology and explanations? In other words, is the nonprofit practicing transparency?

3. If individuals receive salaries, do they seem reasonable? It is difficult to put an across-the-board number on what is acceptable; use your own sense about what is or is not appropriate.

4. If you have followed up with the people behind the financial report—those who are responsible and authorized, not just public relations representatives—for additional information or clarification, are you satisfied that you received timely, straightforward, and complete answers?

5. Are you convinced that this organization will most compellingly maximize your financial impact? For example, many of us want to make a difference for those whose lives are impacted by cancer. But there are many cancer organizations out there. Before you give, consider which one can make the most difference with your funds, in the ways that matter to you.

6. Combining all the criteria, does everything about the organization now seem okay to you, or is there something that still doesn't appear quite right? If a number, or something else, seems "off" to you, trust your gut. Without all of the above considerations, you should not be giving to that fund.

Interestingly, the first-ever mention of financial accountability is in the Bible. When recounting the repairs and maintenance of the Temple in King Josiah's time (late seventh century BCE), 2 Kings 22:7 states:

> But no accounting was done concerning the donations given, because they did their work in a trustworthy manner.

Over the course of time, Jewish tradition changed its approach. The great halakhic authority Rabbi Moshe Isserles (Krakow, 1530–72), basing his decision on an earlier ruling, added the following comment to a law in the sixteenth-century Shulchan Arukh:

> In any event, it is best for them [the managers of a Tzedakah fund] to give an accounting so that they stay "clean" — [as the verse states in Numbers 32:22], . . . *you shall be untainted both as far as God and Israel are concerned*. (*Yoreh De'ah* 257:2)

As people who are immersed in the work of Tzedakah, that should continue to be our goal today.

From the Ziv Tzedakah Fund Final Report (2008)

Commencement speakers customarily mention easily remembered quotes along with their own "Rashi" commentary. Since Ziv's final Annual Report is also a commencement, I will do the same.

> Strengthen the hands that have become weak;
> Make firm tottering knees!
> Say to the anxious of heart, "Be strong, fear not." (Isaiah 35:3–4)

Your Tzedakah money has been used to bring these words to Life. *Everything* we do relates to some part of this verse.

Simcha Shel Mitzvah: The Joy of Doing a Mitzvah

In our work together, sometimes this kind of joy gives us a sense of satisfaction because we "did the right thing" and lived up to our own humanity. At other times, we may feel it as a certain sweetness-of-the-moment. And in some fortunate moments, the *simcha* may be so intense, we feel like we have reached the sublime heights of heaven.

Chief Dan George, a character in the movie *Little Big Man*, says, "My heart soars like a hawk." Imagine this magnificent bird soaring high on the wind. *That* is the hint of the feeling of the *simcha* of doing Tzedakah.

Being

> Tzedakah is not about giving; Tzedakah is about being.
> —Rabbi Bradley Shavit Artson

> *Hachaim haym Mitzvot*—Life is Mitzvahs.
> —The Rabbanit Bracha Kapach

Engaged in Mitzvahs, we need not worry that we are living merely "near-Life experiences." In Mitzvahs, we are *always* in the Real World.

The Long Road Together

> Our long road together has been *basima*/pleasant.
> — Sukkah 52a

We should not restrict the definition of the last word, *basima* ("pleasant"). As my teacher Sharon Halper pointed out to me, it can signify more than "pleasant." The Talmudic phrase could mean, "Being together on this journey has been ever-so-moving, reaching into the very deepest parts of our being."

And it is because of the miraculous power of Tzedakah money, the grandeur of the Mitzvah heroes, and the essence of Mitzvahs themselves that we have been so moved by this joint venture called "Ziv."

From the Report: The Romema Families

When my many visits with Trudi Birger, z"l, come to mind, the first sentence always has an exclamation mark at the end, something like, "Ah, what a woman!" As a young woman, she was saved from death more than once in the Nazi extermination camps. For the rest of her life, until she passed away in 2002 at age seventy-five, she was determined that no child should suffer as she did.

After the war, she and her husband, Zev, came to Israel. Her drive and determination led to two projects that would in fact make life better for so many people: Dental Volunteers for Israel (DVI) and personal involvement, care, and support for fifty families in Jerusalem's Romema neighborhood. These families were locked into poverty, and Trudi believed that education was the key to changing the course of the families' history. For years, while paying their utility bills and purchasing a multitude of necessities from school supplies to heaters for the chilly winters, she, in her unique manner, constantly, forcefully, yet gently encouraged the children to succeed.

Over the years, the way things would work with Trudi, the Romema families, and Ziv was simple: She would contact us periodically to tell us the needs of the moment. To whatever extent we could provide the necessary dollars, we would do so.

Now, Zev has carried on her work with thirty-two of the families as well as with DVI. When his latest request came in, informing us that he was approximately $25,000 short of meeting the needs, we—because of your fine donations—were immediately able to respond with a $10,000 donation. This was one of those many high moments in the history of Ziv. Once again the fund was able to carry out its original mandate: responding quickly and with a substantial sum of Tzedakah money.

Some additional notes concerning the life of this extraordinary woman:

1. I encourage you to read Trudi's autobiography, *A Daughter's Gift of Love—A Holocaust Memoir* (coauthored with Jeffrey M. Green), the story of her years in the death camps. While I believe that the word "gripping" has been overused, this story is truly gripping.
2. Zev has been the Director of the Jerusalem International Book Fair for twenty-six years. Now, a children's book award, the Trudi Birger Prize, has been established in Trudi's memory, to be given to "the author (or author and illustrator) of a book that inspires the reader to selfless devotion to the community."
3. Trudi was laid to rest in a portion of Jerusalem's Har HaMenuchot cemetery reserved for distinguished individuals in the Life of Israel, including Schvester Selma, pioneer chief nurse of Jerusalem's Shaare Zedek Hospital; Viscount Herbert Samuel, High Commissioner during the British Mandate; Gershon Agron, Mayor of Jerusalem and founder of *The Palestine Post* (after Israel's independence, *The Jerusalem Post*); and Naftali Herz Imber, composer of *Hatikvah*.

Ah, what an extraordinary woman Trudi Birger was. *Yehi Zikhrah Barukh*—May her memory be a blessing for all who knew her, and for those who will study her life and be inspired to perform similar acts of Tikkun Olam.

A Smaller World (2020)

Technology must be the point of departure for any discussion of Tzedakah-giving in our day and into the future. That is simply because the advent of the tech age offers us such enormous promise when it comes to giving. Every new device and application has staggering Potential-for-Good. It bends the imagination to contemplate the implications.

The world has gotten so much smaller. I recognize, through my devices, more devastation and suffering around the world. I care more, with my devices, because I perceive more—the impact of a catastrophic earthquake in Nepal, or fires in California. I donate more, via my devices, with a simple click or swipe. Crowdsourcing websites such as GoFundMe detail Mitzvah projects and enable whoever sees them to say "Aha!" or "Wow!" and join in the Mitzvah. And every Mitzvah hero who engages on social media and enables web donations reports greater contributions to his or her work, including varying percentages of what might never have been donated at all.

Of course, the tech terrain also has its downside, dangers, and difficulties.

My brother, Dr. Stanley Siegel, and his coauthors, Scott Donaldson and Chris Williams, address one big issue—cybersecurity—in *Understanding Security Issues* (2018), a review of every type of malware, spyware, phishing (there's even spear phishing—sending fraudulent emails to people from an apparently trusted address), hacking, and all the other evil intrusions on our data and privacy.

Another difficulty arises from the world being at our doorstep and from the needs of people and the earth proliferating so expansively in our consciousness. There is real danger of "hitting the wall"—being so overwhelmed as to become paralyzed and stop giving ("What difference could I possibly make?"). In addition, willing donors have to sharpen their sense of what they *really* want to accomplish with their money and have to have a more acute sense of the ethics of giving—*exactly* who are the recipients, who are the intermediaries handling the donations, and similar issues.

By now, this should have precipitated more discussion in our Hebrew schools, Jewish day schools, and yeshivas—and, for that matter, adult education programs. But that hasn't happened yet in Jewish education. Tzedakah—with its full meaning of the Jewish way of giving—is rarely given the same attention as the holidays, basic rituals, and similar topics. Isn't it time that Mitzvah heroes, Tzedakah and *Tzedek*, and how to personally budget your own funds for ethical giving become standard components of the syllabus for Jewish life?

Perhaps more than ever, there is a profound need to program into our lives time for *slowing down*. Many people find that Shabbat and holidays, opportunities not to use smartphones and computers, are welcome and necessary breaks from being immediately and constantly connected. For those who think they have to be continually connected in order to be creative, consider this quote from Einstein, who worked out great mysteries of the universe with only pencil and paper:

> When I ask myself how it happened that I in particular discovered the Relativity Theory, it seemed to lie in the following circumstance. The normal adult never bothers his head about space-time problems. Everything there is to be thought about, in his opinion, has already been done in early childhood. *I, on the contrary, developed so slowly that I only began to wonder about space and time when I was already grown up.* In consequence, I probed deeper into the problem than an ordinary child would have done.[2]

Making the effort to connect with others in person is critically important in an era when this can be taken for granted. One ironic contemporary development of being able to reach anyone, anywhere, anytime, at least according to my friends who have teenage children, is that many teens no longer rush to get their driver's license as soon as they reach the legal age. This appears to be a direct result of young people texting each other so frequently that they don't feel the same need to see their friends face-to-face.

We need an enormous effort to instill cyberethics—what exactly is right or wrong in the cybersphere—from earliest childhood. This endeavor will require raising up many more trained teachers, professors, mentors, and rebbis. Note to all readers: this would be *our* assignment too, our not insignificant act of Tikkun Olam. In a way, it is an extended implication of the bumper sticker "If you can read this, thank a teacher."

In my hand I hold a smartphone, and I am staggered once again to consider the incredible power that resides within it. Previous generations could never have even imagined the technological power I hold with the mere touch or swipe of a finger. I have instant connectivity to breaking news on every continent; I can instantly listen to any piece of popular or classical music I can name; I can speak with all of my friends and family almost anywhere in the world, individually or collectively. With my dozens of apps, I can accomplish astonishingly more activities in the blink of an eye. It is all so radically amazing . . .

. . . and yet, I know too, it is also used for cyberbullying, slander, extreme self-absorption, and withdrawal. It is radically amazing and dangerous all at once.

In essence, all technology is ethically pareve, not inherently good or evil. This is as true of past technologies as current and future ones. In fact, some of the technological challenges we associate with our times were matters of concern more than a half century ago. As far back as the 1960s, the great Orthodox theologian Rabbi Joseph B. Soloveitchik observed that people were suffering from what he called an "epidemic of loneliness." As he contemplated the postwar space race, he was skeptical that great advances in technology would relieve this existential crisis:

> Who knows what kind of loneliness is more agonizing: the one which befalls man when he casts his glance at the mute cosmos, at its dark spaces and monotonous drama, or the one that bests man

exchanging glances with his fellow man in silence? Who knows whether the first astronaut who will land on the moon, confronted with a strange, weird, and grisly panorama, will feel a greater loneliness than Mr. X, moving along jubilantly with the crowd and exchanging greetings on New Year's Eve at a public square?[3]

Rabbi Soloveitchik, a supporter of space exploration, presciently worried about what could be lost in human relationships as technology became more . . . astronomical. More recently, Senator Ben Sasse has voiced similar concerns:

The same technology that has liberated us from so much drudgery has also unmoored us from the things that anchor our lives. The technological revolution of our time has given millions of Americans the ability to live like royalty, but it has also outpaced our ability to figure out what community, friendship, and relationships should look like in this modern world.[4]

Technology is merely a tool. Whether it is used for connection or isolation, for construction or destruction, remains up to us.

Our agenda for the next generation must be to figure out how to sharpen our relationship with this power at our fingertips, to figure out how to do only good with it. Surely, with the world at our fingertips, so too is the potential to give Tzedakah with it, to heal and repair its broken fragments bit by bit, through a sublime web of interconnectedness.

PART 2

POETRY

6

From *Soulstoned* (1969)

Father Abraham — Genesis Chapter 22 Slightly Changed

Just yesterday
  deciding blasphemy was better
  removing lowdramatic Hollywooden fantasies
        I cut a jagged edge in my Tanach
        just before God's goodygoody angel
          toodivinely grabs the knife
          from Abraham

A welltold story to a point
  believable
        for even those who don't believe
  a threedays silencewalk
        in all or almost all aloneness
          with his and laughing Sarah's longawaited son
  to a mountain
        where the air and mind
          could clarify each other
  and then to build an altar
        thankyou blessings
          for the gift of
            mountains son and airclearminds

But what kind father
  ties a son face-up
        on any altar
  daring staring into Isaaceyes
        slicing deeply fiercely
I can't believe he stared
          and yet in any sense a father
            raised a knife

And so too every Father Abraham
  before he ties the rope

around his preboxed son
     at local maddened drooling draftboards

I like it better
    thinking Father Abraham had said
        forget it Isaac
        let's go home

7

From *And God Braided Eve's Hair* (1976)

The Crippler

I had always been told
my Zeyde cut his own finger off
to escape the 20+ years' exile in the Czar's army
but now I know the truth:
that there was this man in their community
in one-day-Poland next-day-Russia
called the Crippler
who obliged the Jews
by maiming the children
before the officers conscripted them.
And as the game developed
the Jews found
an index-finger was not sufficient —
the Czar would be a laughingstock.
So the cry arose for variety
to give appearance that everything
was from a natural accident.
And so the Crippler got new sticks and saws
and a holy sense of destiny
for it was he who said:
From this one I will take an eye
from that a leg
and those each shall be broken-backed.
Now I think that this
was how
his own Zeyde
came to be a deaf-mute tailor —
a stick in the ear,
acid in the mouth —
and he was free to stay home
bear children

and sail to America
before the last pogrom
robbed him
of his good fortune.
Here he could gesticulate his way
to old age
and pass on the tale
to his grandson
my Zeyde
who would tell me
in an Aleph-plus hotel
in Yerushalayim
how it was back then
     back there
so that I might rise above
the shame
and promise my own children
that there are other ways
     better ways
to be chosen.

A Recent Immigrant Comes from the Soviet Union to His Family in the United States

and asks
   3 questions in shul:
         1. Where
   are the children?
         2. Where
   are the children?
         3. Where
   are the children?
Did I pass through Auschwitz
   to see a synagogue
   too dignified to tolerate
   five-year-olds playing on the bima?
Did I live in Leningrad
   for 30 years
   at minyans
   for the feeble zeydes
   to find a freedom
   empty of the noise
   of unadulterated childhood?
There they hid or died.
There their parents' fear
   turned them into goyim
   and marranos
But here there is no reason.
Without giggling and shouts
   and infants crying
   your sanctuary
   is a vacant temple
   your prayers
   are hypocritical.

Let us have noise and chaos
in the house of prayer
    Lest we cause ourselves
a self-made holocaust
    Lest Berlin and Moscow
win a victory
    we fought
    but lose now
for the sake
    of order
    and a myth of church-learned
        straight proprieties

Selig and the Judge

The following story was told, and perhaps retold many times, in the Yeshivahs of Eretz Yisrael by Reb Yakov Radotchkovitzer. Reb Yakov died miserably not so many years ago, having degenerated from years of brilliance and madness remembered tear-clearly by the students who listened to his strange tales and watched his antics. His story is not unlike a fantasy by Peretz; his biography, as sketched by my Talmud teacher, is worthy of Wiesel:

A certain Jew of everyday appearance came before the Single Heavenly Court, sometime during that warped eternity, after the flames of Auschwitz ceased to be heard and the crematoria of Dachau temporarily closed for repairs. No doubt two groups of divine beings waited outside the courtroom: Gay-clad escorts to Gehennom and togaed, chubby angels in white, the royal entourage to Eden.

When the door closed behind the Jew, he walked neither terrified nor proud toward the Judge's bar. There was no need for God to pound the gavel on the tabletop—all was quiet as expectant Sinai, except for the rhythmic footsteps of Selig.

"Did you study the Torah, my little yid?" God whispered in a well-known still-small voice.

"Nayn, Tatenyu, I did not study Your Torah."

"Did you davvin every day, my little yid?" God whispered, this time louder and with humor and curiosity.

"Nayn, RiboynoShelOylam, I did not davvin," Selig answered, showing neither chutzpah nor forgiveness by his tone.

Sensing the next answer, the Almighty roared mighty as Pharaoh, "And did you keep My Holy Shabbas?"

And, as expected, the Jew again answered the disappointing, "Nayn."

"Be gone! Take him away to Gehennom forever!" screeched the Judge, red-faced and raging for the first time since the Flood. "Get out of here!"

Selig turned to leave, walking out as he had entered, without terror, without pride. At the door, he paused to face his aging God again, saying, "I, too, have a question, an old-time *shylah* for the Rebbi, and then I will go."

The Holy One, surprised but interested, always curious for questions, sat down again on the diamond-and-emerald throne, and listened to Selig, who asked:

"Tatenyu, bei Hitler bin ich a yid—bei dir, nayn?—Father, for Hitler I was a Jew, and for You I am not?"

Astounded and drained, God sat in silence, that divine silence of confusion and mystery, as Selig waited for his answer. At last, God whispered, "Halachah K'Hitler—Hitler was right."

Personal Preference

I think
(now that I look back)
I'd rather drive a taxi
in Jerusalem
than be the King
of all of South Dakota
or the Cantor
in the Great and Ancient Synagogue
of West Rangoon.

I don't know why.

Here the sun sets red,
and there the suns set red.
Here the trees sway with infinite grace,
and there the breeze moves the leaves
with equally gentle fingers.

I don't know why
I'd rather drive a taxi in Jerusalem,

but neither have I come to know
just why the seed becomes a daffodil
and not a rose.

Hebrew

I'll tell you how much I love Hebrew:
Read me anything—
    Genesis
    or an ad in an Israeli paper
and watch my face.
I will make half-sounds of ecstasy
and my smile will be so enormously sweet
you would think some angels were singing Psalms
    or God Himself was reciting to me.
I am crazy for her Holiness
    and each restaurant's menu in Yerushalayim
    or Bialik poem
gives me peace no Dante or Milton or Goethe
could give.
I have heard Iliads of poetry,
Omar Khayyam in Farsi,
and Virgil sung as if the poet himself
were coaching the reader.
And they move me—
but not like the train schedule from Haifa to Tel Aviv
or a choppy unsyntaxed note
from a student who got half the grammar I taught him
     all wrong
but remembered to write
    with Alefs and Zayins and Shins.
That's the way I am.
I'd rather hear the weather report
on Kol Yisrael
than all the rhythms and music of Shakespeare.

Psalm 55

For the Jews of Bnai Isaac,
Aberdeen, South Dakota

Happy are we whose synagogue is small
    because we love each Jew
    because we have to
    because we do
Happy are our children
    who sit in sixes and fours
    learning Torah
    with the rabbi
    for he knows them well enough
    to know them
Happy are our homemade caterings
    our hospitality on Pesach
    our own-washed floors
Happy is the man who walks right in
    day or night
    through the unlocked doors
    to meditate and sit in peace
Happy are we whose house is a shul
    and whose temple is a home

Mashiachtzeit or Davidson from Egged

For Rabbi Jonathan Porath

Right while I was sitting on the balcony
watching the city wake itself
a jag cut in the dirty sky
over the Pentagon complex
and a Golden hand holding a Glittering Dishrag
began scrubbing the Heavens
until they sparkled
like the glasses in an Ivory commercial.
The glare was tremendous
and traffic stopped for a moment
so the drivers could adjust their eyes.
The hearts of many hardened people
unwound so easily
some began to whistle
and everyone felt Just Good
all over.
In the meanwhile
the Hand withdrew
and disappeared into the sawed-out
piece of sky
and a jumbling confused sound
came from behind the Cheerblue screen
as the people below
paused in confusion.
Then the Hand emerged again
holding a White Bus
and a Well-Dressed Gentleman.
The Fingers placed them
on Independence Avenue
near George's Monument

and the city-folks
began to converge
on this one point.
I followed
though the crowds were immense
and in a chilly frenzy
reminiscent of a Tel Aviv soccer mob.

Slowly
slowly
I worked my way downtown
and stood in line
until I was close enough to see
it really was
the J-18
for Yerushalayim.
I took the 40 Grush
from my pocket
smiled at the driver
as I boarded
then took a seat
next to my brother
waiting now only
for the Man
to let out the clutch
and begin the Last Run.

Knife, Birds

Isaac should have knocked the knife away,
slung it down the mountain,
broken it on a rock,
whatever—
as soon as he saw Abraham
unwind the rope from the ass's saddle.
He should have shouted in his father's
sad-eyed face,
"Your sadness is cheap!
too sophisticated,
too programmed,
weeping for Youth Dying Young
according to God's will!
Stop crying! Defy this mystery-laden
Master, this Voice of yours,
and love me, your visible son!"

Would not the birds,
stunned by the near-atrocity of the act,
would they not have burst
into a mighty Psalm-song
to drown the clank of the knife
rolling down the hillside
and the roaring joy of Abraham?

8

From *Between Dust and Dance* (1978)

A Blessing

Berachot 17a, Eruvin 54a

May your eyes sparkle with the light of Torah,
and your ears hear the music of its words.
May the space between each letter of the scrolls
bring warmth and comfort to your soul.
May the syllables draw holiness from your heart,
and may this holiness be gentle and soothing to the world.
May your study be passionate,
and meanings bear more meanings
until Life itself arrays itself to you
as a dazzling wedding feast.
And may your conversation,
even of the commonplace,
be a blessing to all who listen to your words
and see the Torah glowing on your face.

Frumka

In a small town in Hungary, there was a little girl named Frumka Raschevsky. She was born in 1941, the fifth of five children.

Now you know the ending of the story, for it is the same story with only the most insignificant variations: she died before she was three.

Now you want to know how she died, and then you will ask why.

I will tell you half the tale:

Frumka, "The Little Religious One," was the infant who whimpered in the cellar as the Nazis and the Hungarians searched the house.

She is the one whose mother strangled her, life-for-life, so the uncles and sisters and grandfather would not be discovered.

Her mother is the one who sits on Dizengoff, wringing her hands, doing the pantomime on Shabbas—whether or not anyone stops to watch.

She is the one in the books you always wondered about.

Be satisfied you know only half the tale.

II

Once upon a time in a village in Poland there was a lively baby, a Jewish baby.

Now you know the end of the story: she is in Canada, married and childless and weary of her husband's tolerance and understanding.

You will want to know how she got to Canada and why she came.

Frumka was born in 1937, by the grace of God, and her father was a well-to-do merchant who always travelled with his family somewhere abroad during the summer.

In 1939 they sailed for the Fair in New York, but in the carnival of progress Frumka's brother became ill and they delayed their return until October while the boy suffered the humid days in the hospital.

By then it was too late, by the grace of God, and they never went back home.

Frumka met her husband in the Bronx in the Goodtime fifties, and his firm transferred him to Montreal at the next decade's turning.

III

Frumka was lost in the Umschlagplatz, separated from her mother
and father by the animal confusion around the tracks.

A fatherly soldier carried her gently to the boxcar and tossed her
into the crowd. She broke her arm in the fall, but by a stroke of luck
died before the train reached Treblinka.

IV

Once—

Many times, in a town called Katowice, a baby named Frumka
was born.

She died the usual forgotten death of those days.

Why do some infants get buried by their fathers?

Why do some have headstones listing their names and recording
their brief struggle:

Jody Marshall
March 8, 1957–
June 17, 1961

overlooking the West Virginia hills, catching the eyes of strangers
and townsfolk carrying a coffin to some other plot?

Why are they so privileged, when Frumka became a vapor irritat-
ing the eyes of local citizens?

V

Frumka—you know Frumka by now—she is the baby who saw Dr.
Mengele ever-so-briefly, trying to keep her eyes open in the sunlight
she hadn't seen for days.

Frumka liked the Doctor's hands, the way they played in the air,
now to one side, now the other, in funny motions.

VI

God loved Frumka.

God must have a Frumka

God roared at the angels —
a little child with a fine name
to play with Sonia,
who was alone.
So the Seraphs and the Archangels
descended the ladder from Heaven
to Czechoslovakia
and took her from the rope on the tree.
God was delighted
to watch them play
and eat
and to look at their eyes.
They were happy.
So God thought —
If they are so happy as two
if there is yet another
they will be still-more-happy.
So Gabriel shot one
and Raphael dressed the wound
to look pretty
and Michael brought
Shayna to her celestial home.
Over the years
the palaces of God's Golden Cities —
where the Law says you must be happy —
became filled
with the scrapes and bounces
and other sounds
of children
making the Almighty laugh.

9

From *Nine Entered Paradise Alive* (1980)

Surveying the Jewish Multitudes

Rejoice, O Jerusalem,
your streets are filled again
with children! Proud children.
Be joyous, Mother Rachel,
your children have come home!

Home. Such a foreign word
to the refugee from Argentina,
the Vizhnitzer chossid,
the Jew from Bulgarian cities.
That you are home,
and there is no more need to hide
and steal across the border,
is the stuff of Jewish lullabies.
When the planes at Lod
crowd with long lost sons
and daughters,
truth and freedom blur
near disbelief.

Tiberias and Yavneh,
raise your voices!
Masada burst your rocks
with song,
for we are home!

Erev Shabbas

It's so stupid.
Wednesday afternoon,
soaked in the idiotica of errands
and all those "things to do"
that steal a human being's minutes, his years—
I forgot the Queen.
Her Majesty was due at four-eighteen
on Friday, not a minute later,
and I was wasting hands, words, steps,
racing to a rushing finish-line
of roaring insignificance
I just as well could fill
with preparations for the royal entourage;
cleaning and cleansing each act's doing,
each word's saying,
in anticipation of the Great Event of Shabbas.

Who am I that she should wish
to spend the day with me?
I dry out my strengths, cook, move dust,
casually insensitive to all the songs
that remind me that she, the Queen,
in diamond-ruby-emerald-glow tiara,
would come to grace my table.
She comes,
no matter how the week was spent,
in joy or in silliness,
yet she comes.
And I am her host,
laying a linen flower tablecloth
that is white,
that is all the colors of the rainbow.

This is the Jews' sense of royalty:
she never does not spend one day a week
with me, and every Jew,
in the open air of freedom,
or lightening the misery of prisoners
in stinking Russian prisons
or the ghettoes of Damascus.

Come, my Shabbas Queen,
embodiment of Worlds-to-Be:
Your gracious kindness is our breath of life,
and though we once, twice, all-too-often
fail to say, "How beautiful your cape!
How lovely your hair, your Shechina-eyes!"
we will not always be so lax,
apathetic to your grace, your presence.
Touch us again this week
with your most unique love's tenderness,
and we shall sing to you our songs,
dance our dances in your honor,
and sigh for you our sighs
of longing, peace, and hope.

Blessing the Children

(Parents place their hands on their children's heads and recite:)

For the sons —

May you be as Ephraim and Menashe,
   of whom we know nothing
   but their names,
   and that they were Jews.
And may you be as all Jews
   whose names are lost
   as witnesses to God's care,
   love, and presence.
Remember them in your words,
   and live Menschlich lives
   as they lived Menschlich lives.

For the daughters —

May you be as Sarah, Rivka, Rachel and Leah,
   whose names and deeds
   are our inheritance;
   who bore us, raised us,
   guided and taught us
   that a touch
   is a touch of Holiness,
   and a laugh is prophecy;
   that all that is ours,
   is theirs;
   that neither Man nor Woman alone
   lights the sparks of Life,
   but only both together,
   generating light and warmth
   and singular humanity.

The Tree and the Mashiach

Avot deRabbi Natan B, Chapter 31

"If you are planting a tree,
and someone comes and says,
'The Mashiach is coming!' —
then plant!"

No matter what reasonable people
or foaming enthusiastic youths tell you:
this messiah or that messiah
is imminent —
plant!
The Mashiach is in no rush.
When you have patted down the last clods of dirt,
and watered your maple, your sycamore,
your elm,
he will still be wherever he is supposed to be,
and more than happy to admire the sapling with you.
Messiahs don't come to uproot things.
If he wanted to,
he could bundle Eretz Yisrael into a package
and bring it to you,
so you would not have to go wandering again
through many lands.
If he really is the Mashiach,
this One everyone pesters you about,
he can bring you Abraham,
who will sit by your tree
and dispense dates
and the flat bread of hospitality,
as in ancient days.

So plant it now, firmly,
water it well,
whether or not there is a Messiah
today or tomorrow.

10

From *Unlocked Doors* (1983)

Children's Games

Why did we always
want to play dead, Eema,
when we played our backyard games?
You should have stopped us.
You should have scolded us,
telling us that we were Jews,
and Jews don't have
to play dead.

Rav Sheshet and the Angel

Mo'ed Katan 28a

"In the street like an animal?
You would take me here
among the shops and flies?
How dare you!"
Thus did Sheshet scream defiance
at Death.
"Come home with me!
Let me die in my bed
like a Mensch!"

Was it the cry, or
was it because no one
had said such things to the Angel before?
Whichever it was,
Death followed Rav Sheshet
to his home
and waited for his family
to gather his last words.
Then,
and only then,
did he dare
to take his soul.

Carolyn's Last Snow

For my friend Dr. Jay Masserman

I. The Angel of Death
came to the lab
dressed in an artist's oil-specked jacket,
stepping light as a dandy
to the microscope
where Jay sat reading
Carolyn's lifeline,
humming Schumann melodies
and dabbing and flecking the plate
with millions of renegade cells,
all that day and the next,
till the following night
when Carolyn spit out her last,
and Jay tore his shirt and wept,
while the Evil Messenger
cowered in the corner in shame.

II. Ah,
what delicate metaphors we use
to cover the vomit on Carolyn's sheets.
How we could sing
of her day-and-a-half dignity—
now that the autopsy
has cleaned her and cleansed her
of the organs
that suffered Promethean agonies.
What a Norman Rockwell picture
it might have been
had it happened otherwise.

But: it was ugly,
    raw,
as crass as unadulterated pain
    could possibly be.

Ask Jay.
    He still smells the stains of blood
        and   hears the over-morphine screams
        and   sees the terrified ice in her eyes.

11

From *The Lord Is a Whisper at Midnight* (1985)

The Geese and Hoopoes Praise You

The geese and hoopoes praise You;
mantises and dragonflies sing out Your name.

The salmon, bluebirds, squirrels gray and black,
in their own way, proclaim Your glory daily.

Beryl and diamonds,
rubies and coal, ferns and flowers
pay tribute silently to wisdom beyond all wisdom.

I wish I could walk like a zebra for You,
howl like coyotes do,
laugh and make faces for You
like monkeys in a zoo cage,
even shine like a sapphire,
for You.

I think, too, the sway of a cedar branch
swinging in the air just so
can be a gesture of praise,
and the clink of keys in a human hand
carried precisely with just the right rhythm
is somehow holy resonance.

Lions yawn so wide; why, if not for You?
Ibexes dash across the plains, swift, flying, for You.

The heavens are more staggering today than ever.
Why should this be, O Lord,
if not for You?

Number My Days This Way

O Lord—
Number my days this way:

Days of strength to lie,
if the truth brings torment.
Days of weakness,
if strength gives rise to suffering.
Days of noise,
if silence is the cause of loneliness.
And
Nights of disconcerting dreams
if I turn smug to the taste of hunger.

Pursue me,
Discomfort me,
Destroy my own complacency
with paradox and contradiction.

Remind me I am Yours.

A Prayer for Teachers of Torah

Dear God,
Give me the strength, the wisdom,
the something,
to be a teacher.
Give me one child,
a single boy or girl,
who will be an honest judge,
and another
who will have the courage,
because of me,
to stop a wrist from bleeding.

I cannot wash the sky,
but let me find some person
who does not care about the sun,
or for a woman
dying of T.B. in an apartment in Chicago—
let me touch him
and teach him to care,
and let him use his own soul
to clean the Windows of Heaven.

Let me breathe the fire of peace
into a quiet, unassuming diplomat,
so that she may pace the deserts and palaces
of Your earth,
reconciling brothers and sisters
who have forgotten to love.

Is this too much to ask?

No?

Then—

Dear God,

Give me the grandchild of a Hungarian Zeyde
whose ashes rushed down the raging Vistula
from Auschwitz—
a child with beautiful hands,
and let me be the one to say,
"Here is a violin,
it belongs to you.
Go! Make the people dance!"

Give me a joker,
a carpenter who loves his wood and hammers,
a childless mother
who wants so much to love a baby.

Please, O please,
O please.

12

From *The Garden* (1985)

All Red White and Blue, We American Kids

I. All red white and blue, we American kids
fell for it:
Dr. Kildare, Ben Casey, Dr. Handsome This,
Surgeon That, eight minutes each television hour
sweating behind a mask and saving them all
on the table.
Life and death were in their hands
and *only* in their hands. Or so it seemed.
Here a snip, there retract, patches and pumps in the innards
and all kinds of miracles happened right before our eyes.
America's Saviors All: the cardio-neuro-ortho surgeons.

It cut us, the common folk, out of miracles.
           (But Tzedakah saves from
           death.)

II. And then along came Tzedakah
on a snorting white steed, rearing high on its legs.
All of a sudden people bought food,
wrote checks, sat at hotlines, and shopped for the shut-ins.
They drove the lonely to synagogue.
They took in children wandering the streets.
They counselled and pushed
and made shiny wrapped packages called Dignity and Hope
and delivered them to Old Age Homes
complete with a choir of youth group kids,
every age unafraid of wrinkles and bends.
           (Tzedakah saves from despair
           and death.)

The kids brought their pets to the sick
and sick at heart to be petted
and played with, smiled at, cooed over,

and you would be hard pressed, you would,
to tell just who exactly was saved from death:
the pettor or the pettee or the kid with the puppy
who missed a little homework because
he was too busy
at the Home for the Lonely
which is located in All Neighborhoods in Every Town
in America
day, night, snow, sleet, rain and sun times,
shooing away death with a gentle bark and a purr and touch.
              (Tzedakah saves.)

Whole troops of them!
The infinite team of salvation makers
and life restorers:
the teacher, the real estate broker, his daughter,
the toy maker, towel dealer, and mechanic,
the academic by day and spoon feeder by night,
regiments of the fat and short and average,
Cary Grant bodies and nerd faces,
PhDs and twelve-year-olds
              (saving Tzedakah from death.)
Yes. Indeed.
There's a battalion, an army or two out there,
in jeans, and sweatshirts, slacks, blouses,
loafers, scarves and gloves—
just your run-of-the-mill normal people—
squeezing into The
Great Crowded Group Photograph in the Sky.
              (The Tzedakah Photograph.)

Wallenberg I

I'll never know why
and I don't read signs into everything,
but Wallenberg was betting high stakes with Eichmann
in Budapest just when I was born.
My certificates read July 11, 1944.
The tall Swede with the life-saving *chutzpah*
came two days before.
But I was in Washington sleeping, wailing,
being pampered and diapered
(even now I'm "the baby of the family" at 40),
not in Hungary.

So I don't have Survivor's Guilt—
just a multitude of questions
that strike me every time I stop to think:

Had my mother been on the trains,
would he have spotted her,
given her a phony pass,
pulled her off into his limousine
because her baby (me) was so small and weak?

Would our "Safe House" escape the Arrow Cross's arrogance?
Would my murderers live on quietly in Wisconsin
next door to neighbors who found them sweet-and-decent folk?

Wallenberg II

Wallenberg—
no smaller than his myth.
Real, ideal, handsome,
big-hearted, pushy-for-Life, tireless—
all of those.

At long last
I don't have to expect
someone will write a book before I die
tearing apart his Image
like they did to the Kennedys and King.

Hype and wishful thinking, exaggeration won't touch him.
He was, indeed, what he was.

Snows of My Childhood

For Mark Hyman and for Jay Wolke, who
wrote a song to the words of this poem

Snows of my childhood   Snows of my youth
    Snows of myself in the picture
        wrinkled with age
        standing embalmed in the clothing
        of mother
          the scarves
          and the gloves
          and sweaters and coats
          and the hat with the earmuffs
and the rolling in mountains of soft
        with my brother
        fallen and sliding
          the sled on the hill.
Snows of my father
        in chains in a maddening car
        on the way to the sick
and working his labors of life
        Snows of my Zeyde
and the marvelous Lady in White
        in the harbor
          holding her torch
to the Jews on the deck
in the snows of his childhood
        the snows of his youth.
Snows near the Vistula sky
        that was silent and white
      camped in an oven for warm
        and for *ewig*
        and ever

and ever.
Snows of the Angel of Death
in the mockery-robes
of Hitler's magicians.
Snows of the City at dawn
and the dance
of the foolish Chassidim
feeling the feathers of Heaven
whirling and sweeping
in time to the Vistula melody.
Snows of redemption and hope
and the splendor of Israel.

13

From *Before Our Very Eyes* (1986)

Sunflower Seeds and Name-Brand Shirts

Sunflower seeds and name-brand shirts,
milk from Jewish cows.
It's here and it's all ours.
Even the stones taste good
when you rub your fingers against them
and touch your tongue.
You can get cinnamon pastries
flavored by refugees from Budapest.

The downtown triangle of streets is seething with Jews —
loud chattering geniuses, drivers, merchants, and kids,
pharmacists from Germany, scholars,
kibbutzniks on a spree, saints,
men shaking in yarmulkas over a Coke,
the round and the blind, the muscle-bulging
of our people, foaming beggars,
and name-brand open-shirted macho Sabra men.

This is us.
This is me, ours, *my* own, *our* own;
it belongs, and *I* belong.
Jerusalem.

A Certain Holiness

It was that time of Jerusalem day
when the sun chooses
any one of many hills
to wash in gold,
the time of day
the City assumes
a touch of the romantic's magic.
The religious said blessings.
The eloquent called to mind
lines memorized in school
for moments such as these
and wrote new songs
from notes made of beams.
Others still, held hands
and kissed
for all this beauty
whose truest words
are whispers and sighs and half-sounds,
hints of interjections
no one can put to a rhythm—
not Shelley, nor Wordsworth,
nor the grand-sweeping Lord Byron.
And Mozart and Schumann deceive us,
trying to make keys and oboes and strings
say things
only a Jewish heart
in love with the Holiest of Places
can say.

Summer 1976, Wine in the Streets

Either it's me and my *Mazal*
or Jewish History is always happening
in Israel.
Every time I go,
something larger than myself
is going on.
I try to sidestep it,
cutting my time to a month
or twenty-one days,
but still:
>The Eichmann Trial,
>Nasser drops dead,
>A quiet Yom Kippur in shul
>>with too many citizens
>>in fatigues
>>instead of *kittels*,
>And now
Entebbe.
I arrived as the Yeshivahs began
their Psalms and fasting,
and July Fourth we were drinking *Lechayyim*
in the streets
and interjecting God's Name
and the word "miracle"
into every other sentence.

Sometimes I do not feel worthy
of these cosmic junctures.
I am too confused
by the living through of Great Events
and the meanings of the aftermaths.
And the questions of
"What next?"

14

From *The Meadow Beyond the Meadow* (1991)

Anthropology

You do what you have to do.
Some peoples breed fierce horsemen, in antiquity
to defend or attack, now, perhaps more for leisurely sport.
Jews do Mitzvahs.
Some peoples breed parsimony into their children,
otherworldliness, or faith. Or to speak laconically.
We do Mitzvahs. It's what we do.
I would imagine on the solid authority
of *National Geographic* that there are yet
numerous bushman tribes whose breadwinners
can knock monkeys out of a treetop with their darts
far better than we. They have to because it is their dinner.
We do Mitzvahs. It's what we have to do, being our Life
and the length of our days.

With a Kiss

It is the little acts, positioned in the day,
that make us: the kissing of the fallen book
which doesn't feel;
not using the Chumash, the Talmud,
as a thing to lean on for other words, be they poetry books
or tax forms (they take no precedence, watch where
you lean); not mistaking a Pushka for a paperweight;
kissing (again) the Mezuzah as we pass through
or pass from (both passages ordained, be cognizant);
the covering of Challah till the time, wine blessed,
tasted, hands washed, is right; the kissing (again)
of Tzitzit; the kissing of the Torah scrolls when they
are marched by, the kissing (yet again), before closing,
of the Siddur.

From these, justice and Menschlichkeit.
Lifting the fallen book we may, just may some day,
lift the fallen neighbor, the stranger, who feels,
with a kiss.

The Old Tapestry in the Den

We had one of them in the den,
one of those tapestries of the hunt.
I believe a patient gave it to my father, oh,
it must have been sometime in the late Forties
because as long as I can remember, I can remember
it on the wall.
For tapestry artists I am sure it is a common theme,
like for painters who do sailboats on a lake in summer.
Over the centuries they must have made thousands
of them, the remains located now in museums
and castles on the Rhine and college art books.
I hadn't thought about that piece of the old house
in years: the hounds, horses, trumpets,
riders, and, of course,
the fox, whose minutes on this earth are numbered
in small numbers.

If you pick up a book of Jewish poetry, we, too,
have our common themes: the Sabbath, for instance,
our dissatisfactions with how God is supervising
humanity, Israel the blooming land, Israel the refuge,
an age-old distaste for pork, and our own form of the hunt:
the horses, the riders, the dogs, bottles of vodka smashed
on the ground, swords, rifles and clubs, and, of course,
the Jews, whose minutes on this earth are numbered
in very small numbers.

The Imaginary Conference
of the International College of Poets,
Tampa, June 12–15, 1982

Their points of reference: Hamlet and Orpheus,
the sprites of old mythologies, ours:
Goering and Himmler, Queen Isabella's dream of a
judenrein Spain.

Their images: light shining through cathedral windows,
fine cardinals' robes, gold-trimmed, ours:
grabbing a tenth for a Minyan on a plane
(a passenger is saying Kaddish, night is rushing
in the direction of the DC-10; time for Mincha).
It seems that all we have in common, said in humor,
is the Pope's yarmulka.

Their music: Mozart, Schweitzer playing organ
in Europe before departing for the jungles,
ours, those mad orchestras in Auschwitz, the surfeit
of string-players Russia is losing as the Jews, free at last,
stream towards Israel.

We try to explain how
we can't even use the word "crisscrossed"
without hesitating about its propriety.

All this in the first day, everyone cordial.

Theirs, the landscapes of the Russian steppes, Katmandu,
Kilimanjaro's slopes, the laze of the Mississippi's course,
ours: parched deserts blooming, a Polish shtetl so cold
the privileged guest sleeps nearest the stove,
snowfall in Mauthausen.

Cordial became politely distant. All agreed the idea
of a conference, in theory, was a good one, the sharing
and openness, collegiality. What came of it, unforeseen,
was something else: music and metaphor were, in theory,
innocent, in life, a gap
wide as the distance inside the wire at Bergen Belsen
to out.

Spring Storm

It is Shabbat and it is Pesach. A storm moves up
the land from Georgia with its whirlwinds, its path
houses blown apart, trailer parks scattered toy-like
for miles every whichway. It won't be here for hours,
if it all. We have hail; you can hear
the stones against the windows as we sit at Seder.

Pharaoh—what affairs of state did he tend to
through the blood and boils? When the cattle died,
the crops, dust, did he chatter on at the dinner table
about the soaring costs of new uniforms for the palace guards
with his wife, joke with his son? Was it the darkness?
the hail? When? At which number of the ten
was his routine so upset he freed the slaves
and freed himself of the whining Moses?
None of them. None.
Until his child, called to eat, failed to show at the table,
dead, intact but breathless, in his chambers.

The Four Children

We are always proud, forever
speaking of the wise one, the wise child.
What about the bad one (recalling, of course,
Father Flanagan's "There's no such thing as a bad kid")?
If we have none of those, why are so many rabbis
making rounds in the Big Houses across our fair land?
Who are these ghosts in the minimum,
medium, and maximum prisons? Figments?
(We had our Uncle Simcha who hid out
with Grandpa for a few weeks. I think it was
Prohibition and he was mixed up with some,
shall we say, undesirable fellows.)
Now comes the hard part, the special two—
"simple" and "unable-to-ask."
You may say "simple" means "nice" or "easygoing,"
the kid who likes everything, is happy, and
makes no demands. It's the one you refer to
now that he or she is grown up when you say,
"Joe (or Nancy) was an easy child." All right, then—
that's three out of four. But that still leaves
"the one who doesn't know how to ask."
I think the pictures in the Haggadah are wrong,
painting children so small.
They shift; they mislead. It doesn't mean:
"so young they can't formulate the words."
It means . . . We know what it means.
And if we just say it, with the pride of the first,
maybe this year more can come out of their hiding places.

Be Not Irrelevant

Be not irrelevant. Last.
Be hope like camellias on their first day out.
Be the champion who wins and wins
and never retires, and losing, be gracious. Do not slow.
Never be just one more phone call to make
before shutting down for the night. Be here, always.

15

From *A Hearing
Heart* (1992)

King Solomon Asks for a Hearing Heart

(I Kings 3:9)

O God, give me a hearing heart.

Let my heart hear the wings of the hawk,
the crane, the eagle and the owl,
the angelic reds and blues of the macaw,
the angels.

Let my heart hear the tides,
the sap flow to syrup in the trees,
the fires in the rock in the heart of the earth,
the conversations of stars.

Let it hear sweet Torah,
truths unshakable,
prophecy alive.

Let my heart, human, hear tearing hearts
in the final stages of repair,
tears wiped away by kindly hands
soft as irises unfolding.

In whatever my heart hears,
let me hear Your voice.

Above All, Teach This Newborn Child

Above all, teach this newborn child to touch,
to never stop,
to feel how fur is other than the leaf or cheek,
to know through these hands diamond from glass,
Mezuzah from anything else in the world.
The same with Challah and a book.

As the baby grows,
teach this child to embrace the shoulders of another
before sadness brings them inhumanly low,
to stroke the hair softly of one younger who is weeping,
one older who cries.

Let these hands be a gentle Yes
when Yes is the Truth,
and, gently, a No, when No is right.

Whatever these fingers touch—
may they be for new holiness and blessing,
for light, life, and love.

Amen.

Bat Mitzvah Speech of a Fifty-Year-Old Woman

I wanted this to be in public,
no less than an anniversary I celebrate
in the midst of my family and friends.
I wanted my People to see
I have studied and prepared and rehearsed my readings
no less than my children did for their celebrations,
but, for my part, done with no reluctance.
I did this out of love, because I love my People,
and I see myself more clearly — because of my People,
and I am more myself because of them.

I never had a Bat Mitzvah.
I was born in Wartime.
My parents lived through the Depression,
a time of despair and uncertainty I cannot imagine or feel.
Other things were more important then,
and I do not fault them their choices.
I cannot conceive of joblessness or Europe in flames,
cannot understand what it was like to get up day after day
with the smoke and clouds blocking the sunlight.
I think they are proud of me today,
and I do not want them to feel any guilt
that they never sent me to Hebrew school.
They taught me to love Judaism and Jews,
and I suspect they knew one day
I would make up for lost time.
I am doing that now,
and I am proud to be standing here before you,
my congregation,
feeling somewhat like I felt at college graduation:
this is commencement.

After the Kiddush and the good wishes
and the contributions you have made in my honor
I will continue my study of Torah
as I did yesterday and the day before.
I am just beginning,
and I am only a few years behind Rabbi Akiva
who couldn't read Hebrew until he was forty.
To my teachers:
My gratitude.
My soul is warm.

To my husband:
My thanks,
for your patience and help
and your willingness to be my study partner,
not out of tolerance,
and not from a sense that sooner or later
I would snap out of this,
but, rather, out of love.

And to my children:
Know this —
whichever way you go as Jews in your own lives,
this is not just "Mommy's Jewish thing,"
like tennis or wanting to be the best lawyer in town.
It is more than that:
It is Myself, a finer I,
and I wish you the same joy I feel today
all the days of your lives.

Judaism is a jewel, a beautiful diamond.
Jews are the setting for a ring or pendant.
Together, they dazzle the human soul.
I stand here before you dazzled by it all.

May God grant us the greatest gift of all—
peace—
speedily
and in our own time.

Amen.

Mitzvah Therapy

Then let us, troubled, do this:
raise finches and parakeets for all Old Ones living all alone;
tend plants and flowers,
violets and geraniums, impatiens, pansies, and irises,
and roses of every color
to grow to give to the lonely of this world
that they have the will to awaken tomorrow and live;
train dogs to pull wheelchairs
when there is no power in the human's legs
to stand or to walk,
train them to run to their owners
when there is someone knocking at the door
but there is no hearing to hear;
groom horses,
Morgans and Quarter Horses and Welsh Ponies,
that will, in their mass and rhythms, and displaying their style,
trot and canter and gallop
and bring dead limbs back to their rightful lives;
let us clean their stables and pitch their hay
and haul their water to the troughs
so they may be mighty Mitzvah steeds
for, though we drop from exhaustion,
we will have done our part;
tune cars at cost or for free
for all who live so close to the edge of poverty they despair
when all they need
is nothing more than a wreck with four wheels
to take them to work
—for anyone who has only one last chance left;
collect millions of pennies,
count them and roll them and give them away;

be huggers at the Special Olympics,
overcoming our fear of touch;
paint the planes that fly hearts and lungs and kidneys
up and down the coast and cross-country
and everywhere in between,
wherever the desperate are waiting;
clown in the hospitals,
do some things all good.

The Late Bloomer

She had not been much for grades,
and, never one to be a leader,
she had held no synagogue or sisterhood office
all her years as a member.
Comfortably settled on the other side of fifty,
she displayed her daughter's Phi Beta Kappa key
in one of those glassed-in cases guests were required to admire
as a kind of admission fee for one of her dinners.
It was propped up alongside some of the hand-painted figurines
she had collected over the years.
She was proud of it,
though she did not live through this child,
nor, for that matter, through any of her other children.
In turn, they did not look down on her
for being average in the common way of things.
What she was good at, they liked,
though there was never anything so striking in the larger sense:
no big deals or scores of music to her name,
no plans laid—even in remote dreams—for a novel
or to be fabulously rich.
If anything, she was admirable in being so content.

What she did, she did well:
clean house,
even while on the phone and exchanging innocent gossip,
cook the full range of meals
that would satisfy
guests who fancied themselves meat-and-potato he-men
as well as delicacies for the most fastidious gourmand.
And shop a grocery store!—in that, she was no less adept
than a general deploying his troops before battle.

Which is how the free home cleaning-and-cooking service
for people with AIDS all began in our congregation.

And it was in no way out of a sense of boredom or desperation.

One day, the kids being all grown and out of the house,
she just knew she was the best at something
but had been looking in all her Self's wrong places.
In the entire congregation there really was no one
who could straighten a house to the owner's liking
as well and as quickly as she,
leaving more than enough time for light conversation,
no one who could pick up as subtly as she could
on which vegetables were someone's favorites
and which were downed merely to be polite,
and, besides, to know which noshers preferred
to lick the pan with the dough
more than eating the cookies themselves,
and, accordingly, leaving that much more in the raw
and making sure to add extra chocolate chips.

It was in her to recognize these small things
as something of far greater significance,
though they were too often taken for granted.

She is what became known around the synagogue as
The Late Bloomer,
and she went to every funeral and wept for each one of her people
from deep in her heart
—just one more aspect of her genius too long ignored,
and much admired and needed by all of us
who know her and learn her Torah
of the holiness of cleaning bed pans
those extra few special strokes of the rag.

Where Heaven and Earth Touch So Closely, They Appear to Be Kissing

In birth, in love,
and in death;
at the horizon (of course),
in the sun's warming the earth so we might live,
in the green leaves' edges
rusting and turning to gold in the Fall,
in bread and its grains and the rains that raise the seed;
in the sapphire and ruby, the emerald and the diamond uncut;
in fingers barely intertwined;
in the red of blood,
the yellow-on-black of the pansies,
the blue of night waters under the rising and risen moon,
the flesh of flesh;
in Torah, in Mitzvahs,
in candles and forgiveness,
in Your never-ending care.

A Recitation for Students of Anatomy

Forgive us.
Forgive us
for what we are about to do.

We pray that you not suffer because of us.
May the work of our hands cause you no indignity.
We mean no harm.

At this most solemn moment,
we swear we shall not forget you.
Your name will be with us
all our days as healers.

Noble and human even in death,
Teacher,
God rest your soul.

Statement by a Woman Who Has Chosen to Be a Jew

I began this journey because I loved one Jew.
I sometimes imagine that, at least at first,
our ancestor Sarah might have done the same,
following her man from Haran to Canaan
through all the hardships and terrors of ancient travel
because she loved him no matter what his ideas or voices,
or perhaps precisely *because of* his ideas and voices.

Now that is no longer good enough for me.

Now I love not only the man I chose to marry
but also the Jewish People, my People.
Where they go, I will go,
and if that means estrangement and exile,
I choose to be the stranger and the exile with them.

I have left my family to be at one with you.
I would not lie at this most awesome moment
saying it is, has been, or will be easy.
Whether they understand or not is not irrelevant,
for they bore me and raised me,
wished only the best for me, and loved me.
They are my parents.
Whether or not they stand by me
as I assume my Judaism —
they will always deserve my love in return.

But *you* must stand by me, *you*, my People,
for you have known the heart of the outcast.

I have been warned:
when the hate of Jews appears in any of its various faces and dis-
    guises and masks,
each one uglier than the next,

and when it roars and growls in its most grotesque voice,
I know:
the curses and stares,
the primitive arrows of old
and the most modern and sophisticated weapons of destruction
are aimed at me.
I cannot hide any more.

Today I cease to be safe,
as I once was in my other life.
Wherever *you* are shut out, *I* am shut out,
and I accept that
as much as I accept all promised joy
that comes to me as a Jew.

If—sitting across the room at some dinner
to raise funds for threatened Jews—
you see this face,
so different from those all around me
because of my Irish grandparents,
I am not a guest or mere sympathizer.
I *belong* there.

Your tragedies of old and of today are mine;
I take them as I take the Simchas:
the Land of Israel, Mitzvahs, Shabbat in all its glory,
foods no longer permitted
now that I have walked ever so proudly over the line.

This week in the Sukkah,
I will revel in God's care,
remembering how fragile our defense is
against the mighty winds and threatening storms
that often frighten us.

I take the name Ruth as mine.
On this most meaningful day, you are my Naomi.
May I and my children be worthy parents
of the Redeemer of Israel.

Amen.

Commencement Address for Rabbinical School

Understand that all is God's glory,
you, yourselves, an angelic part of it.
Play your part with might, mind, heart, soul and inspiration.
If you will be with God,
God will be with you.

Shepherd your sheep each moment
as if all the world's holiness, all of history's,
depended on you.
It does . . .
on how you sit with a mother at Shiva
whose son lies miles away in no more than pine slats for a bed,
linen for night clothes,
on how you stand close to the bedside
of those who lie in agony and fear of death,
on which ancient words of hope you whisper to the weary of soul,
on how you touch the disheartened,
on the openness of your house, hand and heart,
on how you make peace.
If you are with your people in good faith,
God, Who redeemed us from Egypt and its agonies,
the taskmasters' tortures and whips,
God will be with you.

Teach all students Torah joyously
and as if your life depended on it.
It does;
and bear that responsibility as privilege.
Few are called to interpret,
fewer to enlighten.
You are of that age-old holy assembly
that counts among its members
giants such as Hillel, Rashi, the Baal Shem Tov,

and others whose names are so many
no human mind can hold them in without the outlet of tears.
They are smoke.

Where holiness hides in shadow, bring the light.
Where it cringes, afraid to show itself,
be strong and comforting.
Set it at ease, holiness.
Embrace it, if you must, in all its loneliness,
until, its weeping through,
it walks with you in your own footsteps
when you walk by the way,
and shimmers in your face
when you lie down and when you rise up.
In your being, be for the sake of Heaven.
In this, too, God will be with you.

Give of your money, the tool of justice and compassion,
and stretch your arms full stretch to those who suffer
as the Almighty God did for us
when all Pharaohs were brought low in our own sight.
The ways of Tzedakah are pleasantness,
and all the paths of Mitzvahs are peace.
Give of yourselves and thereby be yourselves.
Be strong.
Love God.
Love the People Israel,
and be you holy unto them.

God is with you.

Speech to the Camp Counselors Just Before the Kids Arrive

I knew some of you in your cribs
when all you could do to entertain yourselves
was stare at a plastic mobile
hanging over your heads in the crib.
I watched some of you play with rattles.
This was before you could say three words.
I used to push some of your strollers to synagogue
as your parents walked beside me teaching me sweet Torah.

Now this camp is yours.
The campers are due to arrive in a few hours,
and if,
in a year,
some wear their Tallis with greater ease,
in five, send you copies of their grades in Hebrew
and flyers from their food drives,
in twenty, send pictures of their children
tasting the lick of honey from their Alef-Bet books,
stand at your bedside in your illness,
stroking your arm gently,
it is *you-in-them* at work.

You are every teacher's dream class:
in commitment, unsurpassed,
craving—far ahead of me at your age—
a world of Menschen, of Menschlich acts,
of Yiddishkeit flourishing and luxuriant
as the most productive field of grain, once sand,
any farmer in the Negev ever dreamed of.
I wish you had been my counselors when I was eight.

I conclude with a photograph:
This is my father, screwdriver still in hand,

and this, the moment of illumination:
At the very instant the picture was taken,
he had just removed the training wheels from my bike,
set me on the seat,
and gave me that cosmic, parental push
we all remember.
In the picture (as you can see),
he has followed me the first few feet,
then stepped back.
Frozen in time in black and white,
you can see his hand still six inches from my shoulder.
This is my father.
This is you.

A Dream: A Touch of Glory

Last night,
what I dreamed was
I was just off my rotation in pediatrics at Hadassah,
and I was exhausted.
Then someone pulled me abruptly out of bed,
and, in a police car, I was rushed to the airport
to one of those mammoth planes taking off every few minutes
for Addis Ababa.
I remember being too tired
to be sick from the terrible air pockets
on the flight all the way down.

Then, all of a sudden, we were on the ground,
and, with the same suddenness,
the plane filled to what I thought was overload,
though it was all done in orderly fashion.
They were sitting on the floor,
packed tightly from one wall of the huge cargo bay to the other.
It was difficult to move among them
to attempt even the most elementary examinations.
While others attended to the births,
I looked at the eyes of the old men and women,
checked for infections and wounds on the nearest limbs
I was able to reach,
and bandaged whatever couldn't wait until we landed.
With two hours still to go,
I found an infant, perhaps six weeks old
(though it was hard to tell for certain
because of how they had been living the last few months).
She had one baby foot over the Line of Death.
I did what I could with the few instruments and ointments
I managed to grab in the rush from my dorm,

and prayed for her,
before moving on to the next one
in this sublime and terrifying scene of family triage.

Then, all of a sudden
(this was a dream)
it was the year 2014,
and the place was some college graduation,
and there she stood,
diploma tucked away safely in her skirt pocket,
scanning the crowd for my miraculous hands.

16

From *Healing: Readings
and Meditations* (1999)

The 23rd Psalm (Adapted) — A Responsive Reading

Because God is my shepherd, I have everything I want,
and, more, everything I need.
I need neither wander for fulfillment nor grope for meaning.

God allows me to find rest in lush meadows and valleys.
Wherever I am — God leads me.

Wherever God leads me,
it is as if I am by a river whose waters are so still,
my mind is at ease, my soul at rest.
God guides me on the right path of Tzedakah,
of justice, right, goodness, compassion, and caring,
for this is of benefit to God
as well as to human beings.

You have set life before me as a royal banquet,
even if there are present those who would harm me.
I am safe.

I am a guest in Your household.
This life is so abundant, my cup of wonder overflows.

I am grateful and bless You for Your generosity.
O, even if I walk in places so profoundly frightening
it feels as though the Angel of Death is in the darkness,
still, I fear no harm, for You, God, are with me,
wherever I find myself.

I am grateful for Your compassion and care, always.
Most certainly I shall continue to live in Your home,
in this life and after.

The Restaurant of Broken Dreams

It came to seem that
wherever he went
everything was broken.
Even when he chanced upon a place,
it was a matter of most everything in pieces,
the largest thing whole being no bigger than a vase
or a small handbag without a tear or scratch.
As he spoke to people,
he heard there, too, lines like,
"This is the street of broken dreams."
"This is the restaurant of broken dreams."
"There is the car of broken dreams."
And so he set himself to find the best carpenters,
experts in porcelain and ceramics, insulation and leather,
people who knew how to mend garden hoses
as well as surgeons fixed arteries, plumbers.
He learned each trade in turn
and drew each of his teachers and friends into
what came to be known as
The Great Fixing in the Land.
When he died,
bits and splinters had become endangered species,
and little children with glue and tape and nails in their hands
surrounded his bed and promised to carry on his work,
and their parents awoke each morning,
their dreams still whole.

17

From *From the Heart* (2012)

Muse

The moment I saw you gather the centerpieces
to take to the hospital,
you became my muse.
Your friend's wedding was over,
and the band members were putting their instruments away.
No one else was left in the synagogue.

I suspect tomorrow you will be sorting clothes
from a drive you organized for the street children,
or calling friends to raise money for a scholarship for camp,
or, perhaps, laying the table for a dinner for New Americans
who need you.

You inspire.
You are alert to cries and outcries
and attuned to the soul's finest moments.
You tend your Mitzvahs
like a home gardener who succeeds—
even with the most wretched soil in a drought—
in bringing forth lilacs and orchids that delight the eye,
yet you leave your guests to discover them on their own.
You are too modest to attribute any of this beauty to yourself.
In your mind, the credit is always due elsewhere.

It makes no difference
if you will ever sit across from me at the table reading the paper
or we ask each other if our days at work went well
or you tell me I look handsome.
Whether or not we ever meet again,
you are mine, forever.

The Bears

It was as if it were Winter
for certain words,
as if, like bears, they were hibernating
in my mind:
"love," "beloved," "dear," "precious,"
and, most of all, "elegant."
It was as if
a Great Warmth spread in the countryside,
and the words awoke, stretched themselves,
then set out, hungry for food
in the setting of a glorious Spring
alive with wildflowers and birds.
Eyes were opening everywhere.
Voices let loose from sleep to sing,
and the bears went seeking their berries and honey,
mighty in their size and force,
my bears seeking you.

In Loco Eshet Chayil

For Friday Night

*(The couple embrace and kiss one another. Then one
partner takes the other's hand and recites:)*

I love you.
What you have done for me this week,
    comforting me,
    challenging me,
    privileging me with your grandeur,
I shall never have the skill, the genius
    to articulate.
Dragged down again and again
    by mundane and commonplace jobs and burdens,
I am raised by your arms once more
    to your visions of
    myself-with-you.
Because of you
    I will never know despair
    or the claws and clutch of loneliness.
You are a constant revelation,
    a reminder of all the Noble
    and the Upright of the Earth,
and I shall never know for what reason
    I have been graced by your love.
Companion. Ineffably precious friend.
    Each moment is a Bracha-blessing
        because of you,
    each day a portion of the mysteries
        of Sinai and Creation,
    each tomorrow a taste
        of Future worlds.

My metaphors are meek
   for you move my soul in ways
   only the eloquence-of-silence can express.

And yet,
   you see,
I must speak.

I love you.

NOTES

1. Mitzvahs and How to Implement Them

1. Personal conversations, newspaper articles, television coverage. In February 1994 John Fling reminded the author of the true story of the eleven- or twelve-year-old who was dying of a brain tumor and who had already become blind. She had said she really wanted a TV. When Sig Friedman, one of Fling's friends, offered to donate one, it was a black-and-white set, but she said she would prefer a color TV. Her reason was that the sound was better on the color set, but Friedman and Fling both understood that it was really for her parents. Many similar tales come from the Make-a-Wish Foundation.
2. Personal conversation on a Shabbat walk.
3. Many of the Mitzvah Heroes described in this 1995 article have moved on to new and different projects in the intervening years. Readers are encouraged to investigate the status of these Mitzvah projects, including how they may have evolved.
4. Personal conversations.
5. Personal conversations with dog owners and their dogs.
6. Meeting, personal conversations, demonstrations.
7. *Baltimore Sun, Ocean City Supplement,* May 16, 1993.
8. Lisa S. Goldberg, "Food for Thought: Four Ten-Year-Olds at Krieger Schechter Are Helping the Homeless, One Fruit Cup at a Time," *Baltimore Jewish Times,* January 29, 1993, 35. On May 18, 1993, an administrator at Ramaz Yeshiva in New York reported that their students were saving sixty pounds of food a day.
9. *St. Petersburg Times,* November 9 and November 11, 1993.
10. A friend, Ari Newman, called the White House kitchen to ask what they do with their leftovers.
11. Ari Newman has the leftovers taken directly to hungry Jews in the Boston area.
12. For a fictionalized biography, see Morton Thompson, *The Cry and the Covenant* (New York: Doubleday, 1949).

13. *Reform Judaism*, Winter 1992, and personal conversations.

14. *First*, April 27, 1992, and personal conversations.

15. William Celis 3d, "Campus Journal: Students Discover Soul of Engineering by Serving the Disabled," *New York Times*, February 24, 1993.

16. *Denver Post*, March 31, 1993.

17. Flyer, personal conversations.

18. *In Jerusalem*, October 1, 1993; *Canadian Jewish News*, March 15, 1993.

19. Jane Gross, "Profile: Laura S. Scher; She Took One Look at the Age of Greed and Made a Quick Left," *New York Times*, November 7, 1993.

20. *Washington Post*, March 21, 1993.

21. Flyer, personal conversations, author's participation in the first Disabilities Faire.

22. Flyer, personal conversations.

23. Flyer, personal conversations.

24. Robert Dallek, *Flawed Giant: Lyndon Johnson and His Times, 1961-1973* (New York: Oxford University Press, 1998), 217.

25. The text is from the Margaliot edition of *Leviticus Rabbah*, the most authoritative critical edition of the midrashic text. Careful readers will note that citations in the Margaliot edition are on occasion slightly different from standard editions of the midrash. *Midrash Leviticus Rabbah*, ed. Mordecai Margaliot [M. Margulies] (New York: Jewish Theological Seminary, 1993).

26. Kavod Tzedakah Fund, Rabbi Yoshi Zweiback, volunteer executive director and founder; 8914 Farnam Court, Omaha NE, 68114-4076; www.kavod.org.

27. The Good People Fund, Inc., Naomi Eisenberger, executive director; 384 Wyoming Avenue, Millburn NJ, 07041; www.goodpeoplefund.org.

28. Yad Chessed; 440 Totten Pond Road, Suite 401, Waltham MA, 02451; www.yadchessed.org.

29. Jewish Helping Hands, Rabbi Joel Soffin, founder; 90 Riverside Drive #4C, New York NY, 10024; www.jewishhelpinghands.org.

30. To Save a Life, Jerry Klinger, president; 6162 Golf Villas Drive, Boynton Beach FL, 33437; www.tsal.org.

31. Hands on Tzedakah, Inc., Ronald L. Gallatin, President; 2901 Clint Moore Road, #318, Boca Raton FL, 33496; www.handsontzedakah.org.

2. Interpretations of Jewish Texts

1. Cited in the Lieberman edition of the Tosefta, the most comprehensive and accurate critical edition of the Rabbinic text: *Tosefta: 'al pi ketav yad*

Yinah ye-shinuye nusḥa'ot mi-ketav yad 'Erporṭ, ḳeta'im min ha-Genizah u-defus Yinitsyah 281, vol. 3, ed. Saul Lieberman, 26 (New York: Jewish Theological Seminary, 1973).

2. Danny Siegel, *After the Rain* (Pittsboro NY: Town House, 1993), 48.

3. "One Man Widely Credited with Saving Chile's Children," *Toronto Star*, March 21, 1992, j6.

3. Portraits of Mitzvah Heroes

1. Samantha Abeel, *Reach for the Moon* (Duluth MN: Pfeifer-Hamilton, 1994).

4. Living a Life of Menschlichkeit

1. See, for instance: Sustainable America, https://sustainableamerica.org/foodrescue/; Food Rescue US, https://foodrescue.us/; and K-12 Food Rescue (especially for schools), http://www.foodrescue.net/.

2. Rock and Wrap It Up!, www.rockandwrapitup.org.

5. How to Give and Why

1. Unique Jewish values and practices relating to Tzedakah are discussed in Siegel, *Giving Your Money Away* (2006).

2. Carl Seelig, *Albert Einstein: A Documentary Biography*, trans. Mervyn Savill (London: Staples, 1956), 71. Italics are mine.

3. Joseph B. Soloveitchik, *The Lonely Man of Faith* (New York: Doubleday, 1965), 37.

4. Ben Sasse, *Them: Why We Hate Each Other and How to Heal* (New York: St. Martin's, 2018), 4.

Other Works by Danny Siegel

Tzedakah, Mitzvahs, Tikkun Olam, and Jewish Values

Angels (1980)

Gym Shoes and Irises: Personalized Tzedakah (1981)

Gym Shoes and Irises: Book Two (1987)

Munbaz II and Other Mitzvah Heroes (1988)

Family Reunion: Making Peace in the Jewish Community (1989)

Mitzvahs (1990)

After the Rain (1993)

Good People (1995)

Heroes and Miracle Workers (1997)

*1 + 1 = 3 and 37 Other Mitzvah Principles
for a Meaningful Life* (2000)

*Danny Siegel's Bar and Bat Mitzvah Mitzvah Book: A Practical
Guide for Changing the World Through Your Simcha* (2004)

*Who, Me? Yes, You! — Danny Siegel's Workbook
to Help You Decide Where, When, Why, and How
You Can Do Your Best Tikkun Olam* (2006)

*Giving Your Money Away: How Much, How
To, Where, and To Whom* (2006)

Tzedakah: A Time for Change (2007)

For Children

The Humongous Pushka in the Sky (1993)

Tell Me a Mitzvah (1993)

*Mitzvah Magic: What Kids Can Do to Change
the World* (with Naomi Eisenberger) (2002)

Midrash and *Halakhah*

*Where Heaven and Earth Touch: An
Anthology of Midrash and Halachah*

Book One (1983)

Book Two (1984)

Book Three (1985)

Source Book: Selected Hebrew and Aramaic Sources (1985)

Combined Anthology (1996)

Poetry

Soulstoned (1969)

And God Braided Eve's Hair (1976)

Between Dust and Dance (1978)

Nine Entered Paradise Alive (1980)

Unlocked Doors: The Selected Poems of Danny Siegel 1969–1983 (1983)

The Lord Is a Whisper at Midnight: Psalms and Prayers (1985)

The Garden, Where Wolves and Lions Do No Harm to the Sheep and Deer (1985)

Before Our Very Eyes: Readings for a Journey Through Israel (1986)

The Meadow Beyond the Meadow (1991)

A Hearing Heart (1992)

From the Heart: Love Poems (2011)

Healing

Healing: Readings and Meditations (1999)

Humor

The Unorthodox Book of Jewish Records and Lists (with Allan Gould) (1982)